D0883692

823.7
Hitchcock, Susan Tyler.
Frankenstein : a cultural
history
2007.

NOV   2007

DATE DUE

FRANKENSTEIN

A CULTURAL HISTORY

FRANKENSTEIN

A CULTURAL HISTORY

Susan Tyler Hitchcock

W. W. NORTON & COMPANY

New York · London

For information about permission to reproduce selections from this book,
write to Permissions, W. W. Norton & Company, Inc.,
500 Fifth Avenue, New York, NY 10110

For information about special discounts for bulk purchases, please contact
W. W. Norton Special Sales at specialsales@wwnorton.com or 800-233-4830

Manufacturing by R.R. Donnelley, Harrisonburg
Book design by Charlotte Staub
Production manager: Julia Druskin

Library of Congress Cataloging-in-Publication Data

Hitchcock, Susan Tyler.
Frankenstein : a cultural history / Susan Tyler Hitchcock. — 1st ed.
p. cm.
Includes bibliographical references and index.
ISBN 978-0-393-06144-4 (hardcover)
1. Shelley, Mary Wollstonecraft, 1797–1851. Frankenstein.
2. Frankenstein (Fictitious character) 3. Literature and society—History.
4. Scientists in literature. 5. Monsters in literature. I. Title.
PR5397.H58 2007
823'.7—dc22

2007025466

W. W. Norton & Company, Inc.
500 Fifth Avenue, New York, N.Y. 10110
www.wwnorton.com

W. W. Norton & Company Ltd.
Castle House, 75/76 Wells Street, W1T 3QT

1 2 3 4 5 6 7 8 9 0

As did Mary Shelley,
so do I inscribe this volume

TO MY FATHER

CONTENTS

FRANKENSTEIN
A CULTURAL HISTORY

INTRODUCTION

And now, once again, I bid my hideous
progeny go forth and prosper.
I have an affection for it, for it was
the offspring of happy days.

——MARY SHELLEY, 1831

Truth in drama is forever elusive.
You never quite find it but the search
for it is compulsive.

——HAROLD PINTER, 2005

As darkness falls on Halloween night, a child stands before a full-length mirror, admiring his appearance, practicing the look, becoming the character one more time before he goes out into the world. His face is greased green, his eyes circled with black. A jagged red scar intersected with black stitches has been painted across his cheek. A crop of fake black hair bulks up his skull. Vague stubs of aluminum foil attach in a homemade way to his neck. He steps back, then walks forward, his arms out, stock straight; his hands blindly groping; his legs clumping with a jerky, heavy, stiff-legged gait. He lets out a deep-throated groan. Perfect.

This is our monster. This is the monster we know so well, the monster we have taken into our hearts and lives, the monster that makes us tremble and cheer, the monster we fear, we seek, and we have become. This is the monster made by man. This is the monster called by his creator's name, if named at all. This is the monster known as Frankenstein.

In the world of gods and monsters, he is not so very old. His origins trace back to a single source. His story has been called the first myth of modern times. It emerged at a turning point in Western history, when the moral universe was shifting and when some dared to believe that advances in scientific knowledge promised humans dominion over that which for centuries had been God's alone. The story of Frankenstein's monster is a myth of claiming long-forbidden knowledge and facing the consequences.

Many belief systems include stories of a hero who dares to stand face-to-face with the powers of the universe on behalf of the human race. In his classic study of mythology, *The Hero with a Thousand Faces,* Joseph Campbell called this the quintessential myth of the search for meaning in human life. The hero is rewarded for his extraordinary courage and sent back to earth with gifts that will enhance human life forever after. The central figure of such a myth shimmers forth in human consciousness and cultural history—Odysseus, Jonah, Beowulf in Western culture; Ramayana in the Hindu tradition; Scarface in the Blackfoot Indian tradition; and many others from around the world. Their stories convey to all that transcendent wisdom and rewards come to those who find the courage to push beyond normal limits and perform the impossible.

Other myths warn against such rash acts. Prometheus, Adam and Eve, and Faust crossed the boundary line that divides the human from the divine, and for that rash act they were punished. In these myths the moral order—the set of rules for playing this game of life—is dictated by the deities, whether Zeus or Yahweh. Even if it is part of human nature to want to, even to be able to, transgress the boundaries set by God, humans must agree to live within limits and follow the divine command. In this moral universe, life presents a perpetual temptation. There is always farther to go, but the reward of a long and serene life comes to those who hang back and toe the line.

These two archetypal myths are essentially human—and essentially contradictory. One inspires a human being to cross over into unknown realms, and congratulates anyone who does so. The other limits human pursuit and experimentation, threatening punishment to anyone who dares. These two ancient myths represent two very different world views with different assumptions about right and wrong, good and evil, the nature and purpose of human existence, and the future of humankind. On the axis formed by these two contradictory myths hang the culture wars of history and of the present day. They reverberate through every debate over life-and-death matters such as cloning, genetic engineering, euthanasia, and abortion. Progressives applaud the human drive to extend knowledge. They can be represented in Prometheus, who risked his own safety to give fire to humankind. Conservatives respect boundaries beyond which human understanding cannot or should not go. They more closely resemble Adam, tempted and fallen but seeking reentry into grace through obedience.

Both mythic views can be teased out of *Frankenstein*, an observation that goes far to explain the novel's everlasting appeal. Frankenstein the man is both hero and villain, applauded for his courage and genius at the same time that he is punished for his pride and transgression. His monster is to be both feared and pitied; for the humans he encounters, Frankenstein's monster is the ultimate other and at the same time a mirror of the deepest self.

All great myths balance irreconcilable opposites. This very characteristic keeps the Frankenstein story alive, retold and reinterpreted through almost two centuries since its original appearance in Mary Shelley's 1818 novel. It is on the one hand so true as to be universal and, on the other, malleable enough to conform to different times, places, peoples, and moments in history. In this story reverberate the monumental paradoxes of life and death, right and wrong, human and divine. They may not register as a trick-or-treater admires his green makeup on Halloween night, yet the monster that the child is portraying remains a player on the great stage of human history because his story continues to raise, not answer, questions.

To the centrally human quandary between risk and obedience, *Frankenstein* adds one more crucial, haunting, modern twist. What if there is no divine source for the rules, no final moral answer, no divine authority to judge, punish, or reward, to create, destroy, or control? In short, what if there is no God? Then what is the story that we can tell ourselves, the myth within which we glimpse our human condition? If there is no God, then what is life? And what is death? The dark possibility of a godless world permeates the novel and carries through every retelling. As if to embody the answer, a monster looms into view. Despite his promise of self-immolation at the end of Mary Shelley's novel—and despite the gruesome deaths he has suffered, over and over, in interpretations, adaptations, spin-offs, and sequels of the novel ever since—this monster lives on, perpetually spawning meaning, an obscene caricature and a god for modern times.

In some ways it is remarkable that Mary Wollstonecraft Godwin Shelley's novel still seems so timely two centuries later. The practice and promise of science and technology were so different in her time than in ours. Yet the name of Frankenstein is invoked repeatedly in the popular press as a reminder of human presumption and its misbegotten consequences. Set an Internet search engine tracking the word through the world press, and you'll get references daily, from Canada to Argentina, Seattle to New York, Glasgow to Singapore. The myth of Frankenstein has accumulated meanings since its birth and has proliferated in the number and ways in which it has been told and retold, in the twists and turns that its plot has taken, and in the transformations through which its characters, especially the monster, have traveled. Compare it to another great work of Shelley's time, *Pride and Prejudice*. Jane Austen's masterpiece may have reached the rank of literary classic earlier and more solidly than Shelley's, but her story and characters have in no way so thoroughly infused the culture and consciousness of the world. The novel remains a period piece, while Frankenstein and his monster have risen from the page and stride through our era as vitally as they did through Shelley's.

In all, Mary Shelley's *Frankenstein* has been published in hundreds of editions, including children's retellings, graphic novels, audiobooks, and e-texts. More than five hundred editions of the novel are in print today, with new editions issued constantly. Fifty thousand or more copies of the novel, in its various adaptations and editions, sell in the United States in a given year, not to mention foreign sales in English and other languages. First translated into French in 1821, three years after its original printing, *Frankenstein* has by now been translated into at least thirty languages, including Hebrew, Turkish, Chinese, Japanese, Basque, Catalan, Malay, and Braille. It is assigned in high school English courses at all levels, in college English lit surveys, and in upperclass and graduate-level courses in English Romantic literature.

With a "stiff, jerky walk" and "slurred, 'AARRRrrr' speech," advised Jenkins in an October 2005 *Mad* magazine, anyone can become the monster.

But such facts only begin to express the twenty-first-century presence of Frankenstein, for today millions know the monster without having ever read the novel, without recognizing the name of Mary Shelley at all. One reason is that, a century after the novel was written, it was embraced in Hollywood, where the monster took on a look that sank deeply into the public imagination. But the general public, at least in Europe and America, knew the monster and his meaning even before 1931. "Frankenstein" was already a household word by the time actor Boris Karloff, director James Whale, and makeup artist Jack Pierce together gave an unforgettable face to the name.

Once embodied in the cultural imagination, the myth and the monster could propagate even more broadly, infusing the popular culture as well as the literate. Toddlers today meet the monster on party plates and trick-or-treat bags at Halloween. He stands tall in the lineup of icons of the Western world, alongside Mickey Mouse, Uncle Sam, and even the haloed Aryan meant to represent Jesus. A short list of features defines today's caricature of our monster: green skin, stitched scars, flat skull edged with black hair, big shoulders, oversize hands, thick-soled feet, and bolts attached to neck or temples. In that familiar form there is a myth that our modern world needs to express. Mary Shelley conjured up the character, and, as in a culturally driven game of telephone in which each new utterance contains new meaning, we make it into the story we need at the moment. Through

The monster is known to young and old. My daughter pieced together this monster collage at the age of three.

Scars, stitches, and neck bolts make many
a monstrous Halloween costume.

almost two centuries the monster has gone through hundreds of
transformations, yet some thread of consistent meaning weaves
through them all.

Using the monster as our guide, this book explores the
Frankenstein story and its evolution in meaning, from Mary
Shelley's dream to the Halloween costumes of today, stopping
often along the way. It has required two years of cultural detec-
tive work, scanning the literary and popular media and following
every lead back to literary references, journalistic analogies,
visual allusions, outright retellings, and chance comments, seeking whatever meaning has been found or expressed in this monster that will not die. My guiding assumption has been that the

monster's story says something important. Otherwise we would not keep telling it.

Two important stylistic decisions bear mention from the start. First there is the matter of italicizing the name "Frankenstein" because it is the title of Mary Shelley's book. In keeping with the observation that the story of Victor Frankenstein and his creation long ago broke free from Mary Shelley's novel and became a myth in its own right, I have reserved the italicized use of the title for references to the novel only, not for the story or myth arising out of the novel.

The second and more interesting decision has to do with the words chosen to name Victor Frankenstein's creation. Quite early in the evolution of the story, the creator's name transferred over to his creation. Most people today call the monster "Frankenstein." The misnomer starts with Mary Shelley's brilliant idea not to give the creature a name at all, leaving his identity an empty cipher, a decision repeated in many artful retellings since.

But you can't get very far in writing a book about a character before you grasp for labels. One student of *Frankenstein,* Chris Baldick, did a tally of the words Mary Shelley gave her narrator or characters to use as names for the unnameable creation. "Monster" appears most often in her novel, twenty-seven times; "fiend" the next, twenty-five; with "daemon," "creature," and "wretch" each used fifteen or more times, and "devil," "being," and "ogre" occasionally. Some who have come to know the character in recent times have strong opinions on this subject. Sara Karloff, daughter of the man who created the twentieth-century image of this character, carefully uses "creature," respecting her father's affection for the role, even though she is surrounded by a world that most often calls him "monster." My own usage balances these two—"monster," expressing horror, and "creature," a softer term, expressing identification and even compassion. Over the course of this book I hope that in the reader's mind the two words will merge into the one paradoxical meaning that the myth conveys.

Like myth and dream, Shelley's tale contains multitudes. A kaleidoscope in which the moral vectors shift with every viewing, the story of Frankenstein manages to balance contradictory views of human nature within one story. Frankenstein, the central character, is both hero and sinner; his creation is both a glorious accomplishment and a horror-filled crime. From this paradox the story derives its power, surging out from a short novel written by an English teenager in the early nineteenth century to become a universal symbol and a myth known around the world.

This is our monster. To know him is to know ourselves.

PART ONE
BIRTH

CHAPTER ONE

CONCEPTION

*Archetypes make their way into the conscious part of
the mind seemingly from the outside and of their own accord.
They are autonomous, sometimes forcing themselves in overpoweringly.
They have a numinous quality; that is, they have an aura
of divinity which is mysterious or terrifying.
They are from the unknown.*

—WILSON M. HUDSON, folklorist

*It would have been naive to think it was
possible to have prevented this.*

—IAN WILMUT, embryologist responsible
for Dolly, the cloned sheep

The weather was strange all summer long in 1816. Twice in April the year before, Indonesia's Mount Tamboro had erupted—the largest volcanic eruption in history—spewing masses of dust into the atmosphere, which lingered and dimmed the sun's rays throughout the northern latitudes. Temperatures stayed at record lows. In New England killing frosts occurred all summer. In Europe crops—deprived of light and bogged down with too much rain—did not ripen. Grain prices doubled. In India food shortages triggered a famine, which very likely led to the cholera epidemic that spread west during the next two decades, infecting thousands in Europe and North America. Fierce storms of hail, thunder, and lightning swept through many regions. It was a dreary season indeed.

"An almost perpetual rain confines us principally to the house," wrote eighteen-year-old Mary Godwin to her half sister Fanny. "The thunder storms that visit us are grander and more terrific than I have ever seen before." She wrote from a house on the eastern bank of Lake Geneva, into which she had just moved with three fellow travelers: Percy Bysshe Shelley, her twenty-three-year-old lover; Claire Clairmont, her stepsister, also eighteen; and little William, the infant son born to her and Shelley in January. Nearly five months old, the baby—"Willmouse," as they called him—would have been smiling and reaching out to grasp a finger offered to him. One calm evening when they had first arrived, just the three of them—father, mother, child—had gone out on the lake in a little skiff at twilight. They skimmed noise-lessly across the lake's glassy surface, watching the sun sink behind the dark frown of the Jura Mountains. Since then, though, storms had moved in. They did at least provide enter-tainment. "We watch them as they approach," Mary wrote Fanny,

> observing the lightning play among the clouds in various parts of the heavens. . . . One night we *enjoyed* a finer storm than I had ever before beheld. The lake was lit up—the pines on Jura made visible, and all the scene illuminated for an instant, when a pitchy blackness succeeded, and the thunder came in frightful bursts over our heads amid the darkness.

Beyond the weather there was an excitement simply in being in Geneva, the intellectual birthplace of the French and Ameri-can Revolutions. Mary described in her letter to Fanny the obelisk just outside the city, built in honor of Jean-Jacques Rousseau, once banished from his city but now recognized as an intellectual hero. Rousseau had declared that the imperfections and suffering in human life arose not from nature but from society. Human beings had only to free themselves from social oppression and prejudice in order to regain their native joy and liberty. A shared commitment to that idea had bonded her mother and father in an all-too-brief partnership; had drawn the young poet Percy Bysshe Shelley to her father, William Godwin, the radical philosopher he most revered; and had flamed the passion between herself and Shelley from the moment they met.

That first meeting had taken place in 1814, when she was sixteen and he was twenty-one. Now, two years later, they were making a household together. She could find pleasure simply in that: In those two years they had been such wanderers. First this odd threesome, she and Shelley and Claire, had sneaked out of London on a dark night in July 1814 and trekked through France and Germany on barely any money. Three months later they returned to London and found themselves roundly shunned. Shelley was, after all, married to another and father to a child. That November, Harriet Shelley had given birth to a second child. Now, in the summer of 1816, the legal Mrs. Shelley was raising Ianthe and Charles—a girl aged three, a boy eighteen months—on her own. Shelley rationalized his behavior with a philosophy of free love. "Love," he would write, "differs from gold and clay: / That to divide is not to take away." His passions—Mary, liberty, poetry, atheism—meant more to him than his responsibility for an estranged and earthly family.

Life with Mary, however, soon developed its own earthly obligations. She had become pregnant during the 1814 escapade and stayed wretchedly sick through it all. In those times, and especially in Mary's own experience, birth and death mingled inextricably. Her own mother, Mary Wollstonecraft, had never risen from bed after giving birth to her. An infection developed, the fever never ceased, and Wollstonecraft died ten days after childbirth. Fear certainly exacerbated young Mary Godwin's condi-

The author of *Frankenstein,* Mary Wollstonecraft Godwin Shelley, in her early forties, a widow and then only recently publicly identified as the author of *Frankenstein.*

tion. On February 22, 1815, a daughter was born prematurely, "unexpectedly alive, but still not expected to live," as Shelley wrote in a journal. One week later parents, baby, and Claire moved from one end of London to the other, from Pimlico to

Hans Place. "A bustle of moving," Mary wrote in her journal on March 2. Four days later she wrote: "find my baby dead——— . . . a miserable day." She managed to write a letter to a friend: "It was perfectly well when I went to bed—I awoke in the night to give it suck[. I]t appeared to be *sleeping* so quietly that I would not awake it—it was dead then but we did not find *that* out till morning—from its appearance it evedently [*sic*] died of convulsions." The child was never given a name.

Meanwhile Harriet Shelley pleaded for help for her two children from the fathers of both her husband and his runaway lover. Timothy Shelley, a baronet of ample means, felt fury over family shame more than anything else and clamped down viciously on his son's access to any inheritance. William Godwin, now remarried, no longer enjoyed popularity as a radical author. He and his wife barely made ends meet by running a bookshop and publishing books for children. They shared the baronet's parental outrage, however, and Godwin turned Shelley's kidnapping, as he termed it, of his daughter and stepdaughter into an opportunity for a gentlemanly sort of blackmail. By the summer of 1816, to meet the demands of Harriet Shelley and William Godwin, not to mention his own household obligations, Percy Bysshe Shelley was negotiating with moneylenders and solicitors for post-obit bonds—loans against his future estate.

Mary, Percy, and Claire moved restlessly, often hiding from creditors, Shelley all the while corresponding frantically with William Godwin about money. On January 25, 1816, though, at the end of a letter full of logistics concerning loans and payments, Shelley wrote: "Mrs. Godwin will probably be glad to hear that Mary has safely recovered from a very favorable confinement, & that her child is well." Mary Godwin and Percy Bysshe Shelley, unmarried, welcomed a son into the world. In a

Percy Bysshe Shelley, the author's lover as she wrote *Frankenstein* and her husband when it was published, did not live to see the novel's popularity.

decision rife with contradictions, they named him William, after her father.

As if that weren't enough, now, in the cold and rainy summer of 1816, there was a new secret to keep from the Godwins.

Claire Clairmont—Mary's stepsister, the daughter of the second Mrs. Godwin—had been the one who selected Geneva as the destination of their upstart band. She was chasing after the outlandish yet irresistibly popular poet George Gordon, Lord Byron. Some speculate that early on Claire, as well as Mary, had had her eyes on Percy Bysshe Shelley. But by 1816 she was feeling like the odd woman out and, presented with the opportunity to meet the notoriously libertine Byron, Claire Clairmont had plotted—and pounced. Exploiting a tenuous personal connection, she approached Lord Byron. "An utter stranger takes the liberty of addressing you," her first letter to him began. It grew more presumptuous with every paragraph: "It may seem a strange assertion, but it is not the less true that I place my happiness in your hands." Rebuffed, Claire wrote again, explaining that she had drafted a play and sought Byron's advice on her composition. "You think it impertinent that I intrude on you," she wrote. "Remember that I have confided to you the most important secrets. I have withheld nothing." Slyly she implied submission even before he pursued her.

Claire was an annoying distraction during a troubled period of Byron's life. He had married Annabella Milbanke in January 1815, but the marriage swiftly self-destructed, despite the birth of a daughter, Ada. The new wife and mother could not ignore Byron's fascination with his half sister, Augusta, and she had heard rumors of his sexual relations with men. She hired a doctor to investigate his mental condition. Byron was diagnosed sane. If he wasn't insane, he was immoral and dangerous, Annabella reasoned, and presented him with separation papers. Evidences of his incest and sodomy were whispered, even published, throughout Britain. "He is completely lost in the opinion of the world," wrote one London socialite. Byron decided to leave England. He

Lord Byron, renegade poet, hosted the dark and stormy June 1816 soiree at which *Frankenstein* was first conceived.

would travel to Switzerland, birthplace of the Enlightenment, tolerant of iconoclasts like Rousseau—and himself.

So when Claire's letters began appearing, Byron was not in a particularly amorous mood. Sometime in late April, though, Claire's plot achieved consummation. As Byron wrote a friend some months later, "A man is a man, and if a girl of eighteen comes prancing to you at all hours there is but one way." It was a heartless fling, Byron said later: "I never loved nor pretended to love her." He probably thought he would shake her loose once he departed from England, but Claire Clairmont did not let go. Learning where Byron was going, she persuaded her friends to head for Geneva, too.

DIODATI ESCAPADES

According to Byron's physician and traveling companion, John William Polidori, the Shelley party first encountered Lord Byron on May 27, 1816. "Getting out [of a boat]," wrote Polidori in his diary, "L.B. met M. Wollstonecraft Godwin, her sister, and Percy Shelley." Byron's fame made the younger poet somewhat diffident, yet Byron hosted Shelley for dinner that very night. Polidori described him as "bashful, shy, consumptive, twenty-six: separated from his wife; keeps the two daughters of Godwin, who practise his theories; one L.B.'s." He got Shelley's age wrong

An 1823 travel book identified this view as Lake Leman (or Lake Geneva) seen from opposite Lord Byron's Villa Diodati—the large building on the crest of the first rise above the water's edge. Mont Blanc's white peaks tower beyond.

by two years but immediately grasped the dynamics between Claire and Byron.

The scene was set for the momentous summer of 1816. Byron rented the Villa Diodati, an elegant estate house above Lake Geneva. John Milton himself, the author of *Paradise Lost,* had stayed in the house in 1638, while visiting the uncle of his dear friend Charles Diodati. Byron must have enjoyed communing with such an eminent forebear. Shelley, Mary, and Claire rented a humbler house down the hill, closer to the lake's edge, and visited Villa Diodati often. One wonders whether Mary ever brought her baby with her into that environment, electric with testosterone and nerves. She hired a Swiss nursemaid, but she still must have felt torn between her duties as a mother and her fascination with her poet friends. Sometimes fierce lightning storms broke open the skies above Villa Diodati. Together with the storms, sharp wit and intellectual sparring may have kept her at the villa longer than she planned.

They spoke of literature, debating the virtues of the writers of the time. Robert Southey, then Britain's poet laureate, had published *Thalaba the Destroyer* and *The Curse of Kehama,* passionate epics set in mysterious Eastern realms and peopled by unknown deities. Shelley so respected these poems that he used them as models, but Byron mocked them for their pageantry and melodrama. William Wordsworth presented an entirely different aesthetic, finding poetry in the language of the common folk— shepherds, idiots, children. Samuel Taylor Coleridge's poems evoked powers unseen and unnamed. Meanwhile Walter Scott, already revered for poems that sang of his native Scotland, was suspected of being the author of *Waverley*. What a shock if it were true—that a popular poet would descend to write a novel, a new and not altogether respected literary form.

Byron leased Villa Diodati, where John Milton had once visited, for the summer of 1816. The house still stands, overlooking Lake Geneva, a private home but a public landmark famous for its place in literary history.

No poet of any renown would write a novel; no elevated person would stoop to read one. Yet in the wee hours of the night, their tongues unleashed by sherry or other elixirs, those present at the Villa Diodati might admit a fascination with an occasional Gothic romance, Mrs. Radcliffe's *Mysteries of Udolpho* or Matthew Gregory Lewis's *The Monk*, perhaps. Set in a dimly imagined past, these popular books of the time pitted established strictures against native human desire, raising the very questions that radical philosophers had been asking about convention and society. Ghosts and spirits haunted the churchyards, vaults, and abbeys; gore, horror, lust, and crime oozed onto the printed page. There was something in the human imagination that made such stories irresistibly fascinating.

Literary fashion was a matter of personal interest to all those gathered at the Villa Diodati, though only Byron was broadly known as a writer in 1816. Polidori had been educated as a physician, but he had fancied a future as a writer ever since pub-

John William Polidori, Byron's traveling companion and doctor, began a story that same June 1816 at Villa Diodati that would ultimately inspire *Dracula*.

lishing an essay against the death penalty, an issue hotly debated in Britain at the time. When he learned that Byron wanted a medically trained traveling companion, he signed on with literary aspirations, believing that a travelogue of his famous employer's antics would be a sure sell. Too soon, however, poor Polidori learned that George Gordon, Lord Byron, cast a long, dark, snide shadow.

That shadow fell on Claire Clairmont as well, whose own literary pretensions soon fell by the wayside. She kept a daily journal, and had once planned on writing a novel—"for years a favorite Plan of mine," she wrote in her journal. "To develop the Workings & Improvements of a Mind which by Common People was deemed the mind of an Ideot [*sic*] because it conformed not to their vulgar & prejudiced views." Her idea echoed a familiar theme of the time—that normalcy and sanity are social constructs—but she produced neither a novel nor the play she had mentioned in her early letters to Byron.

Mary Godwin, on the other hand, was born to write. Her mother, Mary Wollstonecraft, had published novels and treatises, including *A Vindication of the Rights of Woman,* the first feminist tract ever. Her father, although less influential by 1816, had been a brilliantly popular writer in the 1790s. His *Essay Concerning Political Justice,* a tome of political philosophy, gripped the public imagination as intensely as did his novels, *Caleb Williams*, for example. "It is not singular that, as the daughter of two persons of distinguished literary celebrity, I should very early in life have thought of writing," she wrote later in life. "As a child I scribbled; and my favourite pastime, during the hours given me for recreation, was to 'write stories.'" Her father even published a clever rhyme she had written at the age of ten, mocking an Englishman who pretends to know French. Mary's literary heritage appealed to Percy Bysshe Shelley, who was from the first, she wrote, "very anxious that I should prove myself worthy of my parentage, and enrol myself on the page of fame."

Even Lord Byron, celebrity that he was, must have admired Mary Godwin's intellectual lineage. He certainly had nothing similar. His birthright included debt and disrepute on his father's side, and his mother had struggled to support him alone in a flat above a perfumer's shop. On the death of his great-uncle, though, George Noel Gordon inherited the family estate and, at the age of ten, became Lord Byron. At nineteen he assumed his seat in the House of Lords. His first great poem, *Childe Harold's Pilgrimage,* was instantly popular when published in 1812. As he told a friend, he awoke one morning to find himself famous. All of England and much of Europe were taken by his graceful rhythm and rhyme, his charmingly archaic vocabulary, and the story he told of an adventurous young nobleman, ruefully independent and unrepentantly lustful.

> Ah, me! in sooth he was a shameless wight,
>   Sore given to revel and ungodly glee;
>   Few earthly things found favour in his sight
>   Save concubines and carnal companie,
> And flaunting wassailers of high and low degree.

Sultry, brooding, misunderstood, dashing, haunted, elusive, alluring, irresistible—in many ways, the persona created in *Childe Harold's Pilgrimage* crystallized the image of the Romantic hero. And Byron himself lived up to the image.

In the summer of 1816 Percy Bysshe Shelley was also a renegade, though not so widely celebrated for his transgressions. As the son of a baronet, he did not equal Byron in social standing, yet he was born into privilege and presumed to be headed for the

House of Commons. From early on, though, Shelley had made it clear that he would not meet those expectations. He attended Oxford but was expelled summarily during his second term for publishing a pamphlet proving, as it was titled, *The Necessity of Atheism.* Two years later, in 1813, he had published—again at his own expense—a "philosophical poem" dedicated to his young wife, Harriet. Her opinion was that *Queen Mab* "must not be published under pain of death, because it is too much against every existing establishment." (A sign of her personality differences from Harriet, Mary Shelley inscribed her copy of *Queen Mab*, "This book is sacred to me.") With 2,305 lines of unrhymed verse followed by explanatory footnotes that more than doubled the page count, *Queen Mab* was a presumptuous undertaking for a man just twenty. Its contents say a lot about the young Percy Bysshe Shelley, whose imagination balanced fairy queens with planetary orbits, imaginative fantasy with scientific fact.

In *Queen Mab* the spirit of a sleeping girl named Ianthe—in Greek mythology a daughter of Ocean—follows Mab, the fairy queen, into realms beyond the human world to see a larger truth and future. Earth shrinks to the "smallest light that twinkles in the heaven" as Mab and Ianthe whiz past "innumerable systems" and "countless spheres." (To phrases such as this, Shelley attached discursive notes on the speed of light and the distance from Earth to the star Sirius.) From such a vantage point, everything human looks different—history, power, wealth, religion. "Where Athens, Rome, and Sparta stood, / There is a moral desert now," the fairy queen displays. All human power structures crumble; all human moral principles fade. "It is impossible to believe that the Spirit that pervades this infinite machine begat a son upon the body of a Jewish woman," state the notes. "All that miserable tale of the Devil, and Eve, and an Intercessor, with the childish mummeries of the God of the Jews, is irreconcilable with the knowledge of the stars."

As she gazes down on human history, Ianthe remembers a scene from her childhood. "I was an infant when my mother went / To see an atheist burned. She took me there." She felt terrified, but her mother told her not to cry, "for that man / Has said, 'There is no God.'" Mab responds:

> There is no God!
> Nature confirms the faith his death-groan sealed:
> Let heaven and earth, let man's revolving race,
> His ceaseless generations tell their tale;
>
> .   .   .   .
>
> infinity within,
> Infinity without, belie creation;
> The exterminable spirit it contains
> Is nature's only God; but human pride
> Is skilful to invent most serious names
> To hide its ignorance.

The first four words of this stanza caused irreparable damage to the fortunes of the poet who wrote them. Only 250 copies of *Queen Mab* were printed, significantly fewer sold, but for this apparent statement of atheism, Shelley was ultimately denied his baronetcy, refused financial support by his father, sequestered from his children, and generally hounded out of England— although his, like Byron's, was a self-imposed exile.

The direst of such consequences lay in the future, though, as the reckless band haunted Villa Diodati that summer of 1816. By then Shelley had published another, very different poem: *Alastor, or the Spirit of Solitude.* He ordered the printing himself—and took years to pay that bill—then found booksellers willing to bind and sell the volume.

Like Byron's hit poem, *Alastor* chronicled a pilgrimage; but unlike Byron's, Shelley's was an inward journey, set in the wild terrain of a nearly unpopulated world. In his preface to the 720-line lyric, Shelley called it "allegorical of one of the most interesting situations of the human mind," representing "a youth of uncorrupted feelings and adventurous genius led forth by an imagination inflamed." He undergoes a coming-of-age at once spiritual and sexual. His soul "thirsts for intercourse with an intelligence similar to itself" and searches for an earthly equivalent to his ideal partner, "the Being whom he loves." A fruitless quest, it ultimately empties him of life. At the poem's end, "He lay breathing there / At peace, and faintly smiling." The crescent moon sinks below the horizon as the youth takes his last breath and glimpses "two lessening points of light alone"—the two tips of the upturned crescent moon, resembling the eyes of the one he had been seeking.

Years after his death Mary Godwin Shelley wrote that "none of Shelley's poems is more characteristic" than *Alastor*. Written, she noted, after he had recovered from a life-threatening episode of consumption, the poem "was the outpouring of his own emotions, embodied in the purest form he could conceive, painted in the ideal hues which his brilliant imagination inspired, and softened by the recent anticipation of death." In some senses, it was a premonition. The intellectual story line of *Alastor* was to be, in an eerie way, the story of Shelley's life—and a foreshadowing of the myth of Frankenstein soon to be conceived by his companion, Mary Godwin.

ELECTRIFYING SCIENCE

Poetry was much on the minds of those gathered at the Villa Diodati, but science charged the conversation as well. Polidori, after all, had been trained in medicine, and Shelley had intended to become a doctor when he entered Oxford in 1810. A friend described his college quarters as cluttered with chemistry flasks and retorts. Early-nineteenth-century advances in science opened up realms of thought as fantastic as any coming from the imagination of a poet. In fact, to some, philosophy, poetry, and science converged to promise revolutionary changes in human knowledge and worldview.

Erasmus Darwin, for example, grandfather to Charles, had proffered an early theory of evolution. "Organic life beneath the shoreless waves / Was born and nurs'd in ocean's pearly caves," he wrote in his epic poem *The Temple of Nature; or, the Origin of Society,* published in 1803. As Darwin described it, life forms "new powers acquire, and larger limbs assume / Whence countless groups of vegetation spring, / And breathing realms of fin, and feet, and wing." Notions of evolving life forms led logically back to questions about the origin of life itself. Joseph Priestley, discoverer of oxygen, used mold on vegetables to demonstrate the spontaneous generation of life. Darwin saw similar things going on in aging wheat-flour slurry: "In paste composed of flour and water, which has been suffered to become acescent [to sour], the animalcules called eels, vibrio anguillula, are seen in great abundance." The eggs of such creatures could not possibly "float in the atmosphere, and pass through the sealed glass phial," Darwin reasoned, so they must come into being "by a spontaneous vital process." Evolution and spontaneous generation may be concepts difficult to accept, Darwin granted, but "all new discoveries, as of the magnetic needle, and coated electric jar, and Galvanic pile" seemed just as incredible.

Once Benjamin Franklin and others had managed to harness naturally occurring electricity, experimenters went to work on devices to collect, control, and generate electrical power. The

galvanic pile, as Darwin called it—precursor of the electric battery—was named for the Italian scientist Luigi Galvani, whose
famous experiments of the 1790s tested the effect of electrical
current on the bodies of animals. When a charged metal rod
caused disembodied frog leg muscles to move, Galvani glimpsed
that electricity motivated living nerve and muscle. His work
advanced understanding of what was called "animal electricity,"
soon renamed "galvanism." By 1802 the *Journal of Natural Philosophy* announced that "the production of the galvanic fluid, or electricity, by the direct or independent energy of life in animals, can
no longer be doubted." Galvani's nephew, Luigi Aldini, toured
Europe during the first years of the nineteenth century, demonstrating how electrical charges could move not only the legs of
frogs but also the eyes and tongues of severed ox heads as well.

In a famous presentation to the president of the Royal College
of Surgeons, Aldini demonstrated galvanism with the body of a
recently executed murderer. Aldini connected wires from a massive battery of copper and zinc to the corpse's head and anus. As
an eyewitness described it:

> On the first application of the process to the face, the jaw of the
> deceased criminal began to quiver, the adjoining muscles were
> horribly contorted, and one eye was actually opened. In the sub-
> sequent part of the process, the right hand was raised and
> clenched, and the legs and thighs were set in motion. It appeared
> to the uninformed part of the by-standers as if the wretched man
> was on the eve of being restored to life.

London newspapers reported the phenomenon, and Aldini
mounted shows for the public. Even the Prince Regent attended
one. It did not seem farfetched to consider this newly entrapped
natural force, electricity, the quintessential force of life. "Gal-

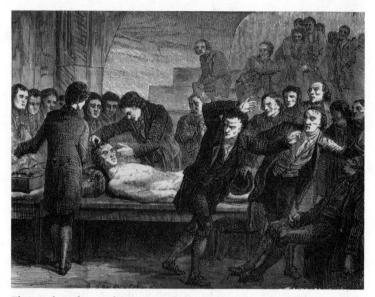

Electrophysiologists demonstrated galvanism, the force of electricity in the body, by animating the corpses of executed criminals like Matthew Clydesdale, pictured here, hanged for murder in 1818.

vanism had given token of such things," Mary Godwin wrote as she later recalled how discussions at Villa Diodati of these scientific marvels had filled her with ideas. "Perhaps the component parts of a creature might be manufactured, brought together, and endued [*sic*] with vital warmth."

THE CHALLENGE

Poetry and science, Gothic horror and reanimation—those topics tingled in the Geneva air that summer of 1816. Somebody pulled out a collection of tales of the supernatural, *Phantasmagoriana,* which became one evening's entertainment. The book had been translated from German into French in 1812 and subtitled *Recueil d'histoires d'apparitions, de spectres, revenans, fantomes, &c.*

traduit de l'allemand, par un amateur—"a collection of stories about apparitions, specters, dreams, phantoms, etc., translated from the German by an amateur." The book must have enjoyed popularity at the time, because an English edition came into print in 1813, with the simple title *Tales of the Dead*. The group at Villa Diodati read the stories to one another from the French edition.

"There was the History of the Inconstant Lover," Mary later recalled—its French title "La Morte Fiancée"—which told of an Italian courtier in love with a woman whose identical twin had died mysteriously the year before. "There was the tale of the sinful founder of his race," as she called "Les Portraits de Famille," in which ancient portraits hanging on cold stone walls assumed supernatural powers. "I have not seen these stories since then," she wrote in 1831, "but their incidents are as fresh in my mind as if I had read them yesterday."

After listening to a few of these tales, chilling yet clumsily written, Byron challenged his companions. Any one of them could do better. "'We will each write a ghost story,' said Lord Byron; and his proposition was acceded to," Mary Shelley recounted in 1831. "There were four of us," she begins, although there were five. The one she left out was Claire Clairmont—maybe Claire was not present, or she simply chose not to write, or maybe Mary was deliberately ignoring her stepsister. Byron only started a story, "a fragment of which he printed at the end of his poem of Mazeppa," Mary reported—a two-thousand-word passage that introduces two Englishmen in a Greek landscape: Augustus Darvell, celebrated, mysterious, and haunted by "some peculiar circumstances in his private history"; and the story's narrator, younger, ingenuous, and mesmerized by Darvell. "This is the end of my journey," Darvell whispers. He has led his young friend into an old Muslim cemetery, full of fallen turban-topped tombstones. He hands him a ring engraved with Arabic characters, with strict instructions to fling it into Eleusinian springs after he dies. A stork alights on a nearby tombstone, a snake writhing in her beak. As she flies away, Darvell breathes his last. The narrator buries him in an ancient grave. "Between astonishment and grief, I was tearless," he says— and at that, Byron abandoned the story.

Percy Shelley appears not to have composed even a fragment in response to the challenge. His wife's explanation, written after his death, was that storytelling was just not his style. Spirits did seem to haunt him—in 1813 he had fled a Welsh cottage, convinced that a ghost had fired a gun at him—but grotesques were not the stuff of his poetry in 1816. Shelley, she wrote, was "more apt to embody ideas and sentiments in the radiance of brilliant imagery, and in the music of the most melodious verse that adorns our language, than to invent the machinery of a story." Ironically, therefore, Byron and Shelley—the two poets destined for the highest echelons of English Romantic litera-ture—fizzled out in response to the ghost-story challenge, but their two companions wrote pieces that would evolve into the two greatest horror stories of modern times.

John Polidori was inspired to write two works, both published three years later. One was a short novel, *Ernestus Berchtold,* little known by anyone but professors of English today. The other, he freely admitted, began with Byron's unfinished story. "A noble author having determined to descend from his lofty range, gave up a few hours to a tale of terror, and wrote the fragment pub-lished at the end of Mazeppa," Polidori explained. "Upon this foundation I built the Vampyre," as he titled his story. "In the course of three mornings, I produced that tale."

Like Byron's fragment, Polidori's *Vampyre* tells the tale of two Englishmen—Aubrey, a young gentleman, orphaned and inno-

cent, and Lord Strongmore, a shadowy nobleman "more remarkable for his singularities, than for his rank." Strongmore suggests,
much to Aubrey's amazement, that the two tour the Continent
together. Repelled by Strongmore's appetite for sex and gam-
bling, Aubrey takes off on his own and falls in love with Ianthe, a
Greek country maid, who soon turns up dead, her throat pierced
with "marks of teeth having opened the vein of the neck." "A
Vampyre! a Vampyre!" the villagers all cry. The assailant turns out
to be Lord Strongmore, who next sets his sights on Aubrey's own
sister. Aubrey warns his family and mysteriously dies at midnight,
leaving others to discover that "Lord Strongmore had disappeared, and Aubrey's sister had glutted the thirst of a VAMPYRE!"
The story, borrowed from a poet and written by a man of little
talent, would in a few years burst back on the literary scene and
then proliferate through the nineteenth century, influencing
Bram Stoker as he wrote *Dracula,* the vampire classic, in 1897.
Thus on the same night in Geneva in 1816 were born the world's
two most famous monsters.

While vampires populated Polidori's imagination, Mary Godwin worried that hers seemed so vacant. "I busied myself *to think
of a story,*—a story to rival those which had excited us to this
task," she wrote fifteen years later. Conscious exertion seemed to
get her nowhere. "I felt that blank incapability of invention which
is the greatest misery of authorship, when dull Nothing replies to
our anxious invocations. *Have you thought of a story?* I was asked
each morning, and each morning I was forced to reply with a
mortifying negative." Her mind remained as if a blank slate, and
discussions between Byron and Shelley concerning "various
philosophical doctrines" including "the nature of the principle of
life" made impressions on it. They cited examples; they speculated as to extremes—sometimes the discussion was detailed

and technical, sometimes visionary. Details of Aldini's galvanic demonstrations may have mingled with descriptions of gruesome phantasms or translucent fairies.

With such ideas swirling in her head, Mary Godwin went to bed. "I did not sleep, nor could I be said to think," she recalled. A story presented itself, as she described it, the life force less in her than in the visions appearing to her.

> My imagination, unbidden, possessed and guided me, gifting the successive images that arose in my mind with a vividness far beyond the usual bounds of reverie. I saw—with shut eyes, but acute mental vision,—I saw the pale student of unhallowed arts kneeling beside the thing he had put together. I saw the hideous phantasm of a man stretched out, and then, on the working of some powerful engine, show signs of life, and stir with an uneasy, half vital motion.

To enter the original moment of the creation of Frankenstein's monster, strip away all the modern imagery created to portray it. No more white lab coat, no more electrical coils and transformers, not even a dank stone tower. The author herself gives us very little: a "pale student," "kneeling" on the floor; beside him, "the thing he had put together"—a "hideous phantasm," "some powerful engine" whose force only made him "stir."

Granted, these few words are themselves just garments wrapped by the author around wordless moments of inspiration. It is as if she, one with her character, had gazed for the first time upon "the horrid thing" standing at the bedside, staring at her with its "yellow, watery, but speculative eyes"—for, at the moment that she glimpsed this kernel of her story, she opened her own eyes "with terror," seeking the comfort of the outside world.

The idea so possessed my mind, that a thrill of fear ran through me, and I wished to exchange the ghastly image of my fancy for the realities around. I see them still; the very room, the dark *parquet,* the closed shutters, with the moonlight struggling through, and the sense I had that the glassy lake and white high Alps were beyond. I could not so easily get rid of my hideous phantom; still it haunted me. I must try to think of something else. I recurred to my ghost story,—my tiresome unlucky ghost story! O! if I could only contrive one which would frighten my reader as I myself had been frightened that night!

Soon the two thoughts merged into one: her waking dream *was* her ghost story. "On the morrow I announced that I had *thought of a story,*" Mary later recalled. "I began that day with the words, *It was on a dreary night of November,* making only a transcript of the grim terrors of my waking dream."

Mary Godwin Shelley's account of the genesis of her novel, written for its 1831 edition, may contain a few fabrications, a few exaggerations, a few skewed memories. But it is still the most reliable rendition we have of how the story of Frankenstein began, and therefore a good starting point.

CHAPTER TWO

BIRTH AND LINEAGE

*Deep within each man and each woman
lie vast shadowed areas veiling ancient and deep-harbored
fears. Man spends his lifetime running from them . . .
never realizing that it is he who casts that shadow.*

—STAN LEE, Marvel Comics creator

The role of the scientist is to break the laws of nature.

—STEEN WILLADSEN, physiologist
and cloning expert

She had seen it—that "hideous phantasm of a man stretched out." Now to turn that vision into a story. The very next morning (as she reported years later), Mary Godwin began by writing those legendary words: "It was on a dreary night in November"—the words that introduce the scene of the hideous being's creation. In her final product the scene occurs midbook, in the book's fourth chapter, but in the author's imagination—and for millions of others nearly two centuries since—the famous story begins as the monster comes to life.

Scholars hypothesize an "urstory," a short work dashed off that summer in Switzerland, but no copy exists. Polidori dates Byron's challenge on June 16, and the week after, Shelley and Byron took an eight-day sail around Lake Geneva, leaving behind a silence in which Mary Godwin began to find the words for her story. Starting with the scene of creation, she spun outward, imagining a plot that would lead to, enfold, and flow out from the dream vision that had so terrified her. It would take her until March 1817 to turn the nightmare moment of inspiration into a completed manuscript: nine months, an appropriate gestation period.

It's a shock, even a disappointment, for today's readers when they actually encounter the creation scene in *Frankenstein*. The physical appearance of the "hideous phantasm" cannot begin to match the grotesqueries constructed for more recent, more sensational renditions of the scene. Although piecing together parts of corpses, the novel's Frankenstein had intended to create an attractive being. "His limbs were in proportion, and I had selected his features as beautiful," he states. Yet the figure that comes to life is anything but:

> Beautiful!—Great God! His yellow skin scarcely covered the work of muscles and arteries beneath; his hair was of a lustrous black, and flowing; his teeth of a pearly whiteness; but these luxuriances only formed a more horrid contrast with his watery eyes, that seemed almost of the same colour as the dun white sockets in which they were set, his shrivelled complexion, and straight black lips.

"Un-human," Mary Shelley added to this passage in a later revision. And, despite the whir, zap, and sizzle of futuristic devices in later adaptations, the novel describes the technology of imparting life very sparsely:

> With an anxiety that almost amounted to agony, I collected the instruments of life around me, that I might infuse a spark of being into the lifeless thing that lay at my feet. It was already one in the

> morning; the rain pattered dismally against the panes, and my
> candle was nearly burnt out, when, by the glimmer of the half-
> extinguished light, I saw the dull yellow eye of the creature open;
> it breathed hard, and a convulsive motion agitated its limbs.

With that a myth was born.

CREATURE MEETS CREATOR

There could be no creature without a creator—the myth
requires them both. Mary Godwin named him Victor Frankenstein. "Victor" echoed a pseudonym used by Percy Bysshe Shelley
in his childhood; some have linked "Frankenstein" to a baronial
German family whose castle stood above the river Rhine. Radu
Florescu, in his 1975 book *In Search of Frankenstein,* presents complex links to an actual Castle Frankenstein near Darmstadt, Germany, suggesting that the author and her companions visited it
during their 1814 European travels, but there is no solid evidence to prove his theory. The character in the novel simply
states, "I am by birth a Genevese; and my family is one of the
most distinguished of that republic."

He enjoyed an idyllic and privileged childhood, adored by his
parents, revered by his two younger brothers, and loved by his
beautiful cousin, Elizabeth, adopted into the Frankenstein home
when Victor was only four. Fascinated by the unseen powers of
nature and the secret source of life, young Frankenstein discovers the work of Cornelius Agrippa, a sixteenth-century scholar
of the occult, and then of Paracelsus and Albertus Magnus,
philosophers in the alchemical tradition whose ideas, as
Frankenstein's father says in the novel, seemed "sad trash" compared with the new sciences of the late eighteenth century. But
some saw value in their writings—William Godwin, Mary's

father, wrote *The Lives of the Necromancers,* biographies of such arcane thinkers, in 1834. They appealed to Godwin, to Mary, and to the character she was conjuring because of the spiritual quest at the heart of their work. The alchemists handled earthly elements, yet they reached for a higher realm. They sought "the philosopher's stone" and "the elixir of life"—alchemical touchstones that symbolized spiritual enlightenment. For Paracelsus and his followers, the goal was to create a "homunculus," a tiny living human being.

In Mary Godwin's fiction two incidents shake Victor Frankenstein's alchemical fascination. First, he witnesses the operation of an air pump, an eighteenth-century laboratory device that created a vacuum inside a bell jar. Air pumps were crucial to the discovery of atmospheric gases and to the understanding of their life-supporting quality. When small animals were placed inside a bell jar and an air pump used to remove all gas inside, the result, of course, was death to the animal, despite no visible change in the jar's interior. Henry Cavendish used an air pump in 1784 to demonstrate that oxygen and hydrogen combine to make water, shattering the age-old theory that water was a foundational element. That a human could create a vacuum was in itself a revolutionary phenomenon; to traditional believers it was an abomination of God's natural order. All these associations resonated through Victor Frankenstein's brief comment that "my utmost wonder was engaged by some experiments on an airpump." Mary Godwin trusted that her nineteenth-century readers caught all the implications.

Second, Victor Frankenstein witnesses a massive lightning strike. Like those at the Villa Diodati in June 1816, he watches monstrous thunderstorms approach Geneva from behind the Jura Mountains. They present a vivid tableau:

The thunder burst at once with frightful loudness from various quarters of the heavens. I remained, while the storm lasted, watching its progress with curiosity and delight. As I stood at the

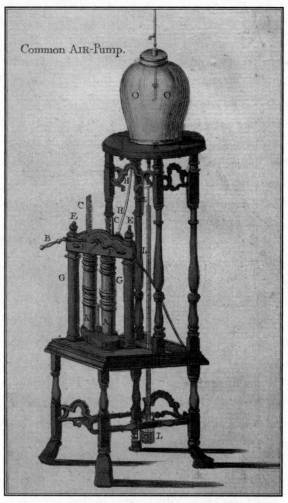

The air pump, essential to eighteenth-century studies of gases and the atmosphere, threatened the metaphysical status quo by suggesting that a human being could create a vacuum.

door, on a sudden I beheld a stream of fire issue from an old and beautiful oak, which stood about twenty yards from our house; and so soon as the dazzling light vanished, the oak had disappeared, and nothing remained but a blasted stump. . . . It was not splintered by the shock, but entirely reduced to thin ribbands of wood. I never beheld any thing so utterly destroyed.

The teenage Frankenstein looks to his father for an explanation. He replies, "electricity," and then, to demonstrate, he "constructed a small electrical machine, and exhibited a few experiments; he made also a kite, with a wire and string, which drew down that fluid from the clouds." These brief science lessons— summarizing electromagnetic science of the day, especially the work of Joseph Priestley and Benjamin Franklin—"completed the overthrow" of Victor Frankenstein's studies in alchemy and the occult.

He turns instead to natural philosophy—his era's name for chemistry and physics, the most thrilling sciences of the day. A generation before, Joseph Priestley had isolated oxygen and other elements, showing the gaseous composition of air—but Priestley was also known as a religious dissenter, an advocate of the American and French Revolutions, and an ally of the most radical of Englishmen. In 1791 royalist mobs stormed Priestley's house and smashed his laboratory equipment, signifying that his democratic politics and his physical science were one and the same threat to society. Modern science and modern democratic political philosophy both sprang from Enlightenment thought, each discipline questioning the prevailing authorities, church and state.

In the same way physicians exploring human anatomy edged into threatening realms of knowledge. Medical dissections of the brain and body implied that personality and emotions, even faith and belief, could be analyzed as physical phenomena. "Anatomical knowledge is the only foundation on which the structure of medical science can be built," argued John Abernethy, a celebrated English surgeon of the time. "Opportunities of dissection should therefore be afforded us." English law allowed anatomists to dissect the bodies of executed criminals, but the demand was exceeding the supply. Grave robbing, even murder, in the service of modern science and medicine was becoming a profit-making venture.

"To examine the causes of life, we must first have recourse to death": these are the ominous words uttered by Victor Frankenstein as he describes the education he received. "I became acquainted with the science of anatomy: but this was not sufficient; I must also observe the natural decay and corruption of the human body." Now thoroughly a rationalist, he holds no superstitious beliefs in ghosts or spirits, no sentimental attitudes toward the dead. "A church-yard," he says, "was to me merely the receptacle of bodies deprived of life." Dispassionate and scientifically minded, he studies the phenomena of death only to discover, as if by revelation, the principle of life:

> I paused, examining and analysing all the minutiae of causation, as exemplified in the change from life to death, and death to life, until from the midst of this darkness a sudden light broke in upon me—a light so brilliant and wondrous, yet so simple, that while I became dizzy with the immensity of the prospect which it illustrated, I was surprised that among so many men of genius, who had directed their inquiries towards the same science, that I alone should be reserved to discover so astonishing a secret.

In that moment, he summarizes, he had "succeeded in discovering the cause of generation and life" and, further, had become "capable of bestowing animation upon lifeless matter." Propelled by knowledge, Victor Frankenstein begins his work, gathering materials from "the dissecting room and the slaughter-house" and piecing together a human body. He makes it eight feet tall to avoid the challenge raised by "the minuteness of the parts" of a normal-size human being.

In Victor Frankenstein's moment of scientific success—the yellow eye opens, the body breathes and shudders—repugnance overwhelms him. "The beauty of the dream vanished," he says, "and breathless horror and disgust filled my heart." Victor Frankenstein turns and runs in instinctive revulsion. He escapes into sleep, but his effort at oblivion is penetrated by the being that he has now brought to life: "By the dim and yellow light of the moon . . . I beheld the wretch—the miserable monster whom I had created. He held up the curtain of the bed; and his eyes, if eyes they may be called, were fixed on me. His jaws opened, and he muttered some inarticulate sounds, while a grin wrinkled his cheeks." Frankenstein flees, then descends into a months-long illness that today might be considered depression, fending off the reality he must ultimately face.

His flight and denial shape the character of his creation. Repugnance is the first human response Frankenstein's creature ever knows, yet he rises above this birthright and develops into an intelligent, articulate, and reflective character. In a sense Mary Godwin's novel was an experiment itself, exploring the psychology of the abandoned newborn giant and borrowing principles from John Locke, the eighteenth-century epistemologist whose *Essay Concerning Human Understanding* she was reading as she wrote *Frankenstein*. Locke argued that the human mind begins as a tabula rasa, a blank slate. Knowledge of the outside world forms as sensory impressions bombard the mind and accumulate into ideas and opinions. Starting from this premise, Mary Godwin composed a life story in the voice of Frankenstein's creature.

His first memories were "confused and indistinct," with "dark and opaque bodies" moving around him. Then—as if his coming of age were a biblical genesis—he learned to separate light from dark, day from night; then to eat, drink, and speak. "Sometimes I tried to imitate the pleasant songs of the birds, but was unable," says the monster. "Sometimes I wished to express my sensations in my own mode, but the uncouth and inarticulate sounds which broke from me frightened me into silence again." Finding a "low hovel" in the countryside (which he compares to "the palaces I had beheld in the village"), he hunkers down, "happy to have found a shelter, however miserable, from the inclemency of the season, and still more from the barbarity of man." He discovers a family—an elderly man, a young man, and a young woman—on whom he spies, thereby taking lessons in human behavior. "The gentle manners and beauty of the cottagers greatly endeared them to me," he recounts; "when they were unhappy, I felt depressed; when they rejoiced, I sympathized in their joys." In the cottagers the creature finds models of love and compassion to counterbalance the repulsion into which he was born.

His knowledge grows, thanks to literature—he listens as books are read aloud, then he learns to read on his own. Mary Godwin carefully crafted the reading list for her maturing monster. First he listened to Volney's *Ruins of Empire,* a controversial social history published in Paris in 1791, just as the French Revolution was beginning to boil. Taking a markedly anthropological point of view, Volney blames religion for much of history's discord and suffering. *"It is not God who hath made man after the image of God,"* wrote Volney emphatically, "but man hath made God after the image of man." Any impressionable young mind would learn from Volney that God was a cultural construct, arbitrary and interchangeable—as if the creature's laboratory birth weren't godless enough.

A few other books shape the hypothetical creature's worldview: Plutarch's *Lives* and Goethe's *Sorrows of Young Werther* were two of the "treasures [that] gave me extreme delight," as he puts it, on which he "continually studied and exercised my mind." Plutarch's *Lives of the Noble Greeks and Romans* sings the praises of mythic and historic heroes, from Theseus and Pericles to Caesar and Cicero. Shakespeare's source for *Julius Caesar* and *Antony and Cleopatra*, it was a familiar classic in 1816. Goethe's *Werther,* published in 1774 and an instant sensation throughout Western Europe, is the quintessential Romantic novel, in which unrequited love turns into an obsession and drives the hero to suicide. "I learned from Werter's [*sic*] imaginations despondency and gloom: but Plutarch taught me high thoughts," says the creature. This pair of readings also spans the extremes of human sociability, from men much in the public eye to an introverted loner, and creates a scale against which to gauge the isolation of Frankenstein and his creation. The son of a civic leader, Frankenstein has only one friend, Henry Clerval, who faithfully tends him during one of his bouts of depressive oblivion but is ultimately destroyed by Frankenstein's lonely obsession, dying at the vengeful monster's hand. In contrast the monster naively seeks kinship with all he sees but, rejected over and over, comes to scorn human society.

Of all the monster's early reading, the most influential book—not only to his character but to the novel that he inhabits—is John Milton's *Paradise Lost,* the seventeenth-century epic poem of the temptation and fall from the Garden of Eden. "*Paradise Lost* excited different and far deeper emotions," the creature says, for in its cosmic characters he found his own dilemma described. He identified with Adam, for, like him,

> I was created apparently united by no link to any other being in existence; but his state was far different from mine in every other respect. He had come forth from the hands of God a perfect creature, happy and prosperous, guarded by the especial care of his Creator; he was allowed to converse with, and acquire knowledge from beings of a superior nature: but I was wretched, helpless, and alone.

Likewise he identified with Satan, "for often, like him, when I viewed the bliss of my protectors, the bitter gall of envy rose within me."

The conventional story of Adam and Eve—the one Milton intended to convey—casts Satan as the arch-enemy. As *Paradise Lost* begins he has mustered forces in heaven to overthrow God. His revolt has failed and, to punish him, God has cast him down though the firmament into hell. But Romantic readers put their own slant on the poem. As the poet William Blake put it, Milton was "of the Devil's party without knowing it." In battle intellectual, Milton's Satan speaks ideas central to the Enlightenment, the French and American Revolutions, English radicalism, and Romantic poetry. "At first I thought that liberty and Heaven / To heav'nly souls had been all one," Satan says. Instead "most through sloth had rather serve"—following established rules rather than challenging authority, thinking for themselves, and embracing the risks that come with personal freedom.

In the Romantic reading of *Paradise Lost,* the Garden of Eden is a prison, not a paradise. "Knowledge forbidden?" says Milton's Satan. "Why should their Lord / Envy them that? Can it be sin to know?" When Satan appears to Eve in a dream, the very smell of the forbidden fruit sends her on a galactic journey during which she, like Shelley's Ianthe guided by Queen Mab, sees "the earth outstretched immense, a prospect wide / And various"—the very sort of knowledge God forbids, Satan tells her. Adam imagines that by eating the fruit, they might become "gods or angels, demigods," even though Raphael has advised him to remain "lowly wise" and "dream not of other worlds." After eating the fruit, Adam and Eve glimpse the great divide between possibilities envisioned by the human imagination and realities imposed by God's will. Enlightened, Adam asks questions that cut to the heart of the human condition:

> O fleeting joys
> Of Paradise dear bought with lasting woes!
> Did I request Thee, Maker, from my clay
> To mold me Man? Did I solicit Thee
> From darkness to promote me or here place
> In this delicious garden?

Milton took a risk in portraying an Adam so cheeky as to question the Deity. In the next few lines, Adam retreats, accepts his fate, and settles into his traditional role as the figurehead of original sin: "I submit," Adam tells himself, for "His doom is fair: / That dust I am and shall to dust return." Freethinkers like those gathered at the Villa Diodati would not sympathize. They valued rebellion, not submission. One can imagine Shelley railing as he read these lines. Mary's more subtle tactic was to go back to Adam's brash moment and clip out two lines for the epigraph for her book: "Did I request Thee, Maker, from my clay / To mold me Man?" Lifted out of their Miltonic context and linked to her iconoclastic story, these words make the creature a presumptuous Adam and Frankenstein a dictatorial God. The question stands, rhetorical and unanswered, strikingly modern and existential.

A giant daring to challenge the prevailing god: The emerging character evoked another mythic hero, the classic Greek Prometheus. Hesiod's *Theogony,* from the eighth century B.C., provides the source for his story. Gaia, the Earth, gave birth to, then mated with Uranus, the Sky. Their children are the Titans, or "the Stretchers," Hesiod explains, "for they stretched their power outrageously and accomplished / a monstrous thing, and they would some day be punished for it." Zeus, king of the Olympian gods, is the son of Kronos, one of the Titans. Prometheus, distinguished by his intellect, is the son of another. In Hesiod's epic, Prometheus tricks Zeus into choosing a sacrifice of bones wrapped in fat, leaving for humans fine meat hidden inside organs; then he steals "the far-seen glory of weariless fire, hiding in the hollow fennel" and gives the valuable gift of fire to humans. As punishment Zeus straps Prometheus to a barren rock, above earth yet below heaven, and sends his eagle every night to feed on the Titan's "imperishable liver." Three centuries later Aeschylus turned the myth into a tragedy, portraying Prometheus as a savior who brought not just fire but language, tool making, agriculture, husbandry, navigation, medicine—all the arts and sciences—to humankind. Of Aeschylus's original trilogy of plays, titled *Prometheus Bound, Prometheus the Fire-Bringer,* and *Prometheus Unbound*, only the first survived in its entirety. The vagaries of literary history, in other words, left Aeschylus's Prometheus eternally bound—until Percy Bysshe Shelley, several years after *Frankenstein,* wrote *Prometheus Unbound,* a lyrical drama promising a total renovation of nature and human experience, symbolized by the release of the Titan from the rock.

Prometheus already haunted the minds of Shelley and his friends in 1816. At the Villa Diodati that July, Lord Byron composed a lyric to him. "Titan!" he wrote, "Thy Godlike crime was to be kind, . . . And strengthen Man with his own mind." Defying Olympian power in favor of earthly mortals, Prometheus becomes an intermediary, neither god nor human but "the immortal prototype of man as the original rebel and affirmer of his fate," "an antigod," in the words of the Jungian analyst Carl Kerenyí. Sociobiologist Edward O. Wilson has suggested that the myth expresses an ancient memory of the stage in human evolution when *Homo habilis* gained the tool- and symbol-making capabilities that turned animals into humans. Of course it would be an anachronism to attribute such ideas to anyone in 1816, but those gathered at the Villa Diodati that summer certainly sensed how this myth expressed the human drive to learn and understand, even if it meant overstepping the status quo.

The Promethean fire, the taste of the forbidden fruit: All these meanings intersected in Mary Godwin's characters. She gave her novel a subtitle: *The Modern Prometheus*. The reference describes Frankenstein, who grants the spark of life to a lower being, but it also describes that being, a giant who turns on the figurehead of power. An eerie, psychomagnetic pull connects Frankenstein and his monster. After the creation the two characters live separate lives for four irritating chapters, during which the reader, along with Frankenstein, almost forgets the creature. Domestic life beckons—a newsy letter from Elizabeth, then a tragic letter from his father. Godwin, a teenage mother, projected her own anxieties as she plotted her novel. Her character's younger brother—named William, the same as her not-yet-year-old son—is found "livid and motionless," with "the print of the murderer's finger" on his neck. All signs point to his trusted nursemaid, Justine, as the murderer: His locket is found in her apron, and she has no explanation why.

Rushing home, Frankenstein recognizes the true identity of the murderer in a flash of lightning, literally. Language and imagery make it a moment of internal revelation as much as a silhouette perceived in the landscape:

> A flash of lightning illuminated the object, and discovered its shape plainly to me; its gigantic stature, and the deformity of its aspect, more hideous than belongs to humanity, instantly informed me that it was the wretch, the filthy daemon to whom I had given life. . . . Nothing in human shape could have destroyed that fair child. *He* was the murderer! I could not doubt it. The mere presence of the idea was an irresistible proof of the fact.

To see him is to know him; to know him is to understand, to be repulsed, and to be terrified. Despite his precognition Frankenstein does not stop the trial and execution of the innocent Justine and thus entwines his own moral condition with that of his monster's all the more intimately.

Soon Frankenstein and the monster come face-to-face, and the intricate strands of mingled identity weave together even more tightly. They meet on the glaciers of Mont Blanc, in icy reaches so barren and remote that they seemed as if "belonging to another earth, the habitations of another race of beings." Venturing alone, Victor Frankenstein now confronts his creation, "the figure of a man" moving "with superhuman speed," surefooted amid the frozen crevices. "I was troubled: a mist came over my eyes, and I felt a faintness seize me," says Frankenstein, but then he looks straight at the other, whose face combines "bitter anguish" with "disdain and malignity." The first word out of Frankenstein's

The glacial heights on which Frankenstein heard his monster tell his tale were bleak, icy, lifeless, and nearly impassable, as this 1823 engraving of the source of the Arve River portrays.

mouth is "Devil!" Next he calls the creature "vile insect" and accuses him of having "diabolically murdered" William.

The monster speaks. At the heart of her novel, Mary Godwin brings the monster center stage, granting him eloquent speeches in which he tells his creator all that has happened to him, including how, when he finally dared to approach his cottage providers, the younger man reacted with horror and violence. "I could have torn him limb from limb, as the lion rends the antelope," the creature tells Frankenstein. "But my heart sunk [sic] within me as with bitter sickness, and I refrained." In fear the family fled the cottage, leaving the creature in solitude and isolation again. For the first time he felt "rage and revenge." He burned the cottage, destroyed the garden, and thus performed his first monstrous act against society. It was, the monster understands, his own fall from innocence. "Remember, that I am thy creature," the being states adeptly to his maker. "I ought to be thy Adam; but I am rather the fallen angel. . . . I was benevolent and good; misery made me a fiend." It is a complicated accusation, full of ambiguities. The analogy to *Paradise Lost* goes two ways. With Victor Frankenstein playing God, his monster could be either Adam or Satan.

Creature and creator, Adam and his maker, Satan up against God: monster and Frankenstein. In the relationship at the center of her novel, Mary Godwin captured an elusive and powerful psychology, self and shadow, described by psychologist Carl Jung more than a century later. According to Jung, the human mind projects universal yet often unrecognized psychic contents, or archetypes, as embodiments and personifications, out of which mythic characters and stories form. One of those archetypes is the shadow. "Everyone carries a shadow," he said in a lecture on psychology and religion, "and the less it is embodied in the individual's conscious life, the blacker and denser it is." The shadow is the converse of man's ideal picture of himself—it is an image of the actual, the primitive, the uncivilized, the less than perfected part of a personality, "consisting not just of little weaknesses and foibles, but of a positively demonic dynamism." It is a remarkable force within the personality, and it must be embraced, not denied or suppressed; otherwise, says Jung, "there emerges a raging monster." In harmony with E. O. Wilson's interpretation of Prometheus, Jung identifies the shadow as the primeval part of the psyche, "the invisible saurian tail that man still drags behind him." The shadow is most likely to emerge in the absence of a ruling god, when a society or an individual turns from conventional religion. The shadow is overwhelming in its power, all the more so when unacknowledged. It is, paradoxically, intimately interior and yet totally other—another way in which the archetype of the shadow, defined by Jung long after the publication of Shelley's novel, still helps explain the power of the mysterious monster character Mary Godwin created.

DEATH, MARRIAGE, BIRTH

Not long after she began composing her story, Mary Godwin embarked with Claire Clairmont and Percy Bysshe Shelley on an excursion into the Alps above Geneva, to explore the glaciers firsthand. Baby William stayed behind with his nursemaid. They traveled as tourists, visiting a different location each day, then returning each night to a comfortable inn. On Monday, July 22, they rode mules up the Arve River, passing through waterfall mist and crossing rickety bridges above the tumbling river, up to glaciers that looked to Mary like "a foaming cataract" at a distance, "pyramids & stalactites" up close. They crested one ridge and looked across to the glacier of Montanvert, the very place where she would locate the encounter between Frankenstein and his monster. Within earshot, a thunderous avalanche tore away part of the mountain they were climbing. They spent that night at the Hôtel de Londres in Chamonix, the village at the foot of Mont Blanc. "I never knew I never imagined what mountains were before," Percy Shelley wrote a friend. "The immensity of these aerial summits excited, when they suddenly burst upon the sight, a sentiment of extatic [*sic*] wonder, not unallied to madness."

Chamonix and Mont Blanc were popular, though demanding, tourist destinations in those days, yet Shelley's travel aspirations were overambitious. He wanted to follow the river Arve back to its source, to climb up to the most desolate ice-covered realms he could find. "The trees in many places have been torn away by avelanches [*sic*] and some half leaning over others intermingled with stones present the appearance of vast & dreadful desolation," Mary wrote in her journal. Torrential rains slickened their path. Shelley tripped—a *mauvais pas* (bad step), he called it, "so that I narrowly escaped being precipitated down the mountain." He fainted and lay for a time unconscious, terrifying Claire and Mary.

On June 25 the three did make their way up the Mer de Glace, the primary glacier coming down Mont Blanc toward Chamonix. "Iced mountains surround it—no sign of vegetation appears except on the place from which [we] view the scene—we went on the ice," wrote Mary in her journal. Shelley's imagination personified the massive mountain. "In these regions every thing changes & is in motion," he wrote Peacock. "One would think that Mont Blanc was a living being & that the frozen blood forever circulated slowly thro' his stony veins." From these visions Shelley composed "Mont Blanc," one of his greatest poems. "Some say that gleams of a remoter world / Visit the soul in sleep," it read. The physical details of this landscape and the fear and awe it evoked bombarded Mary's consciousness. Her imagination made connections between these vistas and her own sleep-divined gleam of a tale. "We arrived wet to the skin," she wrote in her journal. "I read nouvelle nouvelles and write my story."

By late July all involved knew that Claire was pregnant. All knew who was the father, yet Byron considered it none of his responsibility. Shelley wrote his lawyer to change his will and include financial provisions for Claire and her offspring. He tried to persuade Byron, who now found Claire repulsive, to agree to care for the child—a tragically misguided plan, as it turned out. Claire tried to ingratiate herself by copying over Byron's new canto of *Childe Harold's Pilgrimage,* now ready to publish, but the poet still refused to see her. John Polidori drank too much, acted

up, and raised the ire of Geneva authorities, who came out looking for him. Rumors ran rampant in Geneva that the little clan of
English were leading "*une vie du libertinage le plus effronté* [a life of
unbridled libertinism]," as Shelley later wrote a friend. "They said
that we had formed a pact to outrage all that is regarded as most
sacred in human society," he recalled. "Atheism, incest, and many
other things—sometimes ridiculous and sometimes terrible
were imputed to us. . . . The inhabitants on the banks of the lake
opposite Lord Byron's house used telescopes to spy upon his
movements." The scene was so shocking, rumor mongers
claimed, that one woman fainted at the sight.

Mounting scandals, manuscript to be delivered, legal matters
pending, a shortage of money, Claire's growing belly—it was
time to leave Geneva. The traveling party, including the Swiss
nursemaid, arrived in Portsmouth on September 8. Shelley proceeded to London, but the plan was to settle in Bath, in part to
keep Claire's pregnancy a secret from the Godwins. Mary and
Percy took separate quarters from Claire, whose child was due
around the first of the year. But as she worked on her novel
through fall and into winter, melodrama turned to tragedy and
scandal paled in importance.

First there was the death of Fanny Imlay. The daughter of Mary
Wollstonecraft, therefore Mary Godwin's older half sister, Fanny
had always been the darkest of the three girls in the Godwin
household. Born out of wedlock, she never knew her father, and
her mother had died, giving birth to Mary, when Fanny was only
three. Although they spent little time together, to Mary she was
an older sister. To William Godwin and his second wife she was a
burden, even though she had dutifully remained at home while
their other two daughters gallivanted off to the Continent. Ever
since Mary and Claire had returned to England, Fanny had been

planning to visit them. Yet on October 9, alone in Swansea, Wales, Fanny Imlay overdosed on laudanum. She left a note behind: "I have long determined that the best thing I could do was to put an end to the existance [*sic*] of a being whose birth was unfortunate."

Shelley put more effort than Godwin into investigating the particulars of Fanny's suicide, but little information surfaced. Her death reverberated in a muffled way through the lives of all who knew her. Godwin insisted on silence and secrecy. No one in the family saw to her burial. Godwin's wife chose to shield their son, age thirteen, from the gruesome knowledge and did not inform him of Fanny's suicide for months. It threw a pall on the households of both Claire and Mary, who could mourn her only privately.

Writing and reading offered constant solace in Mary's life, as these brief journal entries from November 1816 display:

WEDNESDAY 20TH
Draw and write. read Locke and Curt.—begin Pamela. Shelley reads Locke and in the evening Paradise Lost aloud to me.

THURSDAY 21ST
Drawing Lesson. write. read Locke & walk out—After dinner read Curt.—after Tea S. reads Paradise Lost aloud—Read Pamela—Little Babe not well—S. reads Locke & Pamela.

FRIDAY 22ND
Draw—Read Locke and write—walk—after dinner read Curt. S. reads Locke & Curt—& finished Paradise Lost—reads Pamela aloud

John Locke and his *Essay on Human Understanding*; the Roman historian Quintus Curtius Rufus, known for his life of Alexander the Great; Samuel Richardson's *Pamela,* an English novel designed as a series of letters—each work colored Mary Godwin's writing. Locke offered a model for mental development; Curtius, the classic heroic tale; Richardson, a structure for her novel. Percy and Mary's daily life settled into something of a normal routine, despite a pervading sadness. Claire's needs grew as her pregnancy approached full term. Byron, in Italy, totally ignored her, and Shelley felt obliged to fill the paternal gap. Harriet Shelley's demands on her husband had fallen quiet, but William Godwin's hadn't, and Shelley was preoccupied with raising money for him. Sometimes Shelley went away for days, to London for business or to Marlow, up the Thames, to visit his friend Thomas Love Peacock. Shelley started talking about moving to Marlow. "Sweet Elf," Mary wrote him in early December, "give me a garden & *absentia Clariae* [the absence of Claire] and I will thank my love for many favours." She had finished a fourth chapter of *Frankenstein,* she informed him, "which is a very long one & I think you would like it."

On December 10 a woman's body was found floating in the Serpentine, Hyde Park's lake. It was rumored that she was pregnant. On December 16 Shelley received a letter from his solicitor, Thomas Hookham, in whom he had entrusted the care of Harriet and his two children. Hookham had lost sight of them, the letter began. "While I was yet endeavouring to discover Mrs. Shelley's address," he explained, "information was brought to me that she was dead—that she had destroyed herself." Harriet Shelley had thrown herself into the Serpentine; whether, and by whom, she was pregnant, we will never know. She left behind a letter to her sister, which included a message to "my dear Bysshe": "If you had never left me I might have lived, but as it is I freely forgive you & may you enjoy that happiness which you have deprived me of."

Harriet Shelley's suicide changed everything. Mary Godwin

and Percy Bysshe Shelley married on December 30, two weeks after receiving the news. Mary's father and stepmother were heartened. Shelley assumed that his two children would become siblings to little Willmouse. Add in Claire and her child, too, and he was likely envisioning a household of four children, two women, and himself as an unlikely paterfamilias.

No such arrangements evolved. Considering Shelley immoral and unreliable, Harriet's family refused to put either child into his care. John Westbrook, Harriet's father, presented the Court of Chancery with correspondence to prove that Shelley neglected his wife and children and claimed that *Queen Mab* and other writings demonstrated sacrilege and sedition. As Shelley wrote to Byron, the Westbrooks intended to "deprive me of my unfortunate children, now more than ever dear to me; of my inheritance, and to throw me into prison, and expose me in the pillory, on the ground my being a REVOLUTIONIST, and an *Atheist*." The suit dragged on into the spring of 1817, when the Lord Chancellor denied Shelley custody of his children. He never saw Ianthe or Charles again.

On January 12, 1817, Claire Clairmont's daughter was born. They called her Alba, but in the long run she was given the name Allegra, "joyous"—Byron's choice and, given the arc of the little girl's life, tragically inappropriate. Allegra would stay with her mother for only two years, after which she was delivered to Byron, who soon ensconced her, at the age of four, in an Italian convent. Just two years later, Clara Allegra Clairmont died of typhus.

No sense of this dark future clouded Claire's pride in her newborn, of course. Shelley found a roomy house in Marlow, close to his friend Peacock's, and by the middle of March, a household of six—the three Shelleys, Claire and Allegra, and the Swiss nursemaid, Elise—had moved into Albion House, as their new home was called. In many ways, the situation was idyllic: a long-term lease on an ample country house, near river and woods yet not too far from London.

Buoyed by the pleasures of a stable home, progress on her novel, and spring in the air, Mary invited houseguests. "All your fears and sorrows shall fly when you behold the blue skies & bright sun of Marlow," she wrote Marianne Hunt, whose husband, Leigh, had just published Shelley's poem, "Hymn to Intellectual Beauty," in his journal, *The Examiner*. It was a milestone: the first of Shelley's writing to be published by anyone other than himself. "Come then, dear, good creatures," Mary Shelley wrote the Hunts, "and let us enjoy with you the beauty of the Marlow sun and the pleasant walks that will give you all health spirits & *industry*." The Hunts accepted the invitation and soon arrived, more than doubling the household's numbers, for with them came Marianne's sister and the Hunts' four notoriously unruly children. Two men, five women, six children, one nursemaid— it was a houseful. Marianne Hunt was pregnant, and Mary Shelley was sensing the same signs in her own body. She would have missed her third menstrual period in March; by April her condition was visible to others. A daughter, Clara Everina, would be born at the end of the summer.

At Albion House both Shelleys worked successfully at their writing. Percy was writing a lengthy poem titled *Laon and Cythna* after its main characters, a brother and sister, lovers and leaders of a political revolution in Constantinople. It was ultimately published as *The Revolt of Islam*. Mary was finishing *Frankenstein*. Surrounded by women and children, aware of another growing inside her, it is remarkable how masculine a novel Mary Shelley created. Some read the novel as a story of male birth; some see in it deep-seated fears of pregnancy, childbirth, child death, and the life-sustaining obligations of motherhood. Certainly the women in the novel do not fare well, becoming victims of rage and tools of revenge.

The two primary female characters, Victor Frankenstein's mother and his cousin, Elizabeth, are introduced as cameos of beauty and virtue. They merge in the dream that haunts him right after his creature's yellow eyes open:

> I thought I saw Elizabeth, in the bloom of health, walking in the streets of Ingolstadt. Delighted and surprised, I embraced her; but as I imprinted the first kiss on her lips, they became livid with the hue of death; her features appeared to change, and I thought that I held the corpse of my dead mother in my arms; a shroud enveloped her form, and I saw the grave-worms crawling in the folds of the flannel.

From out of this dream Frankenstein wakes with a start to see his creature, backlit by the moon, peering in on him in bed. It is as if the two visions—grave-worm dream of the women he loves and creature's existence—are one and the same. The monster's existence demands a female counterpart. During their encounter on the glacier, the creature pleads for a mate, promising that a companion will quell his rage. To do this work, Frankenstein travels to a farflung edge of civilization, the northern islands off Scotland. Just short of the moment of animation, though, he faces the horror of what he is doing. "She might become ten thousand times more malignant than her mate," he thinks, or, even worse, "one of the first results of those sympathies for which the daemon thirsted would be children, and a race of devils would be propagated upon the earth." The modern Prometheus would thus have created a modern Pandora. Victor Frankenstein dashes the female body to pieces. An eye for an eye, a tooth for a tooth, a mate for a mate: Seeing what has happened, the creature speaks his dire oath: "I shall be with you on your wedding-night." He follows Victor and Elizabeth to their honeymoon getaway—Evian, in sight of Mont Blanc and the Jura—and finds the moment when a nervous Frankenstein leaves his bride alone in her room.

> Suddenly I heard a shrill and dreadful scream. It came from the room into which Elizabeth had retired. As I heard it, the whole truth rushed into my mind, my arms dropped, the motion of every muscle and fibre was suspended; I could feel the blood trickling in my veins, and tingling in the extremities of my limbs. This state lasted but for an instant; the scream was repeated, and I rushed into the room.
>
> Great God! why did I not then expire!

Frankenstein rushes in to find Elizabeth, cousin and bride, "the purest creature of earth," lying "lifeless and inanimate, thrown across the bed, her head hanging down, and her pale and distorted features half covered by her hair." Having turned once again from the shadowy monster, Frankenstein meets it again in the form of violence against that which he most loves. It is a turning point in the novel, the end of Frankenstein's participation in human society. It is an iconic moment as the myth is retold, over and over, in years to come: a beautiful woman, flung lifeless across the bed, the innocent victim of manmade monstrosity.

MAGNETIC PULL

In composing her novel, Mary Shelley worked from the inside out. She began with the vision, the "phantasm of a man stretched out," and spun a complex fiction around it. Her novel has been compared to a Russian nesting doll, one story fitting inside another.

Polar expeditions of the sort led by Capt. Robert Walton in *Frankenstein* were ongoing during the decade of the novel's composition and after, as suggested by this illustration for a book on later nineteenth-century Arctic discoveries.

We learn the monster's life story when he tells it to Frankenstein on the glacier; we learn Frankenstein's life story as he tells it to another character, Robert Walton, an Arctic seafarer whose letters to his sister frame the novel in the epistolary structure exemplified by Richardson's *Pamela* and other novels of the time.

On a scientific expedition to learn more about the earth's magnetic force, Walton has hired a ship and crew to sail to the north pole. His quest would sound familiar to Mary Shelley's readers. The first serious polar expedition sailed northward in 1773 on a mission, wrote one of its crew members, "to seek new adventures, and to find, towards the North Pole, what our Creator never intended we should, a passage to India." That mission encountered a wall of ice and turned back, but other expeditions continued into the middle of the next century. As Mary Shelley was completing *Frankenstein,* in fact, English whaler and explorer William Scoresby, Jr., was sailing north, collecting information that would appear in his 1821 *Account of the Arctic Regions.*

Walton's early letters clearly establish his polar expedition as a quest as ambitious and obsessive as that of Victor Frankenstein. "I may there discover the wondrous power which attracts the needle," writes Walton on the novel's first page, "and may regulate a thousand celestial observations, that require only this voyage to render their seeming eccentricities consistent for ever." Walton's first reported observations, however, turn out to be the monster and, soon thereafter, Frankenstein.

Summer is ending, and the ice is closing in on his ship. He and his crew gaze out on the blindingly white scene:

> We perceived a low carriage, fixed on a sledge and drawn by dogs, pass on towards the north, at the distance of half a mile: a being which had the shape of a man, but apparently of gigantic stature, sat in the sledge, and guided the dogs. We watched the rapid progress of the traveller with our telescopes, until he was lost among the distant inequalities of the ice.

The next morning another being floats up to the ship on chunk of ice—"not, as the other traveller seemed to be, a savage inhabitant of some undiscovered island, but an European." Walton and the crew nurse him back to consciousness, and soon sympathetic harmonies bring the two men closer. "You seek for knowledge and wisdom, as I once did," says the revived drifter, "and I ardently hope that the gratification of your wishes may not be a serpent to sting you, as mine has been. . . . If you are inclined, listen to my tale." With that, the reader, through Robert Walton, listens to the story told by Victor Frankenstein.

By framing her novel with Walton's Arctic voyage, Shelley staged another round in the debate between the two modes of conduct pitted against each other throughout the novel: self-limiting prudence vs. experimentation and risk. The novel returns to the Arctic scene at its conclusion. Tired of being icebound and fearful for their lives, Walton's crew demands that he give up the expedition and head home. "Are you then so easily turned from your design? Did you not call this a glorious expedition?" Frankenstein himself exhorts them. "Oh! be men, or be more than men. Be steady to your purposes and firm as a rock." The crew is not swayed. The ice begins to crack, a westerly breeze picks up, and Walton relents, turning the ship toward home. Frankenstein does not sympathize. "You may give up your purpose; but mine is assigned to me by heaven," he says. He must end what he has begun. "Farewell, Walton! Seek happiness in tranquillity, and avoid ambition, even if it be the only apparently innocent one of distinguishing yourself in science and discoveries. Yet why do I say this? I have myself been blasted in these hopes, yet another may succeed." With those words, utterly self-contradictory and inconclusive, Frankenstein dies—but the novel's conversation continues. "The tale which I have recorded would be incomplete without this final and wonderful catastrophe," writes Walton. The monster will have the last word.

He boards the ship and, unseen by the crew, approaches his maker. Walton finds him, leaning over "the lifeless form of his creator," lamenting aloud that he "irretrievably destroyed thee [i.e., Frankenstein] by destroying all thou lovedst." The author offers one more look at him: a figure "gigantic in stature, yet uncouth and distorted in its proportions," his face "concealed by long locks of ragged hair," his hand "in colour and apparent texture like that of a mummy." Speaking to Walton, he meditates on his existence. *Paradise Lost* remains central to his moral universe. "The fallen angel becomes a malignant devil. Yet even that enemy of God and man had friends and associates in his desolation; I am quite alone." He restates a radical thesis of the novel, that society made a monster of him: "Am I to be thought the only criminal, when all human kind sinned against me?" And then, reports Walton, "He sprung from the cabin-window, as he said this, upon the ice-raft which lay close to the vessel. He was soon borne away by the waves, and lost in darkness and distance."

With those words Mary Shelley closed her novel. Barely a conclusion, it invites endless speculation. Victor Frankenstein dies, but what of his monster, disappearing eternally into the "darkness and distance" and also looming out there forever, ready to reappear? Hundreds have started where Mary Shelley left off, completing, embellishing, or revising the story—but she was satisfied to leave her monster in a limbo of the imagination, like the dreamland from which he came.

LIVE BIRTH

As her plot moved on toward its bleak ending, a child was growing inside the body of Mary Shelley—an oddly insistent counterpoint to the scenes of despair and destruction she was creating on the written page. The manuscripts of *Frankenstein* show how intimately the Shelleys collaborated on the novel, with an underlying layer of words written in Mary Shelley's large, angular handwriting, touched up in both hers and the slightly more crabbed script of Percy Bysshe Shelley. "I give you carte blanche to make what alterations you please," she wrote him during the final days of proofing. Each reader crossed out, added, rearranged words, neither in a way distinct from the other, as if the two editors worked as one. Then the author set about to transcribe the edited version, spending days on end creating a fair copy that could be submitted for publication. In May, Percy Bysshe took over, copying out the last dozen pages. If we believe Mary's report from fifteen years later, a short preface for the novel "was entirely written by him" yet in the voice of the novelist, begging the reader's indulgence for the fantastical tale. It ends by recalling the circumstances that brought the Frankenstein story into being. Here ghost story competitors number only three:

> The season was cold and rainy, and in the evenings we crowded around a blazing wood fire, and occasionally amused ourselves with some German stories of ghosts, which happened to fall into our hands. These tales excited in us a playful desire of imitation. Two other friends . . . and myself agreed to write each a story, founded on some supernatural occurrence.
>
> The weather, however, suddenly became serene; and my two friends left me on a journey among the Alps, and lost, in the magnificent scenes which they present, all memory of their ghostly visions. The following tale is the only one which has been completed.

With manuscript in hand, Percy Bysshe Shelley went to London to act as literary agent for his wife. It went first to John Murray—Byron's editor and a "courtly publisher" in Mary's eyes—but *Frankenstein* did not interest him. Then Shelley took it to Charles Ollier, a bookseller he had just met through Leigh Hunt. Ollier took only two days to refuse the novel. "I hope Frankenstein did not give you bad dreams," Shelley wrote him, likely hoping that he had not spoiled his own prospects with Ollier. Finally a publisher showed some interest: Lackington & Allen, "Cheapest Bookseller in the World," as their motto read, etched in stone over the doorway of their London headquarters in Finsbury Square. Lackington & Allen specialized in books on magic and the occult: Their list included Francis Barrett's *The Magus; or Celestial Intelligences; a Complete System of Occult Philosophy*; Joseph Taylor's *Apparitions; or, the Mystery of Ghosts, Hobgoblins, and Haunted Houses*; and, oddly enough, the new English translation of *Fantasmagoriana,* the ghost stories that had started it all two summers before.

As they prepared the book for print, editors corresponded with Percy Bysshe Shelley, who now revealed himself as an agent, not the author. "I ought to have mentioned that the novel which I sent you is not my own production," he wrote, "but that of a friend who not being at present in England cannot make the correction you suggest." He kept it secret that the author was young, female, and very much pregnant. He assured them that he would read the proofs and proposed that the publishers split net profits equally with the author. In the end Lackington agreed to a royalty of one-third of net profits on a first printing of five hundred copies. But within days another momentous event took all Mary's attention. "I am confined teusday [*sic*] 2nd," she wrote one morning in her journal. Later that day, September 2, 1817, she gave birth to Clara Everina.

While Mary Shelley tended her human creation, her husband midwifed her literary progeny. "On Monday, Dec. 29, 1817, will be published, in 3 vols., dedicated to William Goodwin [*sic*], a Work of Imagination, to be entitled, Frankenstein, or the Modern Prometheus," read a notice on the front page of London's weekly *Observer* on December 28, 1817. Several such announcements appeared in British papers over the next few weeks. *Frankenstein* sold for 16 shillings 6 pence, on the low side compared to other books of the time. Percy Bysshe Shelley ordered

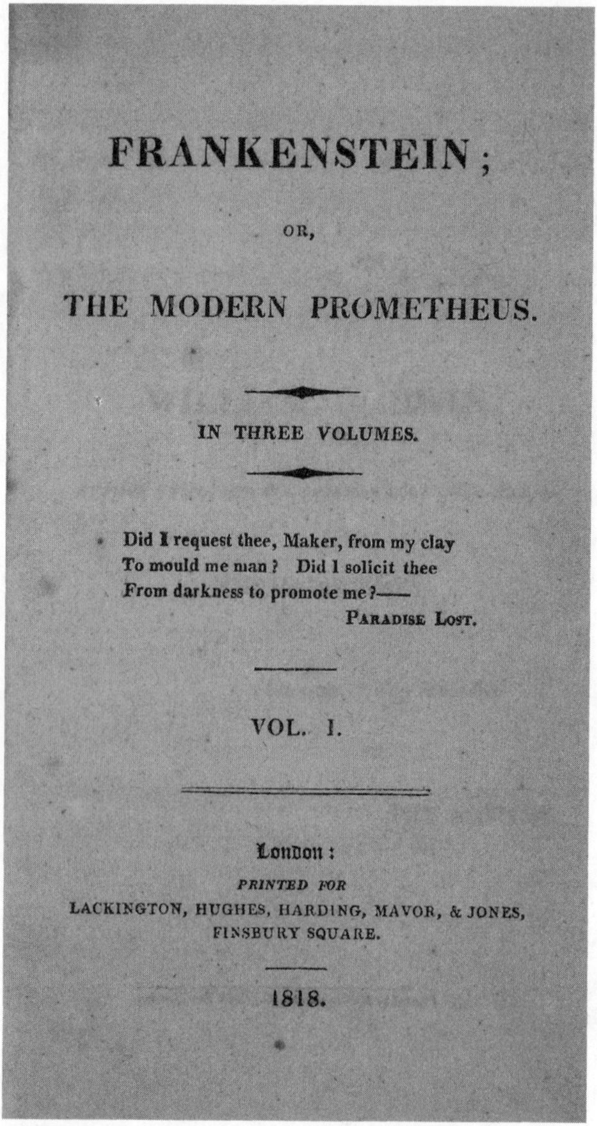

FRANKENSTEIN;

OR,

THE MODERN PROMETHEUS.

———

IN THREE VOLUMES.

———

Did I request thee, Maker, from my clay
To mould me man ?   Did I solicit thee
From darkness to promote me?——
PARADISE LOST.

———

VOL. I.

———

London :

PRINTED FOR
LACKINGTON, HUGHES, HARDING, MAVOR, & JONES,
FINSBURY SQUARE.

———

1818.

It took nine months for Mary Shelley to write her novel and nine months for it to come out in print in early 1818. For several reasons it was published anonymously.

extra copies to send to friends and people of literary influence. "The Author has requested me to send you, as a slight tribute of high admiration & respect, the accompanying volumes," he wrote, sending an early copy to Sir Walter Scott.

On New Year's Eve, 1817, Mary Shelley noted in her journal: "Fran^tein comes."

CHAPTER THREE

RECEPTION AND REVISION

Though you seek to bury me, yet will you continuously
resurrect me! Once I am unbound, I am unbounded!
—BRIAN W. ALDISS, *Frankenstein Unbound*, 1973

The story, doubtless, is familiar enough, and does not need
recounting. Its effectiveness as a thriller lies more
in the idea than in the narrative.
—*NEW YORK POST* film review, 1931

"This Tale is evidently the production of no ordinary Writer," wrote a critic in the April 1818 issue of *Gentleman's Magazine.* "Though we are shocked at the idea of the event on which the fiction is founded, many parts of it are strikingly good." Others responded more harshly. "Waking dreams of horror" in "three spirit-wearing volumes," wrote one; "an uncouth story . . . leading to no conclusion either moral or philosophical," another; "a tissue of horrible and disgusting absurdity," declared a third. The *Quarterly Review* critic quoted three passages at length—the creation scene and Frankenstein's grave-worm dream; the glacial meeting of creature and creator; and the last scene, with monster mourning Frankenstein—all of which the critic declared "nonsense decked out with circumstances and clothed in language highly terrific." The novel serves no social purpose and "inculcates no lesson of conduct, manners, or morality." The critic wondered "whether the head or the heart of the author be the most diseased."

The most positive of all reviews appeared in *Blackwood's Edinburgh Magazine,* its author later revealed as Sir Walter Scott. Scott called it an "extraordinary tale" revealing "uncommon powers of poetic imagination" and congratulated its author for evoking a supernatural event not for its own sake but to explore human nature. Other novelists of the time did not greet the novel so warmly. William Beckford, whose *Vathek* scholars consider a Gothic classic, wrote the following into his copy of *Frankenstein*: "This is, perhaps, the foulest Toadstool that has yet sprung up from the reeking dunghill of the present times."

The absence of a clear moral message troubled many critics. "This is a very *bold* fiction," wrote a columnist in *Bell's Court and Fashionable Magazine.* "Did not the author, in a short Preface, make a kind of apology, we should almost pronounce it to be *impious*." The reviewer filled the troubling void with his own interpretation: "We hope, however, the writer had the moral in view which we are desirous of drawing from it, that the *presumptive* works of man must be frightful, vile, and horrible; ending only in discomfort and misery to himself."

No author's name appeared on the title page of the first edition of *Frankenstein,* a rather common occurrence in those days, but one that nevertheless invited guessing and gossip. The book was dedicated to William Godwin, a clue to its authorship. Scott drew from that fact the idea that *Frankenstein* had been written by Percy Bysshe Shelley, and one anonymous critic hinted that "we have some idea that it is the production of a daughter of a celebrated living novelist." Somehow a writer for the *British Critic*

learned that the author was female, which for him made the
novel's moral vacuum all the more reprehensible. "If our
authoress can forget the gentleness of her sex, it is no reason why
we should," he harrumphed, "and we shall therefore dismiss the
novel without further comment."

UPROOTED

Mary Shelley had no time to brood over the reviews of *Frankenstein,* for by the time the book was published, her Marlow household was disbanding. It had been for Mary a sweet respite of
domestic tranquillity, but that was not the life her husband was
destined to lead. Prone to respiratory ailments, he was adamant
that he needed to abandon England for sunnier climes. He suffered from severe ophthalmia—eye inflammation—through the
winter and felt his entire energy sag. "It is not health but life that
I should seek in Italy," he rationalized to his father-in-law in
December 1817, "for the sake of those to whom my life may be
a source of happiness utility security & honour." Publishing obligations fulfilled and the chancery suit over Harriet's children,
Ianthe and Charles, concluded, on March 12, 1818, the Shelley
retinue departed for Italy. A full household—Mary, Percy, and
their two children; Claire and Allegra; Elise and Milly, two
nursemaids—crossed the Channel and traveled south through
France to Italy. Soon after they reached Milan, a messenger
arrived from Venice, sent by Byron to fetch Allegra, according to
prior arrangements. From Milan the Shelleys kept on moving.
Livorno, Bagni di Lucca, Este, Venice, Bologna, Rome, Naples,
Florence, Pisa—they rarely stayed anyplace long enough to make
it a home. Percy Bysshe Shelley wrote more prolifically than ever
in Italy, completing his finest poems, including *Prometheus
Unbound.* Mary read, copied, and commented on his work but

wrote little save letters. Friends in England kept her current on the success of *Frankenstein* in London. "It seems to be universally known and read," Thomas Love Peacock wrote in August. Even the most damning reviews, he believed, "on the whole have done it service." The Lackington & Hughes first printing sold out, and of the £208 net profit, Mary Shelley received nearly £70—around £3,000 today, not a lot, but more than her husband would ever earn with his writing.

Seeking a respite from the summer heat, Shelley rented a cottage in Bagni di Lucca, a Tuscan spa town in the Appenines, higher and cooler than Florence or Pisa. Clara Everina approached her first birthday. William, two and a half, was babbling English, French, and Italian. They began receiving worried letters from Elise, the nursemaid sent to Venice with Allegra, and a quick decision was made for Claire to travel the two hundred miles to be sure her daughter was all right. "Shelley and Clare are gone (they went today) to Venise [*sic*] on important business and I am left to take care of the house," wrote Mary on August 17. A week later Shelley wrote, urging Mary to join him. She packed up their home and their two small children. En route Clara developed dysentery and a fever. She died in Este, partway to Venice, on September 24, 1818.

Numbly, the Shelleys continued to travel, then returned to Rome in the spring, by which time Mary recognized she was pregnant again. The first symptoms of serious illness arose in three-year-old William in late May. Two weeks later he died, stricken by malaria. "We went from England comparatively prosperous & happy—I should return broken hearted & miserable," Mary Shelley wrote Marianne Hunt a few weeks later. "May you my dear Marianne never know what it is to loose [*sic*] two only & lovely children in one year." It must have been bitter consolation for Mary Shelley to feel the new child begin to move inside her. Death and birth were so closely connected for her: Her own birth had meant the death of her mother. All three of the children to whom she had given birth had died. To hold hope in giving new life seemed futile. Nevertheless, on November 12, 1819, Percy Florence Shelley was born, the only one of Mary Shelley's children to live to adulthood.

And still the sorrows were not over. Percy and Mary had done their best to keep watch over Allegra, shocked at Byron's dictatorial disregard. In April 1822 they received the sad news that she had died. By then Percy, Mary, and their toddler son were living in a dark, musty house in the little town of Lerici, on the Gulf of Spezzia in northwestern Italy. The marriage was foundering. Mary suffered a miscarriage that almost killed her, saved only when Percy plunged her into a tub full of ice. He was generally distracted, too, haunted by a fear of his own death. In early August he and a friend set sail down the coast, intending to be gone overnight. Five days later word came to Mary: Two drowned men's bodies had washed ashore some twenty miles south. Friends, including Byron, cremated Shelley's remains on the beach there.

Tragedy upon tragedy deluged Mary Wollstonecraft Godwin Shelley, while in London her creation was gaining steam. The book sold out, but Lackington & Hughes did not reprint it. It might have faded into history, the name of its author never known, had not, as a journalist put it in 1824, "The Vampyre made considerable noise on its appearance."

The April 1819 issue of the *New Monthly Magazine* included a story of a young man who befriends a mysterious nobleman and then discovers him to be a vampire. It was announced as "The Vampyre: A Tale by Lord Byron." As publisher Henry Colburn well knew, anything labeled "Byron" would sell. He prefaced the story in the magazine with an editor's note, identifying a Russian countess as the owner of three manuscripts given to her by John William Polidori, ghost stories by "Lord B., the physician, and Miss M. W. Godwin." A London bookseller snatched up the vampire story and printed it as a book by Byron as well.

Instantly both Polidori and Byron were up in arms, Polidori claiming authorship and Byron denying it. Polidori, now studying law, wrote angry letters to the magazine and the bookseller, demanding payment and the right to revise. Byron was in Venice, but his publisher railed on his behalf. The book publisher created a new title page, author anonymous, and kept *The Vampyre* in print. Four more English editions came out in a matter of months; translations were printed in French, Italian, German, Swedish, and Spanish. Stage versions started springing up in the United States, France, and Germany.

As he published *The Vampyre,* Colburn also reported possession of an outline "of Miss Godwin" which "has already appeared under the title of 'Frankenstein, or the modern Prometheus.'" That comment cleared up any uncertainty as to the novel's authorship, so that when a pamphleteer parodied Byron that summer, he wrote of the poet's escapades with a "Vampyre crew / Who hate the virtues and the form of man, / And strive to bring fresh monsters in view." Among those monsters, he cited "the wretch abhorred" by the name of Frankenstein. The mistake of calling the unnamed creature by its creator's name therefore goes all the way back to 1819, just a year after the book's original publication. No matter that the book was out of print

Theatre Royal, English Opera House, Strand.

This Evening, FRIDAY, July 20th, 1827,

Will be presented (*First Time this Season*) the Comick Opera of

LOVE IN A VILLAGE.

Sir William Meadows, Mr. CHAPMAN,
Justice Woodcock, Mr. BARTLEY,
Young Meadows, Mr. PEARMAN,
Hawthorn, Mr. THORNE,   Eustace, Mr. J. BLAND,
Hodge, Mr. KEELEY.

Rosetta, by a YOUNG LADY,
(*Her First Appearance on any Stage.*)

Deborah Woodcock, Mrs. WESTON,   Lucinda, Miss HAMILTON,
Madge, Miss KELLY.

In Act I. the STATUTE FAIR and RUSTICK DANCE.

Footman, Mr. IRWIN,   Carter, Mr. LODGE,   Cook, Mr. MINTON,
Housemaid, Miss GOULD,   Country Girl, Miss PHILLIPS,

In Act III. Dr. Boyce's celebrated Duet of "*TOGETHER LET US RANGE THE FIELDS*,"
By Mr. PEARMAN and the YOUNG LADY who will perform Rosetta.

After which (*Third Time this Season*) a Romance of a peculiar interest, entitled

PRESUMPTION!

OR, THE

FATE OF FRANKENSTEIN.

The MUSICK composed by Mr. WATSON.

With WINTER's OVERTURE TO ZAIRA.

Frankenstein,   Mr. BENNETT,
De Lacey, (*a banished Gentleman*) Mr. CHAPMAN,   Felix De Lacey, (*his Son*) Mr. THORNE,
Fritz, Mr. KEELEY,
Clerval, Mr. J. BLAND,   William, Miss SMITH,
Hammerpan, Mr. SALTER,   Tanskin, Mr. MINTON,   Guide, Mr. J. COOPER,   Gypsey, Mr. J. O. ATKINS,
(- - - - - -) Mr. O. SMITH,
(*His Third Appearance in that Character.*)

Gypsies, Peasants, Dancers, &c. Messrs. Bowman, Brady, Buxton, Cooper, Heath, Shaw, Smythers, Willis—Lodge, Miller, Walsh—East, Henshaw,
Irwin—Fuller, Green, Jones, Sherreff. Mesdames & Misses Blackford, Gould, Ebbs, Jerrold, Lodge, Parslow, Perry, Phillips, Reed,
Remmins, C. Remmins, Tennant, Viale, Vidull, Vine, Wells, Willis.

Elizabeth, (*Sister of Frankenstein*) Miss BODEN,   Agatha De Lacey, Miss HAMILTON,
Safie, (*an Arabian Girl*) Miss GOWARD,   Madame Ninon, (*Wife of Fritz*) Mrs. J. WEIPPERT.

WITH AN ENTIRELY NEW LAST SCENE,

Conformably to the termination in the original Story, representing

A SCHOONER IN A VIOLENT STORM!

In which FRANKENSTEIN and THE MONSTER are destroyed.

DRYDEN's revived OPERA, with PURCELL's celebrated MUSICK, will be repeated *twice a week after Miss PATON's Engagement*; and the NEW MELO-DRAMA, continuing also to be received with unanimous applause throughout, will be acted To-morrow.

To-morrow, **Miss PATON** will make her First Appearance this Season, as *Mandane*, in the Opera of ARTAXERXES—

Artaxerxes, (first time) Miss GOWARD,   Artabanes, Mr. H. PHILLIPS,   Arbaces, Mr. PEARMAN,   Semira, Mrs. TENNANT,
With (27th time) LYING MADE EASY, and (17th time) The CORNISH MINERS.

On Monday, The Grand Serio-Comick Opera called **THE ORACLE**, (first produced in this Country last Season at this Theatre) will be performed, for the 20th time.—*Myra*, by Miss PATON. After which, (2nd time this season) The VAMPIRE; or, The Bride of the Isles!

On Tuesday will be produced a NEW MUSICAL DRAMA, to be called

THE SERJEANT'S WIFE!

With entirely new MUSICK, composed by Mr. GOSS.—And new SCENERY by Mr. TOMKINS and Mr. PITT.
The Characters by Mr. PEARMAN, Mr. BARTLEY, Mr. J. BLAND, Mr. CHAPMAN, Mr. O. SMITH, Mr. KEELEY;
Miss GOWARD and Miss KELLY.

After which (29th time) LYING MADE EASY. And (8th time) The CORNISH MINERS.

A NEW GRAND OPERA will be shortly announced; to be rapidly succeeded by, other NOVELTIES.

Stage Manager, Mr. BARTLEY.——Musical Director, Mr. HAWES.——Leader of the Band, Mr. WAGSTAFF.
Boxes 5s. Second Price 3s. Pit 3s. Second Price 1s. 6d. Low Gallery 2s. Second Price 1s. Up. Gallery 1s. Second Price 6d.
Boxes, Places, Private and Family Boxes, to be taken at the Box-Office, Strand Entrance, from 10 till 4.
Doors open at half-past 6, begin at 7. Vivat Rex! No Money returned. [S. G. Fairbrother, (Lyceum Printing Office) Exeter Court, Strand.
☞ All complaints and applications respecting the delivery of the Play-bills to be addressed, (post paid,) to Mr. T. Cooper, Stage Door, Exeter Street.

By 1823, five years after the novel's publication, the story of Frankenstein had been transformed into a stage sensation titled *Presumption,* the first of dozens of dramatic, comedic, and operatic adaptations of the tale. *Presumption* played for years throughout Britain.

by that time. The monster had asserted its identity in the public imagination.

PRESUMPTION

Mary Godwin Shelley and her surviving son, Percy, remained in Italy for a year after the death of Percy Bysshe Shelley. She finished a new novel and began working on a third. At home in England, not only her *Frankenstein* but also *A History of a Six Weeks' Tour,* a travelogue of her 1814 Continental adventures with Percy and Claire, established her as an author. Writing seemed the best way to support herself and her son; London seemed the place to do it. Her father encouraged her. "Frankenstein is universally known," he wrote in March 1823. "If you cannot be independent, who should be?"

Enduring coach travel through France and seasickness on the Channel crossing, Mary and Percy Shelley reached London on Monday, August 25, 1823. That very Friday, the day before her twenty-sixth birthday, she went with her father, her half brother, and a friend to see a wildly popular play now in its second month on the London stage: Richard Brinsley Peake's *Presumption, or the Fate of Frankenstein.* "Lo & behold!" Mary Shelley wrote to a friend. "I found myself famous!"

The monster "bursts on to the stage five minutes after its birth, a tall *light blue* figure, with a white face and long black hair!" wrote a reviewer in the London *Times.* Peake's script called for the monster to sport "dark black flowing hair—*à la Octavian*"—wild and wavy over the brow, like Augustus Caesar's. His bare face, hands, arms, and legs were to be colored light blue or French gray, matching a cloth that wrapped around his torso, "fitting quite close, as if it were his flesh."

The author of *Presumption,* Richard Brinsley Peake, was born

Peake's *Presumption* capitalized on the novel's melodrama and respectfully costumed the monster in light-blue skin and a classical toga.

into London's theater world. His father worked for forty years in the treasury office of Drury Lane Theatre and named his son after the great dramatist-turned-politician, Richard Brinsley Sheridan. By his mid-twenties, Peake was writing plays and continued to do so, ploddingly well, until his death in 1847. *Presumption* was his third play to be staged and his first serious drama. His forte was farce and light comedy, to which he returned after the success of *Presumption*. It is Peake, not Shelley, whom we have to thank for a number of the plot elements that now seem essential to the Frankenstein story. He invented the character of Fritz, a goofball servant in the tradition of Shakespeare's mechanics, and thus began the long line of bumbling assistants, chief among them the hunchback played by Dwight Frye in the 1931 film. In Peake's play, the audience first sees the monster through Fritz's eyes when he stands on a footstool and peers through a window into Frankenstein's offstage laboratory, attracted by a blue light—"the devil's own flame," he calls it. Frankenstein's voice is heard, uttering the words, "It lives! It lives!," whereupon Fritz jumps down and "totters tremblingly," babbling out the words, "There's a hob—hob-goblin, seven-and-twenty feet high!"

Peake's "hob—hob-goblin" does not speak—another feature of his play that entered the Frankenstein vernacular. *Presumption*'s monster uses gestures, grunts, and groans to express the wide range of emotions assigned him in the script: delight, rapture, disappointment, fondness, violent self-defense, agony, hate, supplication, vengeance, treachery. He hears a flute and stands "amazed and pleased, looks around him, snatches at the empty air, and with clenched hands puts them to each ear." Music soothes Peake's savage—a dramatic innovation based on a brief passage in Shelley's novel—and such a scene became integral to future tellings of the tale.

Presumption climaxes at a "Wild Border of the Lake" under "a lofty overhanging mountain of snow," where a band of Gypsies accompanies Frankenstein, armed with musket and pistols to kill the monster. In that snowy setting, Frankenstein and his monster

face off, and then he shoots, causing a stage avalanche that "falls
and annihilates the monster and Frankenstein.——A heavy fall of
snow succeeds.——Loud thunder heard, and all the characters
form a picture as the curtain falls." This finale was a production
challenge, forcing stage managers to get creative. When *Presumption* was staged in Birmingham, stagehands up in the fly were to
throw down a canvas elephant, left over from another play but
now painted all white——the closest thing theater managers could
find to a heap of snow. *"Avalanche* (the Stage Elephant) came
down before the cue was given him," reported one reviewer, "so
that *Franky* and his *Demon* were obliged to seek death from some
other source than excessive *snow-ball."* In his memoir years later,
the actor who played the Monster explained that "the Master
Carpenter being over anxious for the success of the experiment
let go——when down came the elephant with a tremendous crash,
knocked down the platform and scenery and came rolling down
the stage to the footlights where it ran some danger of being
roasted."

No such slapstick marred the production that Mary Shelley
attended at the English Opera House in August 1823. She
approved of the actor playing Frankenstein, James Wallack, who
began "full of hope & expectation." She especially appreciated the
theater's sensitivity to her decision not to name her monster.
"The play bill amused me extremely, for in the list of dramatic
personae came, _____ by Mr T. Cooke," she wrote Leigh
Hunt. "This nameless mode of naming the unnameable is rather
good." Thomas Potter Cooke, a thirty-seven-year-old actor with
a solid reputation on the London stage already, had just caused a
sensation by starring in *The Vampire*, a stage version of Polidori's
story. "Cooke played _____'s part extremely well," wrote Shelley. "His seeking as it were for support——his trying to grasp at the

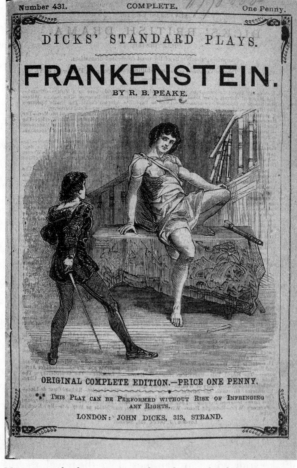

No copyright laws prevented a playwright from scripting another author's story. Peake was one of many stage writers in Britain, France, and the United States who turned Shelley's novel into onstage action and dialogue. Many others departed more boldly from the original.

sounds he heard—all indeed he does was well imagined & executed. I was much amused."

Far from jealously guarding her story, Mary Shelley took personal pride in seeing how "it appeared to excite a breathless eagerness in the audience . . . & all stayed till it was over." It was a commonplace in the theater of the time to stage a story from a popular novel, and in fact, the success of *Presumption* promised the author of *Frankenstein* a living. Reading advance notices of the play, Shelley's father had already arranged for a new edition of her novel to be published before she returned to England. This time advertising and the book's title page declared the author to be "Mary Wollstonecraft Shelley," citing her first, middle, and married names and declaring her kinship with mother and husband.

Reviewers didn't know what to make of *Presumption,* so popular it soon migrated into a larger theater in London. "The piece upon the whole has little to recommend it," one critic wrote, "but that, as times go, will be no great obstacle to its success." The *Sunday Times* reviewer complained that the Muse had abandoned London, since "the moderns may do no more than brandish a tailor's scissors against the leaves of the last romance" in order to come up with a new play. *Presumption,* he snorted, was a "Scissor-born monster." Meanwhile moralizers protested the blasphemous implications of the story, hanging leaflets throughout London, exhorting citizens to stay away from "the monstrous Drama, founded on the improper work called 'Frankenstein.'— Do not take your wives and families." Like the novel, the play was "of a decidedly immoral tendency" because "it treats of a subject which in nature cannot occur." In Birmingham as well, warnings went up throughout the city. "As if the impious description of the NOVEL were not enough," read one, "we must here have the very horrid and unnatural details it contains embodied and presented to the view."

Familiar Refrains

Peake's *Presumption* started a trend, and new Frankensteins haunted the London stage all that summer of 1823. "This evening," read a notice in the *Times* on September 22,

> the performance will commence at half-past 6 precisely, with an Act of Horsemanship by the Indian Phenomenon, Master Juan Bellinek. A favourite Song, by Mr. Bennett. After which, an entirely new romantic melodrama, called FRANKENSTEIN; or, The Danger of Presumption. Juan Bellinek will then go through his wonderful Performance on the Flying Rope. In the course of the evening, the celebrated Stilt Dance by the Madlles. [Mademoiselles] Bellinek. To conclude with a melodramatic spectacle, in 8 sets, called THE LADY OF THE LAKE.

In other words, this was by no means high culture.

Richard Brinsley Peake wrote a farce of his own play, and on October 20, the Adelphi Theatre in the Strand staged "an entirely new outlandish, supernatural, never-to-be-sufficiently-admired or dreaded burletta of parody and peculiar interest, entitled ANOTHER PIECE OF PRESUMPTION." A servant named Frizzy helps a master tailor, Mr. Frankinstitch, a tailor, sew together body parts from nine yeoman tailors, creating a being named Hobgoblin. "Prometheus of old / Wasn't half so bold," he sings. "I'll do all I can / To make this made man." The play crescendos to an encounter between maker and monster in Mrs. Frankinstitch's garden. Hob unknowingly trips a spring gun, set to fend off intruders, and causes an "avalanche of cabbages and cauliflowers." The joke worked because audiences already knew both the story of *Frankenstein* and the staging fiasco required for *Presumption*.

A different comic version of the story opened at the Surrey Theatre, playing as a warm-up for *Antigone*. "THIS PRESENT EVENING," read the notice, "will be presented an entirely New and Original Romance, founded partly on the celebrated Novel, partly on ancient legends, and principally upon modern Dramas, called HUMGUMPTION." This Dr. Frankenstein lives in Hoxton, a village north of London known for religious dissenters and madhouses. The onstage action culminated in "an awful Avalanche of Earthenware, and a tremendous Shower of Starch, and an overwhelming explosion of Hair Powder!"

By the end of 1823 five different retellings of *Frankenstein* had animated the London stage. While there may not have been many copies of the novel on booksellers' shelves, the story had become familiar through its notorious retellings, brought to public attention not only by the stage productions but by the righteous outcry against them. The monster and his story were familiar even to those who had never read the novel. Certain elements remained constant: an ugly and oversize created being, the centrality of lightning and electricity to events in the story, and the intimate psychological relationship between creator and creation. At the same time, though, the story had already begun accruing new elements, foreign to Mary Shelley's version, many of which attached so tightly that they have appeared ever since: an inarticulate monster, a bumbling laboratory assistant, an angry crowd in search of the monster, and a cataclysmic ending in which creature and creator perish together. The public eagerly grasped this monster of a story, told and retold it, reshaping it as they did.

In 1824 the monster entered the political arena. That year the Lord Chancellor opened Parliament by announcing that King

George IV "has not been inattentive to the desire expressed by the House of Commons in the last session of Parliament, that means should be devised for ameliorating the condition of the negro slaves in the West Indies." Having banned the slave trade in 1807, members of Parliament generally abhorred slavery yet feared the consequences of uncontrolled emancipation. George Canning, MP from Liverpool, soon to become prime minister, advocated systematic moral education for all slaves as a condition for emancipation. "In dealing with the negro, we must remember that we are dealing with a being possessing the form and strength of a man, but the intellect only of a child," Canning argued. To explain further, he called up an analogy apparently familiar to his contemporaries:

> To turn him loose in the manhood of his physical strength, in the maturity of his physical passions, but in the infancy of his unin-structed reason, would be to raise up a creature resembling the splendid fiction of a recent romance; the hero of which con-structs a human form, with all the corporeal capabilities of man, and with the thews and sinews of a giant; but being unable to impart to the work of his hands a perception of right and wrong, he finds too late that he has only created a more than mortal power of doing mischief, and himself recoils from the monster which he has made.

"Canning paid a compliment to Frankenstein in a manner suffi-ciently pleasing to me," Mary Shelley wrote a friend later that week. Three years later she was still bragging that Canning liked her book.

Stage interpretations of Frankenstein multiplied through the 1820s and 1830s. *Presumption* was resurrected again and again. A production reached the United States by 1825; the *Evening Post* reported that New York audiences greeted it with "unbounded applause." A French stage version of the story, *Le monstre et le magicien,* opened in Paris in 1826, T. P. Cooke again playing the monster. A greater departure from Mary Shelley's original than ever before, this play portrayed Frankenstein as an infernal alchemist, his laboratory full of "crucibles, alembecks [*sic*], and devil's kitchen utensils." In the grand finale Frankenstein maneuvers a small boat through a tempest and the monster, with "a shout of demonic joy," leaps from the rocky shore into the vessel with him. Lightning strikes the boat, breaking it in two, and instantly man and monster are engulfed in a billow of waves and fire. Parisians loved the melodrama. "Le succès du *Monstre* est monstrueux comme lui-même," wrote a reviewer—the play's success was as monstrous as the monster himself.

Frankenstein; or, The Man and the Monster, written by H. M. Milner, opened at London's Royal Coburg Theatre in July 1826 and challenged the long-playing *Presumption.* Milner's published script clearly cited Mary Shelley's novel and the French rendition as its sources. The scene was Italy, with a manufactured Mount Etna looming upstage. Frankenstein is a husband and father, and when his own son falls victim to the monster, he wails, "Oh! presumption, and is this thy punishment?" "Presumption": the word was appearing more and more often as the formulaic expression of Frankenstein's tragic flaw. Milner played up the story's Prometheanisms. A posse of peasants chases the monster up Mount Etna, trapping him at the crater's edge. "Now I think the best thing we can do is to fasten my gentleman to this pinnacle of rock," says their leader. Using his superhuman strength, the monster loosens the rope and rappels down into the mountain chasm, where he meets Frankenstein. As monster and maker grapple, a fiery volcanic eruption engulfs them both.

BACK IN PRINT

Like a blockbuster film today, the popular dramas of Frankenstein spurred new print versions, and in 1825 there appeared a
two-penny chapbook—small, cheap, and paperbound, the
equivalent of a paperback today—called *The Monster Made by
Man; or, The Punishment of Presumption*. The next year the same
story appeared in a one-penny edition as an issue of *Endless Entertainment: A Series of Original Comic, Terrific, and Legendary Tales*. "The
Monster Made by Man," published anonymously, leaned on
Peake's play more than the original novel, dwelled more on the
creator's errors than the creature's terrors, and ultimately told a
moral tale rather than a chilling melodrama.

The main character enjoys a family background just like that
in Shelley's novel, but his and every other name changes. He is
Ernest Walberg; his doltish assistant is Frantz, who "sometimes
thought his master a madman, and sometimes a wonderful
genius." Walberg infuses an alchemical elixir of life into a
sculpted clay body, which then comes to life during an electrical
storm. The creature's first quivering moments read like an oddly
altered version of the scene in the novel:

> As it gradually arose from the platform on which he had mod-
> elled it, its perfect proportions were enlarged to an unnatural
> size, its regular features were distorted into hideousness, the
> eyelids opened, and displayed two green balls, bedded in a yel-
> low fluid, and the alabaster whiteness of its exterior turned to a
> leaden blue colour; at length it stood erect, every nerve and
> muscle writhing with convulsive agitation.

Frantz falls to the floor, shouting, "A man devil!" Like Frankenstein, Walberg escapes into sleep.

ENDLESS ENTERTAINMENT.

A SERIES OF ORIGINAL
COMIC, TERRIFIC, AND LEGENDARY
TALES.

No. 7.   FRIDAY, JUNE 17, 1825.   Price 2d.

Contents.—THE MONSTER.

See page 101.

THE MONSTER MADE BY MAN;
OR, THE PUNISHMENT OF PRESUMPTION.

IN every age of the world woman's curiosity has been equalled by man's presumption, and one of the most astonishing events produced by the latter quality is related in Germany, that native country of every thing non-natural.

Almost as quickly as the Frankenstein story was retold on stage, it was refashioned into stories written by other authors, who embellished the plot or changed its details but did not hide their links to Shelley and *Frankenstein*.

But in this story, when the creature next gazes in on him, the creator responds lovingly. He wraps a cloak around him and teaches him to eat bread. He treats him like a dog, leashing him with a rope and leading him toward a cage. At that the creature's "whole frame appeared convulsed as if some new sensation within him was struggling to find vent," and then "at length in a hollow voice, in which [were] discernible none of the usual tones of human nature, he uttered, 'I am the punishment of thy presumption.'" Ultimately this monster learns kindness, and the story takes a turn different from either novel or plays before it. "Thou art a sensible monster now, and fit company for those who think they are most learned," says Walberg. Declaring, "I will be thy pupil," he leaves family and friends behind and climbs with the creature into the Alps. There, together, they are destroyed by an avalanche, caused—of course—by a thunderstorm.

In less than a decade *Frankenstein* had penetrated the public imagination and had become a story told, retold, and reinterpreted. Horror exaggerated into melodrama, melodrama overflowed into comedy. Some versions tasted of the tragic, others dripped with pathos. Sometimes the story ended on a high moral ground. Most often the story warned against presumption, the prideful quest to create life and thereby overstep human bounds, but other versions spotlighted an innately innocent creature, turned monster by circumstances and society. Mary Shelley had presented a novel precariously inconclusive as to moral, message, or ending. Its subtle uncertainty matches the famous Romantic definition of "negative capability"—the poetic state of mind described by her contemporary John Keats as the ability "of being in uncertainties, Mysteries, doubts, without any irritable reaching after fact & reason." Among those who took up her story and told it again and again, turning it into a myth of modern culture, few were willing to keep so many uncertainties in the balance as she had. The story invited retelling, but those coming after Shelley shaped it in ways that felt more comfortable to them, to their audiences, and even to their censors.

The most influential retelling of *Frankenstein* came from Mary Shelley herself. Through the 1820s she made a living as a writer, publishing stories, essays, reviews, and novels. She also devoted herself to collecting, editing, and annotating her late husband's poetry. Occasionally interests expressed in *Frankenstein* resurfaced in her later work. In "The Reanimated Man," an 1826 essay, she embellished on reports (later proved false) of a seventeenth-century Englishman buried in an avalanche and brought back to life "upon the application of the usual remedies." In "Transformation," an 1831 story, an Italian suitor trades his handsome body for a gnarled dwarf's riches, an eerie example of mingled identities. "The Mortal Immortal," published two years later, told the story of a student of Cornelius Agrippa's, denied death because he drank an alchemical elixir. By the 1830s, Mary Wollstonecraft Godwin Shelley had published four novels, fifteen short stories, three poems, six translations, and fifteen critical essays. The *Athenaeum,* a respected literary monthly, considered her a leading modern English author. Her reputation—and the continuing public fascination with the story of Frankenstein—meant that in 1831, she was able to sell *Frankenstein* to Richard Bentley, whose Standard Novels series was expanding monthly. Bentley was buying up out-of-print novels by authors including Jane Austen, William Godwin, and Thomas Love Peacock. He sold each volume for a mere six shillings, a third of the price of the original

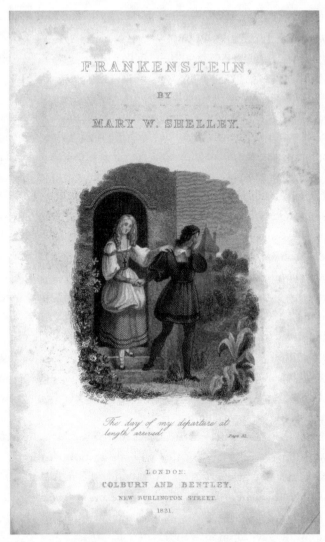

By 1831 the novel—and, more important, the story it told—had taken such a firm stand in British culture that a new edition formed part of a series of "standard novels," with Shelley's authorship clearly indicated.

edition of *Frankenstein*. As one of Bentley's Standard Novels, *Frankenstein* stayed in print into the 1850s.

For the Standard Novel edition Shelley thoroughly revised her creation. Some of her changes were minor: adding missing prepositions, clarifying plot mechanics, fine-tuning word choices. Other changes shifted tone, emphasis, and even moral judgment. Now a widow in her mid-thirties, relying on a writer's income supplemented by a small allowance from her bitter father-in-law, Mary Shelley's life had changed. No longer did the voices of radical atheism and revolutionary rhetoric surround her. Polidori, Byron, and Shelley—all were dead, their idealisms faded with them. Risk and revolution no longer thrilled her. She was a different woman as she revised her novel in 1831.

Determined that her novel not raise the specter of incest—one of the sins associated with the renegade band during that Geneva summer of 1816—Mary Shelley changed the relationship between Victor Frankenstein and his fiancée, Elizabeth. In the 1818 edition Elizabeth was Victor's cousin, adopted at the death of her mother, a sister of Victor's father. In 1831 Elizabeth became an Italian foundling, brought charitably into the Frankenstein home during Victor's childhood.

From the start Frankenstein speaks more moralistically in the new volume, as if Mary Shelley wished her novel to impart a clearer message at every turn. For a while, he tells Walton, he rejected both alchemy and natural science and "betook myself to the mathematics." All too soon he returned to the study of anatomy, he says ominously in this new passage:

> When I look back, it seems to me as if this almost miraculous change of inclination and will [from alchemy and anatomy to mathematics] was the immediate suggestion of the guardian angel of my life—the last effort made by the spirit of preservation to

avert the storm that was even then hanging in the stars, and ready
to envelope me. . . . It was a strong effort of the spirit of good;
but it was ineffectual. Destiny was too potent, and her immutable
laws had decreed my utter and terrible destruction.

With language like this Mary Shelley cast the fate of Frankenstein
into even the earliest pages of her novel. She made Walton more
desperately driven from within. "There is something at work in
my soul which I do not understand," the sea captain writes his sister. "But success *shall* crown my endeavours." Frankenstein
responds moralistically. "Unhappy man!" he says to Walton in passages newly written. He hopes that the polar adventurer will
"deduce an apt moral from my tale; one that may direct you if you
succeed in your undertaking and console you in case of failure."

Mary Shelley made few changes in the monster's narrative
until he begins to explain young William's murder. In the first
edition the creature identifies Justine from afar as "one of those
whose smiles are bestowed on all but me" and, jealous over her
disregard, chooses to "work mischief" by making it seem as if she
killed William. In the language of the 1831 edition, this moment
grows more intimate and ghastly, the scene rife with frustrated
sexuality. The monster bends over and whispers to Justine,
"Awake, fairest, thy lover is near." When she stirs, "a thrill of terror" excites him, and he implicates her in William's murder as
revenge against the human race:

> Should she indeed awake, and see me, and curse me, and
> denounce the murderer? Thus would she assuredly act, if her
> darkened eyes opened and she beheld me. The thought was mad-
> ness; it stirred the fiend within me—not I, but she shall suffer:
> the murder I have committed because I am for ever robbed of all
> that she could give me, she shall atone. The crime had its source
> in her: be hers the punishment!

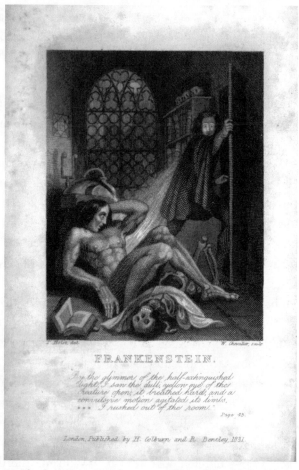

FRANKENSTEIN.

*"By the glimmer of the half-extinguished
light, I saw the dull, yellow eye of the
creature open; it breathed hard, and a
convulsive motion agitated its limbs.
. . . I rushed out of the room."*

Page 43.

London, Published by H. Colburn and R. Bentley, 1831.

For the frontispiece of the 1831 edition, the publisher chose
to illustrate a pivotal moment in the story. Having brought the
being to life, Frankenstein flees in horror and revulsion.

From this point on in the 1831 revision of the novel, new language turns the creature into a monster, hopelessly bloodthirsty
rather than helpless and confused. Playing up the monster as
fiend and Frankenstein as self-aware and repentant, Shelley uni-

fied the moral message of her novel. She even borrowed language from stage renditions to express it, now describing the manmade being as "the living monument of presumption and rash ignorance which [Frankenstein] let loose upon the world."

For the Standard Novel edition, Shelley wrote a new preface, from which we get her version of the scene at the Villa Diodati in June 1816. She calls Shelley her husband (even though he wasn't, then), introduces Byron and "poor Polidori," and leaves Claire out altogether. She recounts Byron's ghost-story contest, the "blank incapability of invention" that she first experienced, and then the vision of "the pale student of unhallowed arts kneeling beside the thing he had put together." It is in this essay, the preface to the new edition, written fifteen years after the fact, that she equates her own moments of creation with those of Frankenstein himself and describes her dream, in which she first saw the creature approach a bedstead with those "yellow, watery, but speculative eyes." A monster met in a dream—it is a scene almost as intriguing as those in the novel itself. Having already given the world one extraordinary myth, she was busy writing another: the story of the creation of her *Frankenstein*.

CHAPTER FOUR

THE MONSTER LIVES ON

The human body is a machine which winds its own springs.
It is the living image of perpetual movement.
—JULIEN OFFRAY DE LA METTRIE,
L'homme machine (Man a Machine), 1748

Remember the Monster is an electrical gadget.
—JACK P. PIERCE, Universal Studios
makeup man, 1939

Mary Shelley died in 1851, probably of a brain tumor. She was fifty-three years old. In the half century that her life had spanned, steam engines had become commonplace, railroads had begun linking cities, and the first steamship had crossed the Atlantic. By 1851 power looms whirred in Britain's textile factories. Michael Faraday had demonstrated his dynamo, or electromagnetic motor, and city streets stayed bright all night thanks to coal gaslighting. A new monarch had been crowned, and with Victoria in 1837 came the new spirit of British confidence and empire. London was the world's largest metropolis. Other British cities had more than doubled in size, too, and in that very year, 1851, the balance of British demographics tipped. For the first time ever, more people lived in the city than in the countryside.

In 1851 Mary Shelley's monster was thirty-five years old, but his life was just beginning. A good seven thousand copies of the novel had been printed and sold—nothing compared to a Scott novel or a Byron poem, but far more than all the volumes of Percy Bysshe Shelley's poetry combined. *Frankenstein* had come out in seven editions, including one French translation. The Standard Novel edition had been reissued in 1849, and two American editions had been published. The story had been told in at least fifteen different stage versions and had played hundreds of times in theaters in Britain, on the Continent, and in the United States. One actor, T. P. Cooke, had donned tunic and blue makeup and played the part more than three hundred times.

MECHANICAL MONSTERS

At a glance, the occurrences seem simultaneous but unrelated—advances in industry and the early evolution of Frankenstein's monster. The original novel gives little grounds for interpreting it as a myth of modern science and technology, as many do today. Aside from the mention of the air pump (which Shelley removed in 1831) and the abstract statement that "the workings of some powerful engine" brought the monster to life, nowhere did Shelley write of any contemporary mechanical or electrical power systems. And yet it took only a few years for the public imagination to associate Frankenstein's monster with machines.

In *Frank-in-Steam,* an 1824 comic knockoff of *Presumption,* creator and creature confront each other aboard a steamship. The grand finale involves not an avalanche or a volcano but a boiler explosion, just after the monster has chased his maker into the hold. The episode echoed real life: In 1803, when English inventor Richard Trevithick experimented with high-powered adaptations of James Watt's steam engines, one of them exploded at

Greenwich, killing four people. Such accidents were happening more and more often. They showed the risks but did not dampen the enthusiasm for the advancements promised by steam power and engines, as the title of Thomas Gray's 1821 pamphlet attests: *Observations on a General Iron Railway or Land Steam Conveyance; to supersede the Necessity of Horses in all Public Vehicles; showing its vast superiority in every respect, over all the Pitiful Methods of Conveyance.*

Power equipment displaced workers in the textile mills, and full-scale mob riots in the second decade of the nineteenth century showed another side of the dangers of industrialization and progress. It was not just the machines themselves, but the effect they were having on human life. By 1849, one pair of playwrights showed the monster as a machine. In Richard and Barnabas Brough's *Frankenstein; or, the Model Man,* the being created is "A mechanical man with skill supreme" whose every joint "is as strong as an iron beam / And the springs are a compound of clock-work and steam." The "model man" in this midcentury version is "put together" with "joint & screw" but brought to life with a potion, half alchemical "Elixir Vitae" and half Victorian-era wonder drug:

> Macassar oil of virtues rare,
> Give a nobby head of hair.
> Grimstone's eye snuff give him sight,
> Odonto, teeth of pearly white.
> Slolberg's lozenge! for the voice,
> Make him speak a language choice.
> Cockle's pills your warmth impart,
> To the cockles of his heart.
> Last & greater than the whole,
> All the others to control,
> Charm vitality to give,

> Charm to bid the patient live,
> Charm of every power rife,
> Parr's life pills shall give him life.

Such a list would surely delight the audiences, whose newspapers were filled with illustrated advertisements for Rowland's Odonto of Pearl Dentifrice, Jean Vincent Bully's Toilet Vinegar, Grimstone's Aromatic Regenerator, and, appropriately, a brand of Medical Galvanism, which promised to treat paralysis, asthma, and indigestion by a method "free from all unpleasant sensation." As Zamiel, the laboratory assistant, says to this Frankenstein, "You may with this Elixer, / Make your Automaton both live & kick sir."

In fact medical galvanism had become a common practice, promising all sorts of results and raising all sorts of philosophical questions. What had been spectacle became practice and often quackery by the 1820s and 1830s. Demonstrations continued

Frankenstein; or, the Model Man, an 1849 stage rendition, forged the link between the story written by Mary Shelley and the concept of a mechanical man.

beyond those of Aldini and his electrically motivated corpses, resulting in ever more remarkable effects. One experimenter connected a battery to the phrenic nerve of a just-dead body and reported that he was able to cause "full, nay, laborious breathing. . . . The chest heaved, and fell; the belly was protruded, and again collapsed." Reattaching the battery to the supraorbital nerve exposed in the corpse's forehead, the experimenter could evoke an array of apparent emotions on its face: "rage, horror, despair, anguish, and ghastly smiles."

Meanwhile Andrew Crosse, an electrical scientist in Somerset, concocted spectacular experiments—bolder and more magnificent even than Franklin's kite—to draw down the power of lightning and store it in Leyden jars, early versions of batteries. Crosse synthesized crystals with electricity as a catalyst and, through the course of one month, claimed to have created life by applying electrical charges to volcanic rock. In fourteen days he observed "white specks or nipples" on the rock; in twenty-six days each speck had grown and "assumed the form of a perfect insect." Then, Crosse recounted, "on the twenty-eighth day these insects moved their legs, and in the course of a few days more, detached themselves from the stone, and moved over its surface at pleasure." Newspapers picked up the story and turned it into a sensation. Some scientifically oriented observers sought rational explanations—the insects hatched from fossilized eggs on the rock, for example—but others were ready to see Crosse's findings as further proof that electricity was the foundational power of life. Some expressed moral outrage at such interpretations, calling them blasphemous and accusing Crosse of playing God. Crosse ignored the charges, but in 1857, after his death, his wife published this statement from him: "I am neither an 'Atheist,' nor a 'Materialist,' nor a 'self-imagined creator,' but a humble and lowly reverencer of that Great Being, whose laws my accusers seem wholly to have lost sight of."

No one replicated insect generation, but doctors and hospitals did use galvanic equipment extensively, believing that the application of electricity had salutary effects on the human body. Plenty of people scoffed, including an 1837 contributor to *Fraser's Magazine,* whose story, "The New Frankenstein," satirized the medical galvanists. The tale is told by an obsessed student of anatomy who, like Crosse, created life with electricity but—"to my infinite regret," pouts the narrator—crushed the creatures as he was handling them. His university professor brings to him "that anatomical man—that identical phantasmagoric hero . . . the human monster—the restored ruin—the living phantom— the creature without a name." Asked to improve on Frankenstein's creation, the student realizes that "instead of his being gifted with the faculties assigned to him by the fair authoress," the creature before him was "a mere automaton—a machine" whose yellow eyes "rolled pendulously in their sunken sockets with a clicking sound not unresembling that of a clock." This creature needed a mind, and thus the narrator resolves to become "a new Frankenstein, and a greater." From the great intellects of his time (including Goethe, P. B. Shelley, and Coleridge) he obtains "mental gases" to insert into the brain of his creature. The narrative swiftly advances to a ridiculous ending involving demons in an ancient Egyptian tomb, and *poof!* turns out to be a dream—a silly yet amusing parody of both literature and science of the time.

With every offbeat parody, the core story of *Frankenstein* was retold and remembered, to the point that many an author could presume general familiarity with plot and message. Sly references to *Frankenstein* pop up in Charles Dickens's 1861 *Great*

Expectations. The novel chronicles the life of Pip, who benefits from a fortune provided by a mysterious benefactor and rises from lowly beginnings to become a gentleman. One of his first projects, having assumed his new identity, is to hire a servant. "After I had made this monster (out of the refuse of my washer-woman's family) and had clothed him," narrates Pip, "I had to find him a little to do and a great deal to eat; and with both of those horrible requirements he haunted my existence." The hired help quickly becomes an "avenging phantom," and Pip abandons the plan of having a servant. Later in the novel Dickens again evokes the story of Frankenstein as Pip discovers the identity of his patron: the escaped convict Magwitch. His presumption undercut, Pip says: "The imaginary student pursued by the mis-shapen creature he had impiously made, was not more wretched than I, pursued by the creature who had made me, and recoiling from him with a stronger repulsion, the more he admired me and the fonder he was of me." Secure that his readers would know the original story, Dickens gave the reference a twist: Now it is the monster, Magwitch, who has created the gentleman.

POLITICAL MONSTERS

By the middle of the nineteenth century, propelled as much by adaptations as by the novel itself, the myth of Frankenstein and his monster had entered the vernacular. The name "Frankenstein" had become a code word for misguided ambition, for new ideas conjured up with good intentions but destined to grow and change beyond all reckoning, ultimately overwhelming those who conceived them. With a swing away from Romantic idealism toward the conservative and pragmatic, the Victorians doubted that the human intellect could understand, control, replicate, or improve the world, whether that world meant natural phenomena or the social sphere. The Frankenstein myth gave them an icon for mistaken idealisms. Variations on the Frankenstein message entered politics, in new incarnations quite different from Canning's comments of 1824 about emancipating the slaves of the West Indies.

The myth fit well, for example, into arguments against the 1832 Reform Bill. The rules by which members of Parliament were elected, based on property ownership and ancient geographical boundaries, disenfranchised the middle and working classes in fast-growing industrial cities like Manchester and Birmingham. Liberal politicians sought to change the law to give more voting power to the masses. George IV and William IV, Victoria's predecessors, had favored Whig calls for social reform, but Tory conservatives fought it all the way. An odd couple—the Scottish radical Henry Brougham and the elegant prime minister, the Second Earl Grey—advocated a compromise bill that would extend the vote to half again as many Britons as before. The situation brought a recently reissued novel to mind, and in 1832 and 1833 several cartoonists referred to the familiar story in comments on the political scene. Brougham became a Frankenstein, the wigged Lord Grey his demented assistant. Together they were bringing to life a monster, a new voting population with the potential of rising up and destroying them—and with them, the old social order.

Cartoonists grabbed hold of the Frankenstein imagery to symbolize a good idea gone wrong. John Tenniel, today revered for his illustrations of *Alice in Wonderland* and *Through the Looking-Glass*, was better known by his contemporaries for political cartoons that appeared in the magazine *Punch* from 1850 to 1901. With his delicate touch and literary sophistication, Tenniel used the myth of Frankenstein over and over. In his "Brummagem

CARTOON.—SEPTEMBER 8, 1866.

THE BRUMMAGEM FRANKENSTEIN.

JOHN BRIGHT. *"I have no fe—fe—fear of ma—manhood suffrage!"*

[MR. BRIGHT's Speech at Birmingham.

"Frankenstein's monster," meaning the newly empowered and now threatening working classes, became a familiar political sobriquet in the mid-
nineteenth century, as in this 1866 cartoon parodying Birmingham's newly
enlarged voting population.

Frankenstein," September 1866, he portrayed populist leader John Bright as a tiny figure, tiptoeing by a giant—an unshorn, pipe-smoking, fist-clenching, working-class man. Typifying citizens of Birmingham (nicknamed "Brummagem"), he glares down at his erstwhile creator. It was Tenniel's response to further efforts to extend voting rights, which he feared would create a working-class monster of unknown strength and disastrous proportions. Similarly, in 1882 Tenniel used Frankenstein imagery to comment on Charles Stewart Parnell and his campaign for Irish nationalism. Here the monster created is the Irish populace, now empowered, yet endowed—thanks to Tenniel's conservative English opinion—with unkempt hair, unshaven chin, predatory fangs, and a simian upper lip, atavistic and threatening. These cartoons settled in on a familiar political theme: Well-meaning reforms often create monsters. In Tenniel's imagination—and presumably that of his Victorian audience—the creature stood in for the Other—the dangerous unknown future force present in a population that is lower-class, newly enfranchised, and potentially threatening to those who have long held power and influence.

Other cartoonists, continuing into the twentieth century, used the Frankenstein myth to comment on war. Tenniel may have been the first, drawing "The Russian Frankenstein and His Monster" for *Punch* in July 1854, three months after Britain and France declared war on Russia in the Crimea. Dominating the frame is a giant figure, a war machine—cannons for legs, a mortar for a body. The monster charges, soulless eyes wide open, bloodied sword and torch held high, as uniformed British soldiers cower. The decision to go to war has made a monster, Tenniel implied: huge, powerful, inhuman, overwhelming.

Most references through the nineteenth century used Franken-

Through the nineteenth century the monster remained a malleable metaphor. In 1854 cartoonist John Tenniel created "the Russian Frankenstein," his monster made of weaponry, as a comment on the Crimean War.

stein's creation to symbolize a monstrous mistake, but radical philosophers in the late 1800s championed the monster, not the creator. On the one hand, the Fabian Socialist movement of the late nineteenth century was the offspring of the Reform Movement half a century earlier, seeking power for the working class; on the other, it entirely reversed the early-nineteenth-century rage against industrial technology, seeing machinery as the friend, not the enemy, of the worker. Members of the Fabian Society tagged playwright George Bernard Shaw to edit a collection of essays, spelling out their argument and social plan. Illustrious radical thinkers each contributed to the book, including Sidney Webb, a barrister and economist who with his wife, Beatrice, helped found the London School of Economics.

In early-eighteenth-century England, Webb wrote, a medieval economy still prevailed. The worker "was apparently better off in 1750 than at any other time between 1450 and 1850," even though the simple, rural, unmechanized world that workers lived in was "a world still mainly mediaeval," "a world of status and of permanent social inequalities." New towns, new classes, new kinds of work had all destroyed those feudal ways. The Industrial Revolution meant "the final collapse of Mediaevalism," and it held hidden promise for the working classes. "Within a couple of generations the squire faded away before the mill-owner," wrote Webb, and now "new motors" are "destroying the individualist conception of property. The landlord and the capitalist are both finding that the steam-engine is a Frankenstein which they had better not have raised; for with it comes inevitably urban Democracy, the study of Political Economy and Socialism."

In this conceit the villainous pair of landlord and capitalist plays the creator, while the steam engine is the monster, capable of shifting power into the hands of the working class, which will then grow in strength and power beyond the creator's wildest imagining. To the Fabian Socialist, the monster, not the creator, is the hero, with his capacity to overturn the old order and grant wealth and power to the working class. Returning to a radical model, the Fabian philosophers of the late nineteenth century picked up the Godwinian strands in Mary Shelley's story—the portrayal of the creature as a victim of social forces, antagonistic because powerless, hostile because unloved. As a champion of the underdog, Webb reorients the moral from a Victorian caution to a socialist ideal. Unknowing creators have brought to life a monster, but he will stand tall and bring forth a brighter day in which the disenfranchised will come to power.

AMERICAN MONSTERS

It did not take long for the imagery of the Frankenstein myth to appear in political commentaries on the other side of the Atlantic. Stage versions of the story had appeared in New York as early as 1825, an American edition of the novel as early as 1833. In the United States, as in Britain and on the Continent, the Frankenstein story first served as code language for mistaken political intentions. Reviewing "a sensible treatise on 'Popular Education,'" a *New York Daily Times* writer in 1852 called adult students—that "host of uneducated human souls"—"as pernicious as the giant of Frankenstein Creation, potent in the capacity for evil; and without sufficient intellectual culture to control the exercise of his physical passions and powers." The educators, this writer implied, must do better than the original Frankenstein and "devise a plan for bringing these people under educational influences. The need is urgent." Seeing the metaphor come to life at a national level, abolitionist Charles Sumner predicted that the Confederacy would operate like "the soulless monster of Frankenstein."

Malleable in its meaning, in 1900 the myth fit the times in other ways. The United States was waging its first colonial war on the other side of the globe, in the Philippines. Many decried the government's imperialist intentions, seeing them as anathema to republicanism, isolationism, and the American commit-

"Our Frankenstein," a political cartoon published in *Life* in 1900, shows the monster of European imperialism coming across the Atlantic to American shores.

ment to free peoples everywhere. The November 1, 1900, issue of *Life* magazine included an oversize page that folded out to reveal a cartoon titled "Our Frankenstein." A giant crowned monarch, ermine cape flying, lurches ashore, menacing a small and startled Uncle Sam. In the distance, across the ocean, a city goes up in flames; on a nearby hilltop, a Greek temple bearing on its pediment one word—"Peace"—stands in ruins. Civilization is crumbling, and the monster causing such ruin is the embodiment of imperialism, clothed in European monarchic garb but arriving on Uncle Sam's shores.

References to Frankenstein and his monster seemed to shift from usage to usage, flinging associations hither and yon. In 1879 a tongue-in-cheek article about America's wealthiest citizenry described A. T. Stewart, founder of New York's first department store, as "a sort of *Frankenstein,* who had constructed a vast machine that was self-moving; but he fell into it, became himself only the central wheel of it, and died when he had worn out." Defending Justus H. Schwab, an outspoken advocate for New York's working class, against charges of inciting a riot in February 1885, a lawyer argued that "Schwab was not the black Frankenstein that he had been painted, but he was an estimable citizen, with theories and pronunciamentos abreast of the able thought of the age." In an 1887 commentary on the present force of munitions, thankfully in the hands of governments and not insurgents, a writer imagined what might happen if "Pekin [*sic*], or Mecca . . . forges Excaliburs successfully!" In his view, "a Chinaman with a repeating rifle which he knew fully how to use would be a Frankenstein against whom the human race might be obliged to unite in order to destroy him." In an Indianapolis campaign speech in 1896, a legislative candidate mixed myths, stirring in Frankenstein with the Greeks for full effect, and promised:

> We deem it wise to pursue an aggressive rather than a negative policy, to be Achilles dragging Hector around the walls of Troy rather than Achilles sulking in his tent. We proposed to make a funeral pyre of the cadavers of Populism and Anarchy. We propose to drag behind our triumphant chariot wheels, in defeat and disgrace, around the National Capitol, the dead Frankenstein personifying their pernicious creed and their turbulent fanaticism.

The more the references, the vaguer the meaning. The name of Frankenstein could refer to creator or creature. The confusion annoyed some readers. One wrote a letter to the editor of the *New York Times* in October 1902:

The mistake is frequently made by writers and orators of describing a monster constructed by man as a "Frankenstein." Mr. James W. Osborne [an attorney] is reported in today's *Times* as being the latest offender in this respect. . . . A reference to Mrs. Shelley's gruesome book will assure the reader that Frankenstein was the man who made the monster and not the monster that was made.

As this correspondent suggested, few of those alluding to the myth of Frankenstein had even read the novel. Indeed, references to Frankenstein proliferated wildly in Europe and the United States through decades when editions of the novel were difficult to find. In England few copies of the novel circulated in the decades between Mary Shelley's death and the 1880s. The last of its editions as one of Bentley's Standard Novels, still priced low at two shillings sixpence, came out in the early 1850s. By 1860 the plates for the novel, as well as others in the series, had been destroyed, but the publisher's copyright kept others from reprinting it for another two decades. Once Bentley's copyright expired, the novel became more widely available, included in series such as the Ideal Library, Gem Classics, and, in 1912, Everyman's Library, published by Dent in Britain and Dutton in the United States, a standard edition still in print today. "Eighty years after its first appearance," writes reading historian William St. Clair, "*Frankenstein* at last became accessible to the whole reading nation," not only in its home country of Britain but in the United States as well.

"The number of writers who should have read 'Frankenstein,' and yet have not read it, is appalling," wrote a *New York Times* book critic in 1901, commenting on the novel's inclusion in the Gem Classics series.

Rarely is any reference made to the book but we hear about "that monster Frankenstein." Now, poor Frankenstein was not the monster at all, yet for years he has done rhetorical service as such. It can only be fervently hoped that the successive editions of Mrs. Shelley's fantastic and tiresome tale may at last stamp out the fallacy.

After decades out of print, now the novel was everywhere. "Apparently no series of English classics, however limited, is considered distinctive or representative unless it includes a copy of 'Frankenstein,'" wrote the same critic, snidely adding, "Why, we are unable to say." Publishers may have wanted to convince the reading public that *Frankenstein* belonged in everyone's library—it was a gem, it was a classic—but for this critic at least, its literary merit was still in question.

PART TWO
COMING OF AGE

CHAPTER FIVE

MAKING MORE MONSTERS

Here comes the point at which we have endeavored to bring out, namely:
That with the strength of Frankenstein's love for his bride and the
effect of this upon his own mind, the monster cannot exist.

——DRAMATIC SYNOPSIS, Edison Films'
Frankenstein, 1910

We are in an area where initial repugnances are hard
to translate into sound moral arguments.

——LEON R. KASS, "Beyond Therapy," 2003

At the turn of the nineteenth into the twentieth century, the myth of Frankenstein resonated with vitality in the imaginations of the British and American public. The word "Frankenstein" evoked a cluster of ideas that required little familiarity with the original novel. The word had gathered up connotations of irreverence and sacrilege, of a renegade willingness to cross ancient boundaries into realms of knowledge meant only for God, of political efforts gone awry, and of the untapped power of the lower classes. The name referred to either maker or monster. The misnomer filled a void left intentionally by Mary Shelley to evoke a figure without human identity, without birth, parents, or family history. "And what was I?" the monster asked in the novel. "Of my creation and creator I was absolutely ignorant; but I knew that I possessed no money, no friends, no kind of property. . . . When I looked around, I saw and heard of none like me." There was no name for his shadowy otherness. The power, the mystery, the utter unnaturalness of Frankenstein's creation required an empty cipher for a name, yet the human brain demands words for the concepts it enfolds. As the monster grew in importance, it usurped the name of its creator.

Visually the monster remained an empty cipher, too, a shape-shifter taking on different costumes and appearances. The toga worn by stage monsters in *Presumption* and other plays of its time seems not to have influenced illustrators later in the nineteenth century. Political cartoonists turned the monster into an Irish commoner, a caped thief, an impish giant, and an ermine-robed monarch. Through the nineteenth century Frankenstein's monster remained a disembodied abstraction in the public imagination, clothed and proportioned to fit each evocation. Mary Shelley's novel had presented few details. Every new interpretation could propose a new appearance. No one knew what the monster looked like—but all that would change soon after he celebrated his centenary.

Authors could make scant reference to the Frankenstein story, knowing that the full meaning would reverberate in every reader's mind. More references like those in Dickens's *Great Expectations* appeared in fiction. In *La recherche de l'absolu,* Honoré de Balzac's main character, a chemist seeking the fundamental element of all matter, comes under the influence of a man whose yellow eyes seem "blazing with the fire of Prometheus." "God help thee, old man," Ishmael says of Ahab in Herman Melville's *Moby-Dick,* "thy thoughts have created a creature in thee; and he whose intense thinking thus makes him a Prometheus; a vulture feeds upon that heart for ever; that vulture the very creature he creates." In "The Birthmark," Nathaniel Hawthorne wrote of "a man of science" during the time of "the comparatively recent discovery of electricity" who seems to forsake his intellectual passions to fall in love and marry, but ultimately destroys his beloved wife when he uses science to try to perfect her beauty. Lesser authors more boldly copied the Frankenstein story, generating their own versions of the classic tale. Such stories appeared in turn-of-the-century British magazines devoted to fantasy fiction of the sort written by H. G. Wells and others of his ilk, fascinated by the potential in the newest technologies of their day.

In 1878 Thomas Edison had patented his first "talking machine." By 1890, he was marketing dolls containing wax cylinders that could be set to project wordlike sounds, seeming to come from the dolls themselves. Ernest Edward Kellett's 1899 story "The New Frankenstein" trumped Edison's accomplishments—in fiction, at least. In it an inventor, Arthur Moore, develops an "anti-phonograph": "a triumph of civilisation" that, in the words of the narrator, can "give the appropriate *answer* to each question I like to put!" Like Edison's, Moore's instrument is fitted out with two tubes, a receiver (or "ear") and a speaker, from which emerges "a sweet and beautifully modulated feminine voice." He installs the anti-phonograph into "a creature that will guide herself, answer questions, talk and eat like a rational being, in fact, perform the part of a society lady." He succeeds so thoroughly that soon two suitors propose to the creature, and she agrees to marry both. One of them learns of the deceit and plunges a knife into his would-be bride. "There was a whirr, a rush. The anti-phonograph was broken," describes the narrator. "I bent over her, and opened her dress to staunch the wound.

Moore had made no provision for her bleeding *there*. As I drew out the dagger, it was followed by a rush of sawdust."At the same moment the creator himself collapses: "He had put his life into his masterpiece; his wonderful toy was broken, and the cord of Moore's life was broken with it."

In Harle Oren Cummins's "The Man Who Made a Man," published in *McClure's* in 1901, it takes only two weeks and one successful experiment to plunge Professor Aloysius Holbrok from the chairmanship of the "department of Synthetic Chemistry in one of the famous American colleges" to "the Rathborn Asylum for the Insane." Holbrok tells a friend, "I am going to do what has never been done in the history of the world, except by God himself—I am going to *make a man*!" Using "only the contents of a few re-agent bottles, a blowpipe, and an electric battery," Holbrok creates "a mass of human flesh." By 1901 public utility networks laced through major American cities, carrying electricity from customer to customer, so it was not farfetched for Cummins to propose that his scientist could draw electricity "from off the mains of the street current outside."A two-thousand-volt surge runs through the uninsulated copper bits attached to key points on the fleshly body, and "then before our starting eyes that thing which was only a mass of chemical compounds *became a man*." The body twitches and sits up, the mouth opens and groans, and—in a matter of three paragraphs—the story ends with some "Higher Hand" using the same electrical current to turn the being into "a charred and cinder-like mass." As if the appearance of the hand of God were not moral imperative enough, the author ends his story with a cautionary scene: "The man who had made a man could not explain, for he was crawling about on the floor, counting the nails in the boards and laughing wildly."

THE MONSTER MEETS THE SCREEN

In 1891 the Edison Company filed for two patents: one for the kinetograph, a camera that captured a series of images on a strip of emulsion-coated celluloid film, and the other for the kinetoscope, a lectern-shaped wooden pedestal topped with a binocular viewer. A person would stand at the kinetoscope, peer down into the viewer, and watch as flashes from an electric lamp illuminated each frame of the film in fast succession. Visitors to the Brooklyn Institute of Arts and Sciences on May 9, 1893, had the thrill of watching the first moving pictures. Three years later methods of projecting the image onto a large screen had been developed, including Edison's Projectoscope. Soon dozens of people could watch a film at one time during showings at the neighborhood nickelodeon. Edison expanded his company to include film production, and for almost twenty years, from 1896 to 1914, the Edison Film Company was a leading producer of silent movies. Limited to a one-thousand-foot strip of film, each Edison picture ran about fifteen minutes. Usually a theater would project several in one seating.

In its heyday the Edison Film Company was cranking out several moving pictures a week. They were black-and-white silents with still title frames offering story contexts and occasional dialogue. "Actuality films" of current events and travelogues were as popular as comedies and melodramas. Edison and others formed the Motion Picture Patents Company, also called the Trust, which kept a grip on the moving picture business by controlling the film and projector technology used by local movie houses. Quickly a competitor sprang up: the Independent Motion Picture Company, led by film producer Carl Laemmle, Sr., and ultimately to become Universal Pictures.

The EDISON
KINETOGRAM

VOL. 2   MARCH 15, 1910   No. 4

SCENE FROM
FRANKENSTEIN
FILM No. 8604

EDISON FILMS RELEASED FROM
MARCH 16 TO 31 INCLUSIVE

One of dozens of silent shorts released by Edison Films in March 1910, *Frankenstein* was promised by producers to be appropriate for all viewers, despite the reputation of the novel and its sensational story.

In the week of March 18, 1910, more than thirty films were released to American theaters from the two manufacturers. Local theaters would choose their own combination of shorts for a full matinee. Titles included *Fruit Growing, Grand Valley, Colorado*; *Her Cowboy Lover*; *A Trip Up the Rhine*; *The Taming of Wild Horses*; *Father's Patriotism*—and the Edison Film Company's *Frankenstein*.

Turning the novel into a fifteen-minute silent film meant stripping away subplots—not to mention various excrescences now attached through stage and prose retellings—and focusing on the heart of the story. The producer's dramatic synopsis called it "a liberal adaptation" of the original novel. A young man bids adieu to family and friends, headed for college. In two years' time, according to the titles, he discovers "the mystery of life." He writes his sweetheart: "In a few hours I shall create into life the most perfect human being that the world has known," the title shows in handwriting—a particularly difficult technical detail that made this film's budget bulge. "When this marvelous work is accomplished," his letter continued, "I shall then return to claim you for my bride."

Sharing his library with a seated skeleton, Frankenstein pours a vial of this, a dash of that into an immense cauldron, then encloses the cauldron in a closet and bolts the door. He views the results of his experiment through a peephole, just as if he were watching a kinetoscopic film. We share his vision: Out of the cauldron emerges, in jerky stages of growth, a smoky being. "Flesh begins to creep over the bones," as the production notes put it. A massive trunk arises; an articulated arm flings up, fingers flailing; a skull with searing eye sockets looms into view— "probably the most weird, mystifying and fascinating scene ever shown on a film," promised Edison promotional material.

The on-film creation of the monster in Edison's *Frankenstein* was a clever photographic trick, an early foray into the realm of film art that would forever be challenged by Mary Shelley's story: special effects. The smoke surrounding the emerging creature

In 1910 the Edison Company's monster was concocted in a steaming cauldron, his haunting emergence created by filming a burning effigy and then showing the sequence of images backwards.

hints at the filmmakers' secrets. Look closely, and it seems to be seething *into* the cauldron, not out of it. Edison Company special-effects artists created a flammable model of the creature, set it afire, filmed its destruction—and then showed the frames backward. The ashes reassemble into a charred remain, then gain bodily substance, and finally assume the form of this Frankenstein's monster. Each phase of the creature's emergence is cross-cut with shots of the creator, more and more alarmed at what he has done. Finally, the creature has come fully to life: a vaguely human torso with two arms and a hairy head. Frankenstein pantomimes his horror in the most melodramatic of gestures, intensified by the eerie appearance of his monster's hand, fingers long and pointed like spider legs, reaching out from behind the closet door.

Playing the monster for the Edison Film Company, actor Charles Ogle was largely responsible for this 1910 interpretation of the monster. Six feet tall and broad of shoulder, Ogle was a well-established New York stage actor when he joined the Edison Stock Company in 1909. His roles ranged far and wide, including Scrooge in *A Christmas Carol,* George Washington in *The Father of Our Country,* and Long John Silver in *Treasure Island.* Working closely with Ogle was film director J. Searle Dawley, known for his risky special effects, like the eagle carrying a baby in its talons in the 1908 film *Rescued from the Eagle's Nest* or the minute devil figures dancing on a dreamer's headboard in the 1906 surrealist film *Dreams of the Rarebit Fiend.*

In the Edison *Frankenstein,* as in the original novel, the newly arisen monster peers through curtains around the bed on which his creator has fainted. Still unclothed, the monster's hairy upper body connects with the exaggerated mass of hair on his head, animal-like. In the next scene he is swaddled in rags from neck to toe. Only his head and his eerie, long-fingered hands reveal the warty, sinewy texture of his skin. His facial makeup accentuates the eyes, with darkened sockets and painted eyebrow arcs. His massive matted wig rises up out of a headband that makes his forehead look broad and tall. His clothing and posture suggest a hunchback. He walks with a shuffle; wrappings around his feet make them unnaturally long and broad.

Early films were limited to just a few stage settings and to a single camera angle for each set. A large part of Edison's *Frankenstein* takes place in a parlor, dominated by a full-length mirror. By using reflections in the mirror as part of the action, the director was able to evoke a second, less solid layer of reality, a special effect that emphasizes the psychological relationship between creature and creator. Taking up a quarter of the frame, the mirror's angle gives the moviegoer a straight-on view of anyone entering the parlor. First, as if to establish its reliability, the mir-

A mirror on the set of Edison's *Frankenstein* not only allowed multiple points of view despite a fixed camera but also suggested the shadowy psychological relationship between the monster and his maker.

ror reflects Frankenstein's fiancée, Elizabeth. The two embrace, she exits, and within seconds, the monster enters, first seen only as a reflection in the glass. Even Frankenstein sees the monster first in the mirror, then turns to confront him face-to-face. Ogle points in the direction of Elizabeth's exit, clasps his hands to his chest, then raises them above his head, pleading. Creator and creature struggle, during which the monster glimpses himself in the mirror for the first time. He throws up his hands in dismay, then "shrinks away in terror," as the stage directions put it.

These scenes prepare for the climax, described this way in the production notes:

Monster enters—business of seeing reflection of himself. Original fades leaving the reflection still in glass. Frankenstein enters

> at door. His reflection takes place over monster's. Monster fades
> leaving Frankenstein's reflection there. Frankenstein [crosses]
> room—sinks in chair as bride comes in. Winds up with Franken-
> stein and bride in each others [*sic*] arms.

It was a sequence of masterful splicing. For a few seconds the
monster looks at himself in the mirror. Then he fades into noth-
ingness, but his reflection remains, suggesting that he was just a
projection of Frankenstein's imagination. As if to confirm that,
we next see Frankenstein gazing into the mirror—yet he is
reflected not as himself but as his monstrous creation. Finally the
image blurs and changes again, resolving into a normal image of
Frankenstein gazing at his own reflection in the mirror. He has
triumphed over the projection of his own evil obsessions and can
now turn and sincerely embrace his beloved, who returns into the
frame. Innovations that would fascinate an audience newly
thrilled by moving pictures, these mirror tricks also supported
the theme of this version of the Frankenstein myth, expressed
in the title that opens this final scene: "The creation of an evil mind
is overcome by love and disappears." Inner evil conjures up monsters; true love makes them disappear. Such a sentimental moral
was sure to satisfy the taste of an audience in 1910.

The Frankenstein story still had the potential to offend cus-
tomers, however, and an article in the *Edison Kinetogram,* the catalog distributed to theater owners, assured them that they had
nothing to worry about:

> In making the film the Edison Company has carefully tried to
> eliminate all the actually repulsive situations and to concen-
> trate its endeavors upon the mystic and psychological prob-
> lems that are to be found in this weird tale. Wherever,
> therefore, the film differs from the original story it is purely

with the idea of eliminating what would be repulsive to a moving picture audience.

We know little about how Edison's *Frankenstein* was received. The phenomenon of theatrical films was so new that no one wrote film reviews. The few articles that appeared cribbed language from the *Kinetogram*. "The actually repulsive situations in the original version have been carefully eliminated in its visualized form, so that there is no possibility of its shocking any portion of an audience," wrote the *Moving Picture World,* a trade publication. "It is safe to say that no film has ever been released that can surpass it in its power to fascinate an audience."

"The entire film is one that will create a new impression that the possibilities of the motion picture in reproducing these stories is scarcely realized, yet they will do much for literature in this direction," said a second commentary published in the *Moving Picture World* two weeks after the film's release. "Very many, for example, will see this picture who have never read the story, and will acquire a lasting impression of its power." The prescience of this comment is uncanny: It would indeed be the film medium (though not Edison's version) that was to carry the myth forward in unforeseen directions, giving it new form and messages that obscured those—or the absence of those—found in the original novel.

While twenty-first-century viewers consider Edison's *Frankenstein* a fascinating treasure, it was just another movie to viewers in its time. Like others it played in theaters and then cycled back to the company warehouse. Other film companies were surpassing Edison's in film technologies, discovering ways to show multiple reels, telling longer stories, and soon synchronizing sound with film as it was projected. In 1914 both the Edison film studio building in the Bronx and the Edison laboratory in Orange, New Jersey, were damaged by fire. The U.S. government clamped down on the Trust Company's film monopoly in 1915. Edison officially closed down his Motion Picture Division in 1920. Amid the drastic demise, archives of the Edison Film Company disappeared. Only the most informed of silent-film aficionados even knew that a 1910 *Frankenstein* had existed. Some have surmised that prints of Edison's *Frankenstein* were destroyed in righteous outrage, too, its subject matter perennially disturbing to moralizers. For whatever reason, the film nearly disappeared soon after its creation. Its reappearance in the late twentieth century is a story worth telling on its own.

In 1980 *Box Office Magazine* published a list of the ten most important films lost to history. The oldest was Edison's *Frankenstein*. Alois Felix Detlaff, a Wisconsin film collector, read the article and discovered what a gem he owned. Detlaff told various versions of the story, but apparently in the 1950s he had obtained a print of the 1910 *Frankenstein*. It was one in a batch of twenty or thirty films he bought together, and his recollection was that he paid about twenty dollars for all of them. "It was in bad shape, it had shrunken about 8%, so it wouldn't run through a regular projector, and it got ripped a little bit," Detlaff told Frederick C. Wiebel, Jr., a freelance artist from Maryland who became devoted to bringing the Edison film back into public view. Detlaff copied the fragile frames onto 35 mm film, losing a few along the way. For years he jealously guarded the film, refusing to deposit copies in any of the national film archives. He showed it occasionally in Milwaukee theaters at Halloween and, delighted with the reception, sought new ways to share it—for a profit. Television networks bought rights to show clips of the film. Receiving more and more invitations to speak at film history and monster movie events, slowly Detlaff warmed to the idea of sharing his precious possession with the larger public. Once films could be reproduced cheaply on DVD, he packaged Edison's *Frankenstein* with F. W. Murnau's *Nosferatu,* a 1922 rendition of the Dracula story, and marketed the pair as "Movies' First Monsters Back to Back."

Alois F. Detlaff died in 2005, but by then his unique copy of the film had reached thousands. Edison archivists and film historians agree that Edison's *Frankenstein* has more importance in retrospect than it did when it was made. To screenstruck viewers in 1910, it was a passing thrill. Today it's another episode in the evolution of the monster that will not die.

Myths of Modern Science

It's ironic that the version of *Frankenstein* sponsored by the so-called father of electricity should in no way rely on lightning or on any electrical apparatus to dramatize how the monster comes to life. The 1910 monster's creation was strictly chemical, suiting the popular science of the time. No longer was electromagnetism the science of the future, as it was when the novel was written. Now biochemistry seemed to promise unimaginable advances. says he can create life, announced a headline in the 1904 *New York Times,* topping a short report of a physician in Indiana who "made the positive assertion that he has succeeded in creating animal matter in the form of insect life . . . by means of a chemical compound and by actual demonstration in his laboratory." The article briefly described his method: "Ammonia, alcohol, and distilled water added to a quantity of salt, and the whole inclosed in a glass tube for a period of about one hour." There appears to have been little follow-up to this experiment, but such news articles primed the public's imagination.

Knowledge about the growth, analysis, and manipulation of tissues in culture provided necessary building blocks for understanding chromosomes, genes, and genetics later in the century. Botanists had already succeeded in isolating and cultivating plant cells; the excitement grew when scientists began claiming similar results on animals. By 1910 the eminent biochemist Jacques Loeb had accomplished in-vitro fertilization and maturation of sea urchin eggs. Loeb's name may be little known today, but he was a hero in his times. Born in Germany in 1859, he immigrated to the United States and worked in the new field of embryology, holding research positions in Chicago and California, at New York's Rockefeller Institute, and with the new marine biological laboratory in Woods Hole, Massachusetts. When Loeb died in 1924 he was eulogized as someone whose "ideas may do more to change mankind's opinion of its place in the world . . . than those of any man of the modern era." He believed that "all living things are chemical machines and that their workings are open to the same mechanistic explanation which explains the operation of any machine made out of inert matter." Newspaper articles popularized his work with phrases like "the elixir of life" and "the creation of artificial life" and quoted Loeb as saying that "Nothing indicates that the artificial production of living matter is beyond the possibilities of science."

While Loeb was exploring life at the cellular level, his Rockefeller Institute colleague Alexis Carrel was pressing the limits of limb and organ transplantation in animals and humans. On March 27, 1910—ten days after the release of Edison's *Frankenstein*— half a page of the *New York Times* Sunday edition was devoted to Carrel's success at what we would now call open-heart surgery on cats and dogs. Experiment after experiment from Carrel's laboratory made the newspapers. He stitched a damaged vein in a newborn's leg to a major artery in her father's wrist, thus creating a live transfusion that, according to the article, saved the life of the baby. He worked with a St. Louis colleague to graft the head of one dog onto the body of another. As his work evolved, he experimented with growing living tissue outside the body. HEART TISSUE BEATS LONG AFTER DEATH, cried one headline in 1912. DR. CARREL ANNOUNCES STARTLING RESULTS OF HIS EXPERIMENTS WITH CULTURES: "PERMANENT LIFE" POSSIBLE. One article even called him a "modern Frankenstein."

Working together at the Rockefeller Institute, Carrel and Loeb seemed destined to succeed at what Mary Shelley's character had accomplished in fiction. Public debate and collegial skepticism swirled around them, but the two scientists used the grandest of language to describe their goals. CLOSE TO MYSTERY OF LIFE, SAYS LOEB, read one headline in July 1912. "The day when the creation of a protoplasm shall be achieved . . . is not far distant," Carrel said in the article. "The day will come, very probably, when science will force into the light of day the mystery of life. On that day we shall be able to create living beings." Three months later, in honor of his work in suturing blood vessels and transplanting organs, Alexis Carrel received the Nobel Prize in Medicine. Reality leapfrogged over fiction, and a process represented in a 1910 film as arcane alchemy now appeared, a few years later, to be authentic laboratory science, triggering the need for an updated adaptation of the myth of a man who succeeded in making life.

PARTNERS IN MONSTROSITY

Associations advanced between the Frankenstein myth and modern technology, too, as the specter of lifelike machinery continued to loom. Assembly lines shaped the work to be done, and human labor became as much the operation of machines as it was the making of products. Factory workers felt as if they were becoming machines themselves. Worse than that, they worried that they could be replaced by machines, which could be designed to do human work, only faster, better, and without any need for food, water, breaks, sleep, or paychecks. The growing anxiety was brilliantly captured in a 1915 play that spawned the universal word for a manmade, manlike machine: "robot," from the Czech for worker or slave. Czech playwright Karel Čapek's *R.U.R. (Rossum's Universal Robots),* written in 1915, dramatized the new future terror, the possibility of manufacturing human beings. The play takes a scientist like Victor Frankenstein and gives him a futuristic twist.

"Cheap Labor. Rossum's Robots," reads a marketing sign at company headquarters. Harry Domin, general manager for the company called Rossum's Universal Robots, cautiously tells a visitor "the story of the invention":

> It was in the year 1920 that old Rossum the great physiologist, who was then quite a young scientist, took himself to this distant island for the purpose of studying the ocean fauna. . . . On this occasion he attempted by chemical synthesis to imitate the living matter known as protoplasm until he suddenly discovered a substance which behaved exactly like living matter although its chemical composition was different.

Rossum used this imitation protoplasm to make human beings. "That old Rossum was mad," Domin continues. "The old crank wanted to actually make people." Domin even calls him "a sort of scientific substitute for God." Rossum's one success took ten years to manufacture and survived only three. His nephew, an engineer, took over the business, but with a new agenda. "If you can't make him quicker than nature, you might as well shut up shop," young Rossum believed, and so he "rejected man and made the Robot"—the new sort of monster made by man, a corollary to Frankenstein's creation.

In the public imagination the two sorts of manmade monsters would intersect and mingle. Soon popular culture adopted Čapek's word "robot," finding it useful to name anything from the metal-limbed automaton servants to the ray-gun-wielding aliens appearing on celluloid. In the mid-1930s, Čapek reflected on all that had been done with his play. "The author cannot be blamed," he wrote, "for what might be called the worldwide humbug over the robots." He wanted the world to know that in his own imagination, the robots of his play "were not mechanisms. They were not made of sheet-metal and cogwheels. They were not a celebration of mechanical engineering" but "were created quite differently—that is, by a chemical path." He had meant for young Rossum to create "a new kind of matter by chemical synthesis," "an organic substance," "something like another alternative to life" that will "reach its fulfilment only when . . . the robots acquire souls." The record corrected, Čapek felt more confident that his public would understand that he "did not invent his robots with the technological hubris of a mechanical engineer, but with the metaphysical humility of a spiritualist." Mary Shelley never wrote such a defense against later misinterpretations, but she might have wanted to had she lived long enough to see what became of her monster. Each author had crafted a story so prescient that it was swept up into the popular culture, adopted, adapted, and reshaped with associations and meanings quite different from those that the author originally and consciously intended.

Both situations offer a lesson in the differences between artist and artwork, between meaning—the artist's consciously intended message—and significance—all the other messages and ideas assigned to a work of art once it has been shared with the world. It is the same lesson learned, ironically, by Victor Frankenstein. Once loose in the world, a creation evolves beyond the reach of its creator. While Čapek intended his play as a "protest against the mechanical superstition of our times," he also presented to the world a word to embody those superstitions and give them life and sustenance. With glum acceptance Čapek watched his abstract meaning take on metallic flesh. "The world needed mechanical robots," he wrote bitterly, "for it believes in machines more than it believes in life." In similar fashion the world needed a monster made by a Frankenstein, and the myth lived on, reproducing ever more monsters through the twentieth century.

CHAPTER SIX

A MONSTER FOR MODERN TIMES

*There is a violent streak in all of us: and if it can be exploded in
the cinema instead of in some anti-social manner
in real life, so much the better.*

—BORIS KARLOFF, 1957

Making "Frankenstein" was the most interesting job I ever tackled.

—JAMES WHALE, 1931

In 1931 something irreversible happened to Frankenstein. Universal Studios released its landmark version of the story, directed by James Whale and featuring a nameless monster played by a relative unknown with the stage name of Boris Karloff. That film's portayal of the century-old story locked in new and indelible imagery for the monster. It had so wide and powerful an influence that ever since, renditions of the story have either depended on, ricocheted off, or actively defended against associations with it. Those sunken cheeks, that square-topped head, and the neck bolts developed by makeup artist Jack Pierce for Boris Karloff came to stand for Frankenstein's monster to everyone, even those who had never heard the name of Mary Shelley. For the monster it was the best of times, it was the worst of times. He attained worldwide celebrity, but his story got wrenched into a simplistic fable.

The Precursors

London theatergoers had thrilled to a portrayal of the monster by entrepreneur and actor Hamilton Deane, whose production of a new *Frankenstein* opened in 1927. Deane had successfully staged *Dracula* earlier that year, introducing as the vampire an unknown Hungarian actor who took the stage name Bela Lugosi. *Frankenstein* seemed the obvious follow-up. Deane tried to convince the playwright John Balderston to adapt Shelley's novel, the two of them having had such success with *Dracula*. Balderston declined, and Deane partnered instead with playwright Peggy Webling, who had just composed a new stage version of *Frankenstein*.

British-born Webling had moved to Canada and by 1927, at about age forty, had published more than a dozen novels and a children's book, *Saints and Their Stories*. Described by one contemporary as "a gentle little gray-haired lady," she interpreted Shelley's novel as a morality play about the limits of human knowledge: "I warn you, solemnly, against the sin of vain presumption. From God alone is the breath of life," utters Dr. Waldman, Frankenstein's professor and the voice of moral conservatism in the play. But Frankenstein has already fed the "elixir of life" to the body he has prepared, and he watches with awe as it begins to move. As the stage directions describe it, the creature "slowly clenches and unclenches his hand, and raises it over his head. He draws a breath with a groan, lifts his head, opens his eyes and glares at [Frankenstein], then sinks back with another groan, while the men watch him in speechless dismay."

Webling switched the first names of scientist and friend, so that the obsessed creator became Henry and his friend became Victor.

Some believe that the change commemorated London actor Henry Hallatt, who played Frankenstein in Deane's production. Whatever the reason, the switch found its way into the 1931 film and many more thereafter. Webling took another liberty with Shelley's original: "I call him by my own name," the creator says early in the play. "He *is* Frankenstein." It was not simply a decision about names, however, for the guiding theme of Webling's play is the identity of monster and maker, a continuation of the mirror imagery explored in the Edison film. When Frankenstein's fiancée first sees his creation, for instance, Webling's stage directions call for the two male figures to "stand facing the girl in exactly the same attitude." She exclaims, "Henry, who is this? You are both alike!" Photographs from the London stage performance show that maker and monster wore identical Regency-era costumes: blousy shirts, greatcoats, and boots.

Hamilton Deane's monster differed from his maker in height and in face, though. Deane, more than six feet tall to begin with, wore lifts in his heels. His makeup was "a strange mixture of blue, green and red," according to Ivan Butler, a film historian who played Victor with Deane onstage and whose memories are chronicled in David J. Skal's *The Monster Show*. Butler's memory, along with every publicity photo of Deane as the Frankenstein monster, emphasizes Deane's lips. Thick to begin with, they became even more so thanks to bright red greasepaint. His makeup may have been garish, but his interpretation was tender. "Except for the final moments of the play there was little horror as the word is usually understood," Butler told Skal. Deane "played the monster very much for sympathy—indeed, he could bring tears to one's eyes."

Webling's play called for such a passionate performance. By the end of the first act Frankenstein reveals that he has threatened his

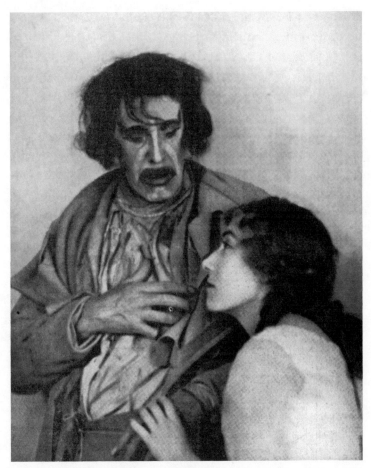

Hamilton Deane, early-twentieth-century London impresario, revived
Frankenstein on stage and played a thick-lipped monster. Written by Peggy
Webling, the play introduced Katrina, a pale young girl whom the mon-
ster unknowingly drowns.

creature into submission. When Waldman points out the greater
physical strength of the being, the younger scientist responds
rhetorically: "What is the courage of a wild beast compared to the

cruelty of man?" By the end of the play, he becomes the victim of his own creation, as the monster "leaps at Henry's throat, like an animal" and, after a short struggle, kills his maker in fury over his own loveless existence. "He is dead who brought me to life, and I—shall be dead soon—and find—God. Rest! Rest! Dead—very soon," he stammers. He "groans and moves blindly" across the stage, as if losing any human acuity. A "vivid flash of lightning" strikes the monster dead, and "he falls, instantly, shattered." Both deaths seem fit moral conclusions. The prideful monster maker is punished and, his creator gone, the creature devolves until destroyed by the forces of nature. Peggy Webling's *Frankenstein* concluded with all again right with the world.

CORPORATE BODY

It is not simply a coincidence of history that the most famous Frankenstein film of all was created during the Depression. World War I had shown the terror as well as the triumph of new technology—its mechanized military maneuvers causing ghastly physical deformations if not outright slaughter. The twenties roared with optimism, but the crash of 1929 left people tottering precariously. They wanted entertainment to take them into a realm of fantasy, to raise their heart rates without reminding them of real-world dangers. The continuing flow of immigrants into the cities looked like competition to those already feeling disenfranchised from the American dream. All these feelings played out on the movie screen. As film historian David Skal points out, in this one year, 1931, American moviegoers reveled in *Dracula, Frankenstein, Dr. Jekyll and Mr. Hyde,* and, oddest of all, *Freaks,* Tod Browning's sideshow drama featuring physically deformed actors. Commentators of the time saw what was going on. "People like the tragic best at those time[s] when their own spirits are depressed," wrote an industry analyst in the *Motion Picture Herald,* "and the economists tell us that even more than their spirits are at a low ebb." Columnist Nelson B. Bell wrote a February 1932 front-page opinion piece in the *Washington Post,* "Thoughts on Horror Era," connecting "this disquieting and startling manifestation of public preference" for the new genre of horror film with the "trying period of economic stress" throughout the world:

> Many are without employment, many are employed only by virtue of having accepted drastic curtailment of income, many live their daily lives in a state of constant dread of the disaster that may overtake them at any minute. This is a state of mind that creates a vast receptivity for misfortunes more poignant than our own. There is, paradoxically enough, a distinctly heartening effect in the sorry spectacle of someone worse off than ourselves.

A monster myth let moviegoers identify, escape, and comfort themselves that life was not as ugly as it could get.

In 1931 *Frankenstein* suited the times in other ways as well. In the two years before its release, references to the myth had resurfaced in the public forum. In the March 1930 issue of the *American Mercury*—the influential magazine founded by H. L. Mencken and published by Alfred A. Knopf—California attorney and poet Mitchell Dawson published an article titled "Frankenstein, Inc.," a survey of corporate law in the United States. Dawson evoked the myth to characterize the newly emerging American corporation, threatening to "monopolize the 'law business'" and sound "the knell of the small tradesman." He cited a 1913 article in the *Yale Law Journal* that predicted, "The lawyer is being devoured by his own Frankenstein." He quoted his friend Carl Sandburg, an observer of the law since he was a cub reporter working the labor beat, who described the problem as an unwise extension of the power of lawyers. "Perhaps they knew too much when they played with the divine fire—long before the advent of the tel-electric man—and created an artificial person who could exer-cise many human functions, with the advantage of relative immortality and the soullessness of a robot," wrote Dawson. He referred to the corporation as "a legal organism—built up of indi-vidual cells like the human body, but having a separate existence of its own."

The same analogy arose in a book, titled *Frankenstein, Incorpo-rated,* and published in October 1931, two months before the first screening of the Karloff movie. The author, I. Maurice Wormser, hastened to explain that he had chosen the Frankenstein motif without reading Dawson's article, yet he, too, used the myth to characterize the corporation. "We all are familiar with Mrs. Shel-ley's thrilling tale of Frankenstein," wrote Wormser,

> the modern Prometheus, who artificially created a vitalized monster which became the terror of "all living things" and threatened the security and well-being of mankind. The fable is not without its application to the corporate business organi-zation of to-day. Corporations are not natural living persons, but artificial beings, *corpora ficta.* They are created by the nation or state, which endows them with distinct personality in the eyes of the law, special privileges and comprehensive powers. Frankenstein's creature developed into a deadly men-ace to his creator.

Wormser argued for government regulation of corporations, lest "a few all-powerful corporate creatures may destroy or at least overpower their creator."

Dawson and Wormser both established an association that

lives on to the present day: the corporation as an entity created by society, intended to behave like an individual but in fact growing into a monster that menaces and may ultimately overwhelm its maker. Metaphoric usages like these revived the name "Frankenstein" in the early 1930s and readied the public consciousness for what was soon to come.

UNIVERSAL HORROR

In Hollywood, the Carl Laemmles, father and son, were building their own corporate monster, although in the 1930s Universal Pictures was the studio underdog, its name a presumption of grandeur yet to be. The Laemmles had been trying to find a niche in which their company could thrive. They enjoyed some early successes—*The Hunchback of Notre Dame* starring Lon Chaney, released in 1923, and *All Quiet on the Western Front,* which won the Academy Award for Best Picture in 1930. Like other American businesses, though, the film company struggled to survive during Depression-era times, losing money, forced into layoffs, and even halting production for six weeks in March and April 1931. Two horror films soon resuscitated the business, though—the old familiar pair: *Dracula* and *Frankenstein.*

Bela Lugosi brought the bloodthirsty nobleman from stage to screen, and *Dracula*, released in February 1931, became an instant classic. It soon brought in the money that Universal needed to revive operations. Lugosi assumed that he would star in the studio's next horror film, no matter what that film would be. Forces converged and—despite some skepticism from the Universal creative team—Mary Shelley's *Frankenstein* was selected. Robert Florey, already well established as a writer and director in Hollywood and London, presented a brief proposal to the Laemmles, articulating how he would film the novel. In his vision of the story, the monster's violence arose from a criminal brain implanted in him. His script climaxed inside a burning windmill—an image, Florey later recounted, that came to him as he gazed out his window at a rotating display atop the Van de Kamp bakery building nearby. At the same time Carl Laemmle, Jr., bought the film rights to Peggy Webling's play. Universal paid $20,000, promising Webling 1 percent of gross receipts worldwide once the film was released, and engaged John Balderston to Americanize the script, just as he had done for the *Dracula* that Hamilton Deane had staged in London. Half a dozen scripts of *Frankenstein* whizzed around the Universal offices during the months of April and May, representing the enthusiasm and chaos that the project excited. The ultimate story was a synthesis with words and ideas from Florey, Webling, Balderston, other writers working at Universal, together with on-the-spot decisions by director James Whale and his actors, especially Boris Karloff, as they brought the script to life.

James Whale, a young actor, director, and stage manager, had come from London to the United States in 1929 to bring his successful production of R. C. Sherriff's World War I drama, *Journey's End,* to Broadway. Starring as Capt. Dennis Stanhope, the nerve-wracked company commander, was Colin Clive, who traveled to New York with the show as well. Together Whale and Clive shuttled from East Coast to West and made the harrowing play into a film. Laemmle noticed the young new director—*Journey's End* placed fourth on the *New York Times*'s Ten Best Films list in 1930—and wooed him to Universal. Whale's first Universal film was *Waterloo Bridge*; *Frankenstein* his second. It secured him success that should have lasted a long lifetime.

Whale saw the promise in Mary Shelley's story. "It was the strongest meat and gave me a chance to dabble in the macabre," he told the *New York Times* in 1931. He found it especially "amusing" to make a film unraveling the story of something that "everybody knows to be a physical impossibility." From the first glimpse of the creature, Whale wanted the film to be believable—therefore gripping—and popular. He spoke as if he considered the Frankenstein story wide open to interpretation, "with a subject which might go anywhere—and that is part of the fun of making pictures." Whale chose key cast members, starting with Colin Clive. "I see Frankenstein as an intensely sane person," Whale wrote his fellow Englishman, "at times rather fanatical and in one or two scenes a little hysterical, [but] never unsympathetic, even to the monster." Whale exhorted Clive to modulate his diction and "get that looseness, instead of what Americans think of as English tightness, in speech." They were dramatizing a "medieval story," Whale believed, but he wanted the result to be "a very modern, materialistic treatment."

For a time, all involved had assumed Bela Lugosi would play in *Frankenstein*. Robert Florey envisioned him as the scientist, but Laemmle and fellow producers were thinking otherwise. Once a monster, always a monster; cash in on brand continuity. Lugosi condescended to a screen test but argued with studio makeup man Jack Pierce over what his monster look should be. They compromised on a clay-caked, expressionless look inspired by the manmade man in the 1920 German film *The Golem*. Someone along the way said that Lugosi looked more like a doll from *Babes in Toyland*. In the long run Lugosi refused to play the part. "I was a star in my country, and I will not be a scarecrow over here!" he shouted. Ultimately both he and Florey got squeezed out of the project and together created *Murders in the Rue Morgue*, which screened in 1932 but never matched its monster predecessors in renown.

As the script gelled, a vision was forming in the director's mind as to the sort of monster the film needed. "It does not walk like a Robot," Whale's final script specifically stated. His would be a creature of flesh and bones, not a Čapek-inspired machine-man. A number of established actors, including the solemn-faced John Carradine, were invited to screen for the part, but over and over, actors saw the role as beneath them. Hidden under makeup, not allowed to speak, subhuman in gesture and intellect—why would any actor stoop to play such a part?

A New Monster Discovered

As the story goes, James Whale was eating lunch in the Universal Studios cafeteria when he spotted the man who fit the monster. "Boris Karloff's face has always fascinated me," Whale said a year later. A January 1931 casting directory includes a photograph of Karloff in Howard Hawks's film *The Criminal Code,* produced that year. There are the features that sparked Whale's imagination: high forehead; straight, shelflike brow; dark eyebrows looming over deep-set eyes, points of darkness peering out from large pools of white; sculpted cheekbones; straight, downturned nose; and a stern line for a mouth.

"Suddenly he caught my eye and beckoned me over," Karloff, then a little-known actor, later recalled. "I leapt—he was the most important director on the lot. He asked me to sit down. I did, holding my breath, and then he said: Your face has startling possibilities." It was a mythic moment, and who knows if it really occurred. Elsewhere Karloff told this story differently: It was a "studio executive" who noticed him, with his "ugly cropped hair" and "gruesome make-up" for *The Criminal Code,* and then tested and signed him on for the part of the monster. No matter what the circumstances, it was surely the face, more than any particular acting talent, that first drew Whale to the man who would shape the monster forever.

Boris Karloff was born William Henry Pratt in England in 1887. His career as a character actor on the dark side had begun with his first stage appearance, in a school play of *Cinderella*. "I donned black tights and a skull cap and rallied the forces of evil as the Demon King," he remembered. "From then on I resolved to be an actor." He immigrated to Canada in 1909 and starting working with local theater troupes for fifteen dollars a week. Along the way he took up a stage name. "Karloff came from relatives on my mother's side," and "the Boris I plucked out of the cold Canada air," he told interviewers in 1962. In the late 1920s he made a smooth transition to the talkies, despite a stutter and a lisp. He played bit parts in the shadows of Douglas Fairbanks, Sr. and Jr., Wallace Beery, Lionel Barrymore, John Barrymore, Edward G. Robinson, James Cagney, and the comic duo of Stan Laurel and Oliver Hardy. By the time he met Whale, he had been acting for nearly twenty years and had played in nearly eighty movies, at least a dozen already in 1931 alone. He was shooting a film called *Graft*, a cub-reporter-blows-politician's-cover drama with Karloff cast as the gangster. At forty-four years old he was, by his own description, "an obscure actor playing obscure parts," no star but at least making a living. "For the first time in my life I had been gainfully employed long enough to buy myself some new clothes and spruce up a bit—actually, I rather fancied meself!" recalled Karloff later. "Now, to hide all this new-found beauty under monster-makeup?" But if Karloff was anything, he was humble—and eager. "I said I'd be delighted."

Whale immediately started sketching Karloff's features, adding "sharp, bony ridges where I imagined the skull might have

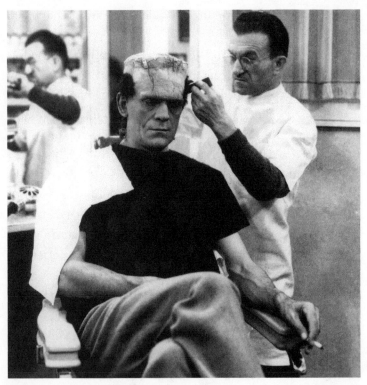

For Universal's first three Frankenstein films, makeup artist Jack Pierce spent hours before and after every day's shooting, working with Boris Karloff to create and then remove the intricate skin, scars, reconstructed face, and body parts of the monster.

been joined," and projecting his natural features out to monstrous dimensions. Meanwhile makeup artist Jack Pierce had been three months at his research on the proper appearance of a monstrous creation such as might have been made by Frankenstein. He began by reading the novel and then plunged into the study of anatomy. "I made him the way textbooks said he should look," Pierce told a reporter in 1939.

My anatomical studies taught me that there are six ways a surgeon can cut the skull in order to take out or put in a brain. I fig-
ured that Frankenstein, who was a scientist but no practicing
surgeon, would take the simplest surgical way. He would cut the
top of the skull off straight across like a potlid, hinge it, pop the
brain in and then clamp it on tight. That is the reason I decided
to make the monster's head square and flat like a shoe box and
dig that big scar across his forehead with the metal clamps holding it together.

The studs attached to the monster's neck Pierce explained as an
"inlet for electricity—plugs such as we use for our lamps or
flatirons." The "lizard eyes," as he called them, were evoked by
attaching rubber upper eyelids. Pierce molded cheesecloth over
Karloff's face and caked it with greasepaint to deepen the pores.
He sculpted strips of cotton batting soaked in collodion—a toxic
plastic lacquer—and attached them to his hands and forehead,
emulating scars. Karloff's own face added certain key features to
the look: His naturally thin lips and his indented upper lip and
chin needed only to be emphasized with makeup shading. He
removed a dental bridge, exaggerating a sunken cheekbone on
the right. The face thus created became a cultural icon.

A costumed Karloff strode onto the Universal set, lifted a
good three inches beyond his six-foot-three height, his clothing
dark, nondescript, and ill fitting. His big hands stretched beyond
his jacket cuffs, especially when he reached for the sunlit window, implored pity from his maker, or approached a victim.
Pierce used shoe polish to blacken Karloff's fingernails. Double-
quilted padding bulked up his torso; two pairs of trousers thick-
ened his legs. Through jacket and trouser legs ran steel rods,
which enforced a stiff stride and posture. The boots, steel and
leather, borrowed from an asphalt worker, weighed somewhere

between ten and eighteen pounds each—estimates varied from one account to the next. Karloff himself called his costume "full horrifying armor," complete with "metallic overalls." For the sake of the lights and camera, Pierce painted Karloff's face a shadowy blue-green, a hue concocted to ensure a lifeless gray on the black-and-white screen. Mae Clarke, who played Elizabeth, recalled that on the film set her fellow actor's skin tone provided "a sudden inspiration" that "awed us and gave Boris and the rest of us a different feeling about the whole concept."

NEW TWISTS

Universal's *Frankenstein* was a spectacular success. Audiences lined up for hours in order to see it. It grossed $53,000 in the first week and more than a million Depression-era dollars through the first release, making it one of the film industry's first blockbusters. No longer would cartoonists be free to shape or clothe a Frankenstein to suit the message of the day; Edison's hairy beast and Deane's lipsticked misfit faded from view. Boris Karloff's portrayal locked certain elements into the physical appearance of the monster—high forehead, flattop head, sunken cheeks, neck bolts, oversize limbs and undersized clothing, a lumbering gait, grunts and groans for speech—and created the gestalt that is still instantly recognizable.

Other features of the 1931 classic became necessary elements in the cultural icon. To orchestrate the dramatic creation scene, Universal hired Hollywood's up-and-coming special effects genius, Kenneth Strickfaden, for $3,000. A mechanical whiz who had turned his teenage fascination with electricity into a career, Strickfaden worked first at Coney Island, where he added sparking saws, flashing lights, and a calliope to the Temple of Music. As sound came to the screen, Strickfaden saw his niche

Not only the face but the full figure of Karloff's monster set the standard: padded shoulders and torso, long arms and fingers, superhuman height, and a gait made heavy-footed by asphalter's boots. His dark, ill-fitting suit became the norm as well.

and went west to Hollywood. He made the engines roar and the
machine guns fire in *Wings,* in 1927 the first film to receive an
Academy Award as Best Picture. Presented with the challenge of
creating machinery for Frankenstein's laboratory, Strickfaden
combined real science with futuristic fantasies. He took inspiration from the technological inventions of engineering visionary
Nikola Tesla, whose turn-of-the-century electrical inventions
were revolutionary, essential to future technologies, and often
labeled mad. So just as in 1818, when Aldini's demonstrations of
elevating corpses with electricity backlit the reading of Shelley's
novel, in 1931 movie audiences thrilled to see Tesla coils dis-
charging intense lightning bolts of power and cathode-ray tubes
focusing high voltages of energy to animate the dead.

Webling's play had not included an assistant for Frankenstein,
but the Universal film reestablished the stage tradition. Dwight
Frye created the part of Fritz, a dimwitted hunchback who operates on animal instincts more than the monster does. Despite
central roles in both *Frankenstein* and *Dracula* in 1931, the handsome young actor never rebounded from such typecasting.
Fritz's bumbling mistakes redirect the moral of the story in the
1931 *Frankenstein.* Sent by Frankenstein to fetch a brain for the
body, he drops the brain labeled "Normal" and carelessly fetches
the "Abnormal—Criminal" brain instead. That one scene muffles
most speculation about cause or motive in the monster's character, for the search for culpability threads inevitably back to Fritz's
mindless error. Sympathy for the monster might well have
shrunk with this plot decision, but Whale's artistry, combined
with Karloff's acting, rescued him from one-dimensional evil.

Horror trumped psychological exploration or theological debate
in this production. It was the genre that was keeping Universal Studios afloat. The Laemmles made sure that some scenes were created

for just that purpose. Whale left his audience in suspense longer than usual, for example, as they awaited the first glimpse of the creature, now brought to life and walking with eyes open. As Frankenstein and Waldman sit and argue the ethics of the situation, a door slowly opens. Through it walks a darkly clad figure, back to the camera. Slowly it approaches, walking backward. The camera moves in as the figure turns around. First a neck bolt, then a scar beneath the chin, then the heavy-lidded eyes come into view. The camera moves in even more closely, framing just the facial features. Karloff's eyes show more white than color, the irises roll up; the flesh of his cheeks and chin seems to cling to the bone. This is a face closer to death than life. Some audience members, it is rumored, fainted at the sight. Some of them, the rumors continued, had been hired by Universal.

Yet neither Whale nor Karloff was satisfied to make simply a scary monster. They understood that a myth must resonate with paradox and contradiction, and that the creature must win hearts as well as cause shivers. After obediently sitting down to Frankenstein's gestural command, the creature notices a shaft of daylight coming in from a window in the stone tower. He turns toward it, then stands, lifts his hands, and reaches toward the light. His muscular forearms stretch out of the too-short sleeves; his face yearns upward. These instincts are natural and familiar—at once plant seeking sunlight, animal seeking warmth, and human seeking the divine. Ordered by his maker to sit down again, the creature strikes an imploring pose. Palms up, eyes focused, head hunched forward, and mouth expectantly open: it is a universal gesture of dependency, vulnerability, and need. In those few minutes, we learn to care for this monster.

Filmmaking decisions about the monster's moral character continued up to the last. In one of the most controversial scenes in the film, the monster encounters Maria, a clear-eyed girl from the village whom he meets on a flower-strewn bank of the lake. At this point in the film, the creature has killed two men: Fritz, who took cruel delight in prodding him with a flaming torch, and Dr. Waldman, who intended to destroy him. Since each murder contains an element of self-defense, viewers can remain sympathetic. The limits of sympathy are tested, though, with the introduction of Maria, the 1931 film variation on the novel's William Frankenstein: Both are naive and loving young characters who cross paths with the monster at just the wrong time.

Maria shows the monster the simple pleasure of tossing flower blossoms to float on the water. Child is mother to the monster, and for the first time in the film, the beleaguered character smiles. In the earliest version of the film an elated monster reached for Maria and tossed her in, too. A momentary scene showed the water bubbling where Maria sank. According to Boris Karloff, he and James Whale argued over this episode, the actor advocating for more ambiguity and innocence on the monster's part.

> My conception of the scene . . . was that the Monster would look up at the little girl in bewilderment and, in his mind, she would become a flower. Without moving, he would pick her up gently and put her in the water exactly as he had done to the flowers— and, to his horror, she would sink. Well, Jimmy made me pick her up and do *that* [motioning violently] over my head, which became a brutal and deliberate act. By no stretch of the imagination could you make that innocent. The whole pathos of the scene, to my mind, should have been—and I'm sure that's the way it was written—completely innocent and unaware.

Once the film was filmed and edited, neither interpretation won out. The sequence cut from the monster's joy over floating flowers to bubbles in the stream, leaving much to the viewer's imagination, until a later scene shows her father carrying his daughter's limp body through the streets of the village. Some state film censors cut the entire episode.

An equally disturbing—and iconic—scene comes immediately after the riverbank scene. As the village celebrates the wedding of Henry Frankenstein and Elizabeth, the monster hovers. He leers into Elizabeth's bedroom, and his face twists into a diabolical half-smile. Whale chose not to show the actual interaction between the monster and Elizabeth. Like Henry and his wedding guests, the audience simply hears her scream. The next frame freezes in time. The monster stands, leering, outside the casement window. A vase of flowers and an overturned table mark the disarray. The body of Elizabeth sprawls, breasts upturned and neck vulnerable, blond hair cascading and wedding gown draped across the floor.

What in fact had happened? The scene invited lurid interpretations. One reviewer outright stated that "Frankenstein's own sweetheart is a victim of his [the monster's] lust," although nothing on film confirms that. At a glance the sprawling Elizabeth could also be interpreted as dead—in keeping with the plot of the novel—yet Whale and Universal chose not to take the story in that direction. He lets the audience linger with that prospect in mind, then the scene cuts quickly to the tragic parade in which the unshorn peasant father carries his little Maria, flung backward in a position that mirrors Elizabeth's. The sight rouses villagers to mass vengeance.

As the villagers gather into a mob, the demographics of their community change before our eyes. Those who wear alpine smocks and leather knickers are joined by men in felt hats, suits, and ties—the prototypical boss men of the 1930s. The mob divides into two, one led by the bereaved father into the woods, the other led by Frankenstein to the mountain. "The fiend must be found!" cries out the pinstriped burgomaster. Baying hounds catch the scent and strain at their leads. Frankenstein splits off from the group and confronts his monster alone. They grapple. Frankenstein falls, bleeding from the mouth, and the creature heaves him over his shoulder and carries him up the mountain slope and into an abandoned windmill. As Frankenstein regains consciousness, the identities of creature and creator balance precariously. The two figures stand opposite each other, divided by the great wooden gear turned by the windmill blades. Echoing the mirror scene in Edison's 1910 *Frankenstein,* more realistic yet more surreal for the movement and chiaroscuro, Whale counterposes facial portraits of Henry Frankenstein and the unnamed creature, one after the other.

Even in their last moments together, agency is in question. Does Frankenstein climb over the rail and jump from high up in the windmill, as one man in the mob yells out for him to do? Or does the creature push him? A rag-doll effigy plummets, caught momentarily by a turning windmill blade, then slides to the ground. Half the mob tends to the fallen Frankenstein. Others torch the aged wooden structure, which erupts into flame. Inside, heavy beams crash down on the creature, who groans in pain as Whale cuts to a long shot of the mountaintop inferno, the windmill blades turning, engulfed in flame.

It would have been a finale in keeping with the novel. The creator devastated, the creature destined for destruction—that precarious, indeterminate ending in a landscape not of ice but of fire this time, as the creature in Shelley's novel had promised. But before releasing it to the general public, Universal screened the film at a press preview. The Laemmles, Jr. and Sr., sensed discomfort verging on outrage. The elder producer insisted on some changes, and a new final version of the Whale-Karloff

Frankenstein ends on an incongruously saccharine note. A finale was created. A gaggle of maids converses with Frankenstein's father, the buffoonish baron, outside a bedroom door. Through it we glimpse a recovered Elizabeth tending her bedridden husband. "Mr. Henry doesn't need this," says the baron to the maids, referring to a carafe of wine that they have brought to revive their young master. His father pours himself a glass of the wine and lifts it, saying, "Here's to a son to the house of Frankenstein." The ending placated the audience and allowed Universal Studios to continue the saga in sequels to come.

Producers were also concerned about the film's affront to religion, a recurring risk in telling the story going back to Shelley's time. A critical scene in Whale's version raised those objections all over again. The created body has been pulleyed up the tall stone silo to receive the life force of lightning. Brought down again, it appears not to move—until one of its oversize hands shivers and raises a telltale finger. "It's alive!" Henry Frankenstein cries out. "It's alive! It's alive! It's alive!"

"Henry—in the name of God!" blurts out his friend, seeking to calm him.

"Oh,—in the name of God?" Frankenstein repeats hysterically. "Now I know what it feels like to be God!"

Lines like these were sure to rattle religious moviegoers, and Universal executives wanted to please the broadest audience possible. They consulted with Roman Catholic priests in Los Angeles, who suggested that a palliative introduction to the film be added. So as they had for *Dracula,* they created a prelude, an old theatrical trick, for *Frankenstein.* It would deflect judgment from the production company and admit from the outset that the film contained material of questionable moral fiber.

A brief script was composed. Edward van Sloan, the actor

who also played Waldman, slipped out from behind curtains, clothed in evening attire, and addressed the camera as if greeting the audience before a play. "Mr. Carl Laemmle feels it would be a little unkind to present this picture without just a word of friendly warning," he said, announcing himself as an emissary of the film producers themselves.

> We are about to unfold the story of Frankenstein, a man of science, who sought to create a man after his own image—without reckoning upon God. It is one of the strangest tales ever told. It deals with the two great mysteries of creation. Life and death. I think it will thrill you. It may shock you. . . . It might even—horrify you! So then, if you feel that you do not care to subject your nerves to such a strain, now is your chance to—well—well—we've warned you!

In the days just before its release, the film's beginning and end had been finetuned to suit the moral temper of the times. With that accomplished, it was time to let the monster out into the public and see how he survived.

They Love to Tremble

Outrage was inevitable. "It has no theme and points no moral," stated a review in Britain's *Film Weekly*. "It is the kind of film which could only induce nightmares." Some municipalities banned its showing. Several state censorship boards demanded cuts so significant that they eviscerated the story altogether. The Kansas State Board of Censors required that four minutes of critical footage be cut. Massachusetts demanded that Universal "eliminate [the] scene showing body on slab coming to life." English censors objected to the scene of Elizabeth sprawled like a victim in her boudoir. Audience members fainted in Detroit, and ambulances rushed to the theater. "Chicagoans must be a pretty brave lot," wrote a reviewer there. "'Frankenstein,' the much heralded spine-chiller which has been causing a dozen or so Detroit folk to require smelling salts and other revivifying remedies daily for the past three weeks opened here yesterday with nary a fainter in the audience." He reported "some squeals, one or two near-shrieks and much hysterical giggling," but "the nurses which Universal and RKO had so accommodatingly provided for lobby hospital service had an easy time of it on the whole."

Plenty of reviewers praised the film, though, warning audiences of its grotesqueness but congratulating actors and director alike. "We needed a weird, shadowy, spooky picture," wrote film reviewer Irene Thirer in the *New York Daily News* on December 5, 1931. She thrilled to the horror but appreciated the happy ending as well: "It's a study of a chemical experiment— one which clutches at you icily and holds you until the romantic ending guarantees satisfaction after an hour's worth of gripping, intriguing horrors." Mordaunt Hall, writing in the *New York Times* on the same day, told of the conscientiously chosen ending and compared it to his sense of the ending of Mary Shelley's novel:

> As a concession to the motion picture audience, Frankenstein is not killed, but he is badly injured. Two endings were made for this production, and at the eleventh hour it was decided to put in the one in which Frankenstein lives, because it was explained that sympathy is elicited for the young scientist and that the spectators would leave disappointed if the author's last chapter was adhered to.

One month later Hall placed *Frankenstein* on his list of the ten best, the "Blue-Ribbon Pictures of 1931," along with Charlie Chaplin's

City Lights and David Butler's production of *A Connecticut Yankee in King Arthur's Court*.

WEIRD THEME PICTURED, read the front-page headline in the *Washington Post*. "This 'Frankenstein' is a thriller supreme," the article said, "for it deals with a scientist who strove to become a 'god'—and, in a curious, bizarre sense, did!" One reviewer called Karloff's monster a "great, gangling automaton" and the film "a carnival of morbidity." Few reviewers compared the film to either the novel or the 1910 Edison film a generation before, more often citing Universal's *Dracula* as its precedent.

Negative or positive, all the attention made James Whale's *Frankenstein* a sensation. The excitement assured Universal not only profits but a star-studded future in the Hollywood horror business, with the monster leading the way. One reviewer expressed regret, however, that "one of the best features of the book, the pathos of the lonely and puzzled monster, has been omitted from the adaptation." In fact, Karloff's film portrayal of Frankenstein's monster evoked more sympathy than many coming after him would achieve.

CHAPTER SEVEN

THE BRAVE NEW WORLD
OF MONSTERS

Original plans called for the horror in the films to be "played down"
in all advertising, until . . . showmen realized that people instead of being
terrified away from the theatre could be terrified into it.

——*NEW YORK TIMES,* 1938

We know exactly how much these pictures are going to make.
They cost so much. They earn so much. Even if we spent more on them,
they wouldn't make a cent more. So why change them?

——UNIVERSAL PICTURES PRODUCER,
quoted by Boris Karloff, 1962

Between 1931 and 1948 Universal produced eight Frankenstein films. The look, the walk, the grunts, and the character of Karloff's monster became the standard, and their once-presumptuous company name became a more apt descriptor for the success achieved by its horror films. Scriptwriters wove ever more preposterous plots that liberated the monster from his origins and propelled him into a world populated by other Universal horror greats like Dracula and the Wolf Man. The monster progressed into the cultural imagination with a new look, soon calcified by less imaginative sequels and repeated screenings around the world. Variants proliferated, emphasizing one feature or another, yet key characteristics linked back to the 1931 Hollywood original. Everyone knew Frankenstein—yet relatively few had heard of, let alone read, the novel.

The two-decade evolution of Universal portrayals—from Karloff's primeval 1931 *Frankenstein* to a slapstick encounter with comedy greats Abbott and Costello in 1948—encapsulates the monster's path into the middle of the twentieth century, starting with artful renderings but progressing—or regressing—into the grotesque or the comic. Push the monster farther toward horror or, in the other direction, farther toward lovability, and you enter the realm of either/or: right or wrong, good or evil. Lost in the process is that delicate interplay of horror and sympathy, the ambiguous moral universe of the original novel. For all its chiaroscuro, and despite the abnormal brain, Whale's 1931 *Frankenstein* likewise shimmered in a zone of moral uncertainty, which is part of its lasting power. Without the added final scene—the cheery toast to the house of Frankenstein—the film would have ended in even more of a moral limbo, with creature and creator hovering between life and death against the background of the flaming windmill. To create a sequel, in fact, Universal scriptwriters disregarded the scene tacked on to the end of *Frankenstein*. The monster did not die, they hypothesized: He fell into the well at the center of the mill, ready to clamber out for another thrilling episode.

THE MONSTER PHENOMENON

Between *Frankenstein* in 1931 and its first sequel, *Bride of Frankenstein,* in 1935, the monster phenomenon reverberated around the world, inspiring a return to Mary Shelley's novel. Australian-born showman George Edwards created a thirteen-part radio serial. Each twenty-minute segment was framed by episodes of an ongoing conversation between Robert Walton, captain of "the good ship *Voyager,* on its way home from the North Pole," and Victor Frankenstein, played by Edwards adopting a thick Swiss accent. Grosset & Dunlap published a new edition of the novel in 1932, part of its occasional series of "photoplay editions." As a frontispiece the publishers chose a shadowy portrait of Karloff's monster. Five other black-and-white studio shots punctuated the text: the classic image of Henry Frankenstein, poised at the controls and gazing upward, ready to throw the switch; and a photo of Frankenstein, Waldman, and Fritz hurling themselves on the monster, captioned, "Hold him! Hold him! He has the strength of ten men." Of course the novel contained no such scenes, and no rationalization for the mismatch was given. As dust-jacket art, the publishers commissioned a painting reminiscent of Universal's movie posters. A sickly green monster face fills the upper half of the cover; a red-headed Elizabeth sprawls lifelessly below. Between them, in brilliant yellow, reads the one simple word: "Frankenstein." Garish in yellow, red, and green, the book jacket was downright alarming, but it joined the film and its marketing regalia in solidifying the icons of the monster and his helpless victim.

The film had revitalized the sense that every home library should include a copy of *Frankenstein,* and American publishers went to great lengths to produce new editions. Three collectors' editions appeared in the next two years, each with original illustrations. First out of the gate was the Illustrated Editions Company, with its 1932 "De Luxe Edition." Nino Carbe, a Hollywood artist who had just produced elegant Beardsleyesque engravings for a new edition of *Cyrano de Bergerac,* was commissioned to illustrate it. A young man in 1931, Carbe would continue as an illustrator and animation designer for five more decades, contributing to Walt Disney's *Fantasia* in 1940, Walter Lantz's Woody

The monster, the mad scientist, the beautiful victim: Three figures told
the entire story on this movie poster, whose imagery inspired the jacket
design for a 1932 Grosset & Dunlap edition of Mary Shelley's novel, illustrated with film stills of scenes that never occurred in her original.

Woodpecker cartoons in the 1970s, and Filmation's *She-Ra: Princess of Power* in the 1980s.

Nino Carbe envisioned Frankenstein's monster as diabolical: fleshly in form and evil in expression, with a sinewy physique, sharpened nails, foreshortened forehead, upraised brow, humped nose, and vampire incisors, top and bottom, revealed by a slack lower jaw. Vignettes of the monster's leering face appear as ornamentals in the book's design. And while the creation scene contains tubes and alembics—Carbe's was an archaic, not a futuristic, portrayal—makeup artist Jack Pierce's influence reveals itself in the bolts protruding from the monster's neck in several of the illustrations.

It was early in Lynd Ward's career as well when publishers Harrison Smith and Robert Haas asked him to illustrate their 1934 edition of *Frankenstein*. Ward had studied at the Leipzig Academy for Graphic Arts and, at the age of twenty-six, had already illustrated a dozen books, including Goethe's *Faust* and Oscar Wilde's *Ballad of Reading Gaol*. He had also created two of his own wordless books, forceful contributions to the genre we now call the graphic novel. Influenced by the German expressionists, his distinctive style combined strong planes, rich textures, and thought-provoking perspectives. For the Smith-Haas *Frankenstein*, Ward created sixty-five illustrations—chapter openers, chapter enders, and full-page plates. Like Carbe, he reveled in the monster's muscularity. He gave the creature long legs, broad shoulders, and a protruding spine that heightened his animal nature. Ward's illustrations evoked sympathy for the character, though, especially the striking portrayal of his first self-awareness: The figure gazes down into a mirror of water, and his reflection stares, shocked and round eyed, straight out from the page.

To illustrate one of several deluxe editions of Shelley's novel published in
the wake of the 1931 Universal film, Nino Carbe pictured a lank, naked
man-monster with sunken eyes and slack lower lip, perpetually scowling.

Another illustrated edition appeared in 1934 as well, this one for the Limited Edition Club, a members-only book series established by George Macy in 1929 that specialized in newly illustrated versions of the classics. *The Travels of Marco Polo* and Dostoevsky's *The Brothers Karamazov* had already been published; Dickens and Shakespeare would join the list in the year to come. Two-color illustrations were created by Everett Henry for this edition of *Frankenstein,* more literal and realistic than those of his contemporaries. True-crime journalist Edmund Lester Pearson—famous for arguing the guilt of Lizzie Borden—contributed a ten-page introduction to the Macy edition. Pearson had researched Shelley and her novel extensively, so that his introduction contained details like the history of Polidori's vampire story, the wording of the 1818 title page, and references to stage performances of *Presumption*.

"In 1931 there appeared the talking-picture *Frankenstein,*" Pearson wrote, bemoaning how little credit the film gave to the novel's author:

> In the manner of the movies, the name of the gentleman who adapted the story for the screen was flashed before the spectators in large letters. In still larger ones, and in solitary grandeur, appeared the name of the director. Then followed, for an instant, a group of those who were "also present" at the birth of this film drama. One of this group, along with costumers, camera-men and electricians, was the young girl to whose genius all these modern artists owed so much. She was mentioned as "Mrs. Percy B. Shelley," and was probably set down, by spectators who noticed it at all, as "someone, out in Hollywood."

Pearson considered the film "a dignified and adequate treatment" of the novel's primary plot and suspected that both Shelleys would have been delighted with the spectacles of the creation scene.

Lynd Ward created a fleshly and ambiguous monster for another deluxe illustrated edition of the novel in the early 1930s. In this scene, Ward's figure combines taut sinews and protruding vertebrae with wide-open eyes that suggest awakening self-awareness.

Some literary types believed, wrote Pearson, that Shelley had spawned an entire genre with her novel. He cited Dorothy L. Sayers, who, recently anthologizing short stories of "detection, mystery and horror," had categorized a group of them under "the Frankenstein theme." Pearson savored his part in reintroducing this "once famous but almost forgotten romance" to the general public. Public tastes had changed in a hundred years, he granted. For audiences of the now ubiquitous "talking-picture," English rhetoric of the early nineteenth century might not read so easily. For that reason Pearson ended on a slightly apologetic note: "Readers can be relied upon to discover in what places it now seems antiquated and bombastic, and wherein it still keeps the power which, on the day I am writing this, is crowding the moving-picture theatres, more than a century after Mary Godwin, a girl of nineteen years, began her story." This renewed interest in the historic moment from which *Frankenstein* emerged was to make an impact on the way James Whale shaped the next film he made about the monster.

THE RETURN

As the Laemmles began planning another Frankenstein film, they called it simply *Return of Frankenstein*. Again scripts abounded. Robert Florey had written a sequel in December 1931, as *Frankenstein* first hit the theaters. Up through 1934 that script went through at least nine versions. Universal records list eight people as authors—including Edmund Pearson, the author of the introduction to the 1934 illustrated edition. No matter who wrote the screenplay, when James Whale finally stepped back on the set to direct the film, it was his hand more than anyone else's that shaped this more-than-sequel.

Both Whale and Karloff had moved swiftly on to other horror

films, classics like *The Invisible Man* and *The Mummy*. Whale
thought he was done with the monster. "They've had a script
made for a sequel, and it stinks to heaven," he told R. C. Sherriff
in 1933. "In any case I squeezed the idea dry on the original picture, and never want to work on it again." Yet when he finally
joined the project, he found many juicy elements remaining in
the story. He handpicked the cast and crafted a film that more
closely mirrored his own sardonic personality, edging toward
nihilism as the years went by. "He knew it was never going to be
Frankenstein," Whale's longtime partner, David Lewis, told film
historian Paul M. Jensen. "He knew it was never going to be a
picture to be proud of. So he tried to do all sorts of things that
would make it memorable."

It took an imaginative twist to bring the monster back to life
from within the incinerated windmill. Soon after the release of
the 1931 *Frankenstein,* producers realized "they'd made a dreadful
mistake," recalled Boris Karloff. "They let the monster die. In
one brief script conference, they brought him back alive." Let us
suppose, the scriptwriters hypothesized, that there was a pool of
standing water at the base of the mill. If the monster fell into it,
he might have survived the fire. This plot device required Jack
Pierce to enhance Boris Karloff's makeup, creating burn scars on
his right cheek and pushing back his hairline to reveal sutures and
staples at the crown. According to Jonah Maurice Ruddy, a Hollywood reporter who visited the set, the new costume weighed
nearly twenty pounds more than the old, and the makeup sessions took five hours instead of three and a half, but such details
were ripe for exaggeration. Early during the shooting, as Karloff
slogged around in the water, he dislocated a hip but kept going.
He was dedicated to the film—and to the monster. "I am genuinely glad to have had the chance to do the monster," he told

Ruddy. Throughout the rest of his career, he spoke of the monster as a dear old friend, and his affection for the character shines through in the 1935 sequel.

In *Bride of Frankenstein*, the monster comes into his own as a living, feeling being. He smiles, he dances, he weeps, he speaks. His limited vocabulary evokes a distinctive worldview. First he learns "friend," "bread," "good." Later "bad" joins the list, and the last words spoken by the monster in the film represent the full extent of his verbal development. He speaks a primitive sentence: "We belong dead." Karloff knew that Mary Shelley's monster had spoken eloquently, but he questioned the wisdom of giving the film monster speech at all. "Time and time again I argued that the monster shouldn't speak," Karloff reflected nearly thirty years later. "If he spoke, he would seem too much more human, I thought. . . . It would have been better had the monster not spoken at all." This and related concerns meant that Karloff would play the monster in only one more Universal Frankenstein film sequel after *Bride*. "When the monster did speak, I knew that this was eventually going to destroy the character," he wrote in 1957. "It did for me, anyway."

Perhaps James Whale went back and read the novel between the first two Frankenstein films he made. The 1931 film credits stated that it was taken "from the novel by Mrs. Percy B. Shelley," but the 1935 credits more accurately expressed that the script was "suggested by the original story written in 1816 by Mary Wollstonecraft Shelley" and "adapted" by Balderston in partnership with William Hurlbut, whose screenwriting credits already dated back twenty years. Whale certainly used the second film to reclaim many of the novel's elements left out in the first, and he created the character of the novel's author herself to set the

scene. *Bride of Frankenstein* begins in a much Gothicized Villa Diodati, portraying Mary, Percy Bysshe, and Byron living a lush aris-
tocratic life. A starched-apron housemaid leads four Afghan
hounds through the vast sitting room for no reason other than
spectacle. Mary sits on a love seat, sewing, dressed in a splendid
gauze-and-sequin gown that "cost a fortune," according to Elsa
Lanchester, the actress who played both Mary Shelley and the
Bride. In this, as in many other details of the film, Whale was
given a generous budget and full artistic power.

From the very start the 1935 *Bride of Frankenstein* more
bluntly parsed out the values of good and evil than the 1931
Frankenstein ever did. Whale used the opening scene at Villa Diodati to establish the film's moral universe, gathering steam from
the celebrated naughtiness of the authorial threesome. The
obligatory thunderstorm flashes through towering casement
windows. Witty conversation swirls. "I should like to think that
an irate Jehovah was pointing those arrows of lightning directly
at my head," trills actor Gavin Gordon, playing the part of Lord
Byron. His comment slyly marries mythologies and establishes
the Judeo-Christian ethic as a moral setting for this film's story.
It is not Jove but Jehovah, not the ancient Greek but the Judeo-
Christian deity who hurls the thunderbolts of punishment at
those who disobey. Lanchester's Mary Shelley speaks as if the
earlier film had been her novel, misunderstood by any who considered it immoral or sacrilegious. Those who cast judgment
against it, she says to Byron and Shelley, "did not see that my
purpose was to write a moral lesson of the punishment that
befell a mortal man who dared to emulate God." One imagines
Laemmle and Whale speaking through her, molding the censors'
opinions in this more sophisticated version of the prelude tacked
on to the 1931 film. And, Mary Shelley adds, there is more to

the story. "I'm all ears," responds an admiring Byron. "While Heaven blasts the night, open up your pits of hell." The audience tunes in for a story of good and evil.

And evil Whale delivers, embodied in a new character, Dr. Pretorius. Played by Ernest Thesiger, a fine-featured, bitingly cynical English actor, Pretorius is the epitome of libertine amorality, glibly disdainful of any attitude involving traditional social conscience or the affirmation of life. His work, he explains, involves even more advanced science. "While you were digging in your graves, piecing together dead tissues," he tells Frankenstein, "I grew my creatures, like cultures. Grew them, as nature does, from seeds." Pretorius practices a biological rather than a technological science, reminiscent of the in vitro fertilization techniques perfected by Jacques Loeb and his colleagues in the 1920s—and of the test-tube assembly lines envisioned by Aldous Huxley in his *Brave New World,* first published in 1932, between the appearance of Whale's first and second Frankenstein films.

James Whale used the display of Pretorius's creatures as an opportunity for humor. Out of a casket-shaped box, Pretorius dramatically pulls six glass bell jars containing human figures. Pretorius's miniature creations recall the homunculus, the legendary goal of medieval alchemists: Film allowed the illusion of a six-inch being living inside each jar. There are a king and a queen, an archbishop and a devil, the last one Pretorius's favorite. "Sometimes I have wondered whether life wouldn't be much more amusing if we were all devils, and no nonsense about angels and being good," he offers as an aside.

Set against this new foil, Henry Frankenstein appears an old-fashioned tortured soul, rationally seeking good yet subverted by inner drives he cannot control. Playing Henry Frankenstein once again was Whale's friend Colin Clive, whose own personal life

had been unraveling since 1931. More than once Clive came
onto the *Bride* set drunk, according to other cast members. With
his face more wrinkled, his dark eyes sunk more deeply, Clive
easily assumed an agonized look. That haunted presence played
perfectly for the character who, surviving his plunge from the
burning windmill, intended domestic tranquillity but found himself still haunted by laboratory ambitions. "I have been cursed for
delving into the mysteries of life," Henry Frankenstein says to
Elizabeth in their lush bedchamber. "I dreamed of being the first
in the world to give man the secret that God is so jealous of—the
formula for life." His eyes begin to glisten again.

"No, no! It's the devil that prompts you," responds Elizabeth,
the voice of popular religion and the social norm: "It's blasphemous and wicked; we were not intended to know those things."
The dialogue sets the stage for another quest beyond God-given
limits.

Icons of Christianity glimmer suggestively in *Bride,* and
repeated associations between Karloff's character and the cruci-
fied Christ champion the monster. First a mob surrounds him,
corralling him back to town and justice. They lash him to a tree
trunk, his hands tied above his head, and hoist him into a hay
wagon. The camera dwells on the bound figure, whose face
breaks into a near-smile of helplessness in the midst of this quasi-
crucifixion.

After escaping the town prison, the monster approaches a
country cottage, attracted by a mournful violin rendition of
Schubert's *Ave Maria,* resurrecting the motif of music's enchant-
ing effect on him. The musician is a blind elder, the epitome of
charitable love without concern for appearances. The old man
feeds the monster and urges him to rest. The scene all but fades
out, and—for just one second—a crucifix glows above the

reclining monster. When the blind man's son returns home, he assumes the worst of such a grotesque monster and attacks him ruthlessly. Cast out, the monster roams a graveyard and angrily topples a saintly effigy. In the misty background, a Christ figure hangs from a cross over all. An early version of the screenplay had the monster mistaking the statue as alive and struggling to free him from his suffering. The final edited film exchanged misguided charity for sheer animal attack.

The moviemaking climate had changed since 1931, and while Universal may have given Whale more leeway, the film board censors would not. Film censorship had been in place five years earlier, but by 1935 procedures had become mandatory and rigorous, organized by the industry but taken seriously by all involved. For every film in production, a script was screened by officials from the Motion Picture Producers and Distributors Association—MPPDA, also called the Hays Office, reflecting the huge control exerted by William Harrison Hays, president of the Motion Picture Association of America. Industry censors combed over every script, dictating what could and could not be included in the film under way. Moving pictures exported to England and other countries underwent further scrutiny by foreign boards, whose standards were just as rigorous but often not identical to those of American censors, resulting in further censorship of films with international appeal.

THE MONSTER'S BRIDE

The chosen title, *Bride of Frankenstein*, suggests the venture into which Pretorius seduces Frankenstein: to create a female. An act interrupted in Shelley's novel, the very idea of a mate for the monster has prompted myriad interpretations through the decades. The bride conceived in 1935 was once again a collaboration between director, actor, makeup artist—and studio marketers department. "Can you imagine the advertising you can do on this one?" read a trade flyer sent out in advance of the film. "The mere thought of the monster seeking a bride makes a showman's fingers fairly itch. . . . Add the bride idea to all you've had before, and you've got a 'tremendousity' of appeal." The flyer's illustration depicted a Karloffesque monster with his arm stretched, almost affectionately, around a startled blond beauty, as if Mae Clarke, Elizabeth in the 1931 film, might become the monster's bride in 1935. And, in fact, that was Whale's first idea: He wanted the monster to kill Elizabeth, then force Frankenstein to use her body to make him a mate. Scriptwriters, actors, and studio executives insisted he reconsider, and in the long run the film implied that this second monster was made by the same techniques as the first, using the very same laboratory equipment created by Kenneth Strickfaden in 1931. Besides, Mae Clarke was unavailable, her career complicated by an auto accident and competing contracts. "Who will be the Bride of Frankenstein? Who will dare?" read movie theater publicity. Early press releases reported that Bette Davis would play the part. In the long run Elsa Lanchester—described by film historian Gregory William Mank as an "elfish Bohemian"—was hired for the highly charged role.

As Lanchester told Mank in 1979, a psychological principle informed Whale's vision. "James's feeling was that very pretty, sweet people, both men and women, had very wicked insides . . . evil thoughts," she said, expressing an idea akin to the shadow archetype, a concept that psychiatrist Carl G. Jung was developing in these same years. These evil thoughts, Lanchester continued, "could be of dragons, they could be of monsters, they could be of Frankenstein's laboratory. So, James wanted the same actress for both parts to show that the Bride of Frankenstein did, after all, come out of sweet Mary Shelley's soul." Lanchester's on-screen presence amounted to little time—four minutes as Mary Shelley at the beginning and another four as the Bride at the end—yet in *Bride of Frankenstein* she established a new icon, as vital and nearly as recognizable as Boris Karloff's monster.

The brief opening in which Lanchester appears as Mary Shelley establishes the stereotype of woman as delicate, fearful, and frail. The first words spoken of her are: "She's an angel." The Byronic dialogue that continues contrasts her feminine character with the monstrous story she has written. Her sparkling white gown draped like a bridal veil, she stitches daintily at the lace she is making. Byron describes her as frightened of thunder and fearful of the dark. Lanchester cocks her head and lifts her eyebrows, then gasps as her sewing needle pricks her finger and draws blood—a brief moment of domestic inconvenience crafted to contrast with the gross sweeps of violence and agony soon to fill the screen.

It was again the job of makeup artist Jack Pierce to turn an attractive human being into a monster from beyond the human fold. Scars, eyebrows, and hair were the most important. Every morning Pierce created the one long scar that slices across the underside of the bride's chin, visible only twice in the film as her head cranes jerkily around, looking at the world into which she has awoken. "For a whole hour he would draw two lines of glue, put a red line down the middle, then start making up the white edges of the scar—*meticulously* done," said Lanchester. The scar took him an hour; the rest of the makeup could take another three. Her dramatic hairdo—uplifted as if she is in perpetual shock and shot through with two lightning bolts of white—was her own. "I had it lifted up from my face, all the way around," Lanchester explained, and "then they placed a cage on my head and combed my own hair over this cage." Her floor-length costume, bridal white, combined muslin wrappings that extended her fingertips and a square-shouldered robe, full of skirt and majestic in flow. Under it, lifts raised Lanchester to nearly seven feet tall to match her man.

The look was magnificent, and Whale designed scenes that presented her as if she were in a fashion show: full length, framed by her two admiring creators, then head-and-shoulders studies, the actress snapping her head from one pose to another to create a series of portrait vignettes. Lanchester's movement style suggests either the precariousness of a newborn colt or the limited repertoire of a programmed robot. She develops in minutes from an ingenue, eyeing the world, to an adolescent, terrified by the advances of a sexual partner. The courtship between monster and bride lasts little more than a minute. He reaches out to her, saying in his kindest voice, "Friend." She leans back and lets loose a bloodcurdling scream. Background music suggests romance. His gruesome hands cradle hers, still wrapped in bandages. His face broadens into a smile more human and heartfelt than Karloff had ever allowed the creature to show on film before. The bride makes no sound. Her eyes widen with terror, accentuated by arching eyebrows. The monster grunts in reply. He reaches out—to comfort her? to assault her?—it is difficult to know. She screams and falls back into the arms of her creator. "She hate me," the monster utters. "Like others."

In the film's few remaining minutes, Whale treats us to two more close-ups: Elsa Lanchester as the bride, hissing (copying a startled swan, she said later); and Boris Karloff as the monster, a tear running down his cheek. The moral universe shifts on its axis, and the monster voices the judgment that closes the film. "You live," he says to Henry Frankenstein and his still-adoring fiancée, Elizabeth. "You stay," he commands Dr. Pretorius. "We belong dead." The monster pulls a giant lever, and he and his intended, together with Dr. Pretorius, the film's embodiment of evil, die in a series of explosions caused by the same equipment that gave the monsters life. Long shots show a suggestively tall, erect stone tower, site of the ghastly laboratory, bursting from within and crumbling to rubble and ruin.

GENERATIONS OF FRANKENSTEINS

When Karloff was first hired to play the monster, he was a minor actor in his forties, certainly not a well-known Hollywood name. He was not even invited to attend the premiere of *Frankenstein*. "I was just an unimportant free-lance actor, the animation for the monster costume," he said years later. With the phenomenal success of that first *Frankenstein,* though, he swiftly gained stature in the industry and in the public eye. By the second Frankenstein film he had become a phenomenon. By the third he could have his way at Universal, and the monster regressed, losing what ability to speak he had gained in *Bride of Frankenstein* and reverting to inarticulate groans. But the repeat performances were beginning to wear thin for the actor. Frankenstein's monster was becoming a caricature. In several ways Karloff's third and final Frankenstein film was a bittersweet swan song for the era of the great horror classics.

Despite the boost from their horror success of the early 1930s, Universal Studios experienced an economic downslide by the middle of the decade. *Bride of Frankenstein,* while praised by reviewers, was not the moneymaker that the Laemmles needed, and the company changed hands early in 1936. Colin Clive's alcoholism and mental instability drove him to death in 1937. James Whale directed a handful of hits, but by 1940 he, too, was grappling with inner demons, resulting in isolation and professional inactivity. The sad end of Whale's life is portrayed poignantly in Christopher Bram's novel, *Father of Frankenstein,* made by director Bill Condon into the 1998 film *Gods and Monsters.*

All these changes brought new producers, new directors, and new actors into the effort of keeping a Universal Frankenstein alive. In the midst of all this scrambling to save the business, the original *Frankenstein* was revived. In 1938 a newly configured Universal Studios lit up the neon and rereleased the 1931 film as a double feature with the studio's 1930 hit, *Dracula.* REVIVAL OF THE UNDEAD, read the headline of a *New York Times* article announcing the horror extravaganza on October 16, 1938, just in time for Halloween: "After having scared a couple of million dollars out of humanity for Universal," Drac and Frank, as they were now dubbed, had been "reverently coiled up in their tin cans like a pair of anchovies and interred in dead storage to sleep the sleep of the just"—until this double-feature plot was hatched. Movie house managers, the article reported, "were looking for something to liven up a jaded bill of fare," "reached back into the charnel house," and started showing "the grisly pair." *Frankenstein* was markedly less grisly than it had been seven years before, however. Universal obeyed stringent MPPDA demands and excised a number of morally precarious scenes, notably Henry Frankenstein's claim to godlike feelings.

The double feature proved an instant hit. Even in Salt Lake City, the Victory Theatre was sold out by ten in the morning. "Four thousand frenzied Mormons milled around outside, finally broke through the police lines, smashed the plate glass box office, bent the front doors and tore off one of the door checks in

Crowds thronged theaters across the United States in 1938 to
see Universal's two favorite monsters in a double-feature
showing. Remarkably Frankenstein's monster and the suave
vampire both traced their origins to the same June 1816 night
in Geneva.

their eagerness to get in and be frightened." The Salt Lake entrepreneur rented a second theater across the street to accommo-
date the crowds. In Cincinnati, Indianapolis, and St. Louis
crowds thronged the theaters. New York's Rialto ran ten sold-out
showings a day.

Such success came as a surprise to Universal marketing executives, whose original plans "called for the horror in the films to
be 'played down' in all advertising." Soon they realized what a
winner they had, and they fashioned trade advertising to promote it. "Throw away the book! Forget all you ever knew about
showmanship! Because horror is paying off again!" they alerted
theater managers. "Smart showmen all over the country are cash-
ing in on it!" "It" was the monster and the vampire, united
again—as they had been in the Villa Diodati in 1816, on the London stage in the 1820s, and in the minds of scriptwriters, screen-
writers, and the Laemmles at the start of the decade. "The public
came, shrieked with delicious, safe terror, and loved it," wrote
the *Times* reporter. The *Frankenstein-Dracula* double feature
became the jewel in the Universal crown of horror.

Europeans looked askance at Americans and their apparently
unquenchable thirst for horror. The British Board of Film Censors approved only the most thoroughly whitewashed *Frankenstein*. Even some stateside observers wondered why the nation
lapped up so much horror; they asked whether Hollywood was
feeding or inciting the hunger. *Look* magazine attributed the fascination to an underlying sense of an impending war in Europe:
"'Nightmares for everybody' is the Hollywood slogan for a more
horrible 1939."

Son of Frankenstein, released in that year of 1939, represented
the third and last of Boris Karloff's performances as the monster
made by Frankenstein. An early scene establishes the moral vectors of the creator this time around. Wolf von Frankenstein, son
of Henry Frankenstein—played by the suave and respectable
Basil Rathbone, who got top billing, even over Boris Karloff—
has left behind an academic career in America to return to his
ancestral home. He and his wife and child move into the ruins of

Castle Frankenstein, a turreted building pushed toward Gothic cliché that stands on the outskirts of a vaguely Germanic town now bearing the family name. This next-generation Frankenstein is determined to "clear the stigma from his father's name," as the film production notes put it. "It was the unforeseen blunder of a stupid assistant, who gave his creation the brain of a killer instead of a normal one," the heir tells his wife as they approach his family home. "How my father was made to suffer for that mistake!"

A generation has passed, but the monster hasn't aged much—he was, one character explains, created immortal. Now scriptwriter Willis Cooper and director Rowland V. Lee assigned the monster a nearly unalloyed tendency toward violence. "A horrible creature," Universal publicity promised, "waiting to pounce upon the unwary to satisfy his lust to kill!" It was not just a marketing exaggeration: In *Son of Frankenstein* the monster has little conscience and an animalistic urge to attack. Nightmares for everybody, uncomplicated by moral ambiguities.

No longer does the monster stretch beyond a nondescript man's dark suit; this monster's costume has definitely gone retro. He wears a fleece tunic, a shapeless overshirt that Boris Karloff considered nothing but "furs and muck," which links him to a new character: Ygor, a morose peasant who lives as a squatter in the ruins of the Frankenstein castle. The actor playing this creepy part was none other than the man who considered himself too good to play the monster in 1931: Bela Lugosi, breaking out of the Dracula mold. Jack Pierce fitted Lugosi with a crooked hump atop his right shoulder, a vestige of a hanging he has survived. "I shtole bodies—they said," Ygor tells Wolf von Frankenstein when they first meet in the stone tower, his father's abandoned laboratory. "They wouldn't bury me in holy place, like churchyard," he laughs, rapping on his misaligned neckbone. "So—Ygor is dead." If anyone approaches the *Bride's* Dr. Pretorius as the embodiment of evil in *Son of Frankenstein,* it is Ygor. "Is my friend," Ygor says with a leer as he shows Frankenstein the prone body of the monster, now lying unconscious in the laboratory. "He . . . does things for me." The plot unrolls to reveal that Ygor has been targeting the judges, one by one, who sentenced him to hang. His friend, the monster without a conscience, dutifully carries out his evil orders.

The dark and dirty looking Ygor—with teeth crooked and rotten, coarse clothing, and unshaven presence—represents an entirely different social class compared to the Frankenstein family, dressed glamorously and served by maids and butlers in proper attire. The Frankenstein household itself, all swoops and shadows, achieves its artful sophistication thanks to the expressionistic set designs of Jack Otterson. There are three worlds here: the attractive human world, the grimy underworld of peasants and monsters, and the scientific überworld, in the towertop ruins of the old laboratory where a new Dr. Frankenstein goes to work.

Wolf von Frankenstein quickly takes up the challenge of reviving the ailing monster. Wearing rubber gloves and a mirrored eyepiece, he measures the blood pressure (300 over 220, "three times normal") and pulse (250 times per minute, "completely superhuman"). The scene highlights two diagnostic technologies just coming into their own in the 1930s: X-rays and blood tests. First Frankenstein examines the monster's heart as revealed on a glowing X-ray screen: "Two bullets in his heart, but he still lives," he observes. Then he peers into a microscope, and an image of cells streaming by fills the screen. Today the microscopic clips look hokey, but contemporary audiences would have been thrilled.

New knowledge about blood was revolutionizing medical practice. Blood types had been established in 1909; diagnosis by serum analysis started in the early 1920s; and the first hospital blood bank opened in 1937. "I've never seen blood that looks like this," says Frankenstein as he peers into the microscope, footnoting his comment with pseudomedical terminology: "Polymorphous cellular. Extreme hemachrosis. The alpha leukocytes apparently do not dissolve," he mutters. "The cells seem to be battling one another as if they had a conscious life of their own." Even at the microscopic level, the monster is a walking contradiction.

The film proceeds for almost an hour—two-thirds its total length—before Boris Karloff rises from his coma. Again he plays a nonverbal monster, as he preferred, which highlights his talent for gestures, facial expressions, and emotive grunts. Other details, though—his shepherd dress, his heftier body, and intimations of a post-coma haze, not to mention the witty savoir-faire of his foil, Rathbone's Wolf von Frankenstein—make Universal's Monster No. 3 more a dumb animal than anything else. Karloff managed to rescue his character in a few scenes, especially when he insists that Wolf von Frankenstein stand and look into a mirror alongside him—a scene of self-awareness, self-loathing, and entangled identities that links this film to all preceding celluloid Frankensteins. Face-to-face with the undeniable differences between himself and humanity, the monster pauses, studies, then erupts in rage, unable to change his own ugly fate.

Two more new characters propel the melodrama of *Son of Frankenstein*. Curly-topped Peter, the third-generation Frankenstein, played by Donnie Dunagan, becomes both friend and victim of the unaging monster. Adorably precocious, like a male

Shirley Temple, Peter plays the perennial role of the trusting child, walking right into the monster's grip. His salvation comes in the figure of Inspector Krogh, a military officer with an artificial right arm that he hoists with his left into a salute or a handshake. Explaining his disability, he tells Wolf von Frankenstein that "I was but a child at the time—about the age of your own son," when the monster attacked his family and ripped off his arm. "One doesn't easily forget . . . an arm torn out by the roots." Krogh's history makes him the righteous avenger, boy and soldier, victim and hero, all in one. The drama mounts. Angered when Frankenstein shoots Ygor, his one and only friend, the monster kidnaps young Peter. Although he releases the boy, Inspector Krogh and Wolf von Frankenstein—military courage and sophisticated intellect—team up to shove the creature into the boiling sulfur lake now conveniently located at the base of Castle Frankenstein.

Plot, point, and character all took a plunge toward mediocrity in this third Universal Frankenstein film, yet it was a popular success. It opened in Hollywood in January 1939, on Friday the thirteenth. Record crowds lined up to see it in Boston and Los Angeles. "For its type, the new horror film is well done," wrote Kate Cameron in the *New York Daily News*. The *Motion Picture Herald* called the film a "masterpiece" of "literary melodrama." Even the British reviewers, so judgmental over the monstrous films that came before, applauded. Perhaps the push toward melodrama made this version of horror less risqué; perhaps a decade of horror films had dulled their senses.

Despite the applause, Boris Karloff mourned the demise of his favorite character. "He was going downhill," he later told an interviewer. "We had exhausted his possibilities. He was becoming a clown." He felt compassion for the character. "My dear old

Monster," Karloff said. "He's my best friend." His sense of the character involved psychological analysis and empathy stemming from his days on the set in 1931. "Whale and I both saw the character as an innocent one," he recalled. "This was a pathetic creature who, like us all, had neither wish nor say in his creation, and certainly did not wish upon itself the hideous image which automatically terrified humans whom it tried to befriend." This empathy infused Karloff's portrayals with a depth of character and gave the films in which he played the monster all the tension and ambiguity needed to keep the myth alive.

After his third Universal film, Boris Karloff never again played the monster in a feature film, despite the scores of Frankenstein movies made after 1939. In his view he was not the one abandoning the monster; the producers and scriptwriters were. They wanted a flat, one-dimensional character—a clown, to use his expression—while he saw a figure full of contradictions, moral qualms, love and hate, good and evil, hope and despair. His monster embodied the existential loneliness and uncertainty of the twentieth century. "The most heartrending aspect of the creature's life," believed Boris Karloff, "was his ultimate desertion by his creator. It was as though man, in his blundering, searching attempts to improve himself, was to find himself deserted by his God."

PART THREE

OUR MONSTER

CHAPTER EIGHT

THE HORROR AND THE HUMOR

In an instant the monster was engulfed by the icy black waters of the Arctic!
He plummeted. The end was at hand . . . but perhaps it was only right
that such a creature should die at Nature's hand . . . for its
very existence had been an affront to her sovereignty.

—*THE MONSTER OF FRANKENSTEIN,* Marvel Comics, 1974

Precisely because the new knowledge and the new powers
impinge directly upon the human person, and in ways that
may affect our very humanity, a certain vague
disquiet hovers over the entire enterprise.

—PRESIDENT'S COUNCIL ON BIOETHICS, 2003

By 1940 a second world war loomed, producing its own Frankensteins. Screen monsters must have seemed clownish reflections of
real-life horror. The metaphor stalked the editorial pages. "Are
WE Frankensteins?" asked the diminutive figures of Mussolini and
Stalin, shocked to see a cleat-booted, high-stepping Hitler, three
times their size. The cartoon appeared on June 6, 1940, in a Washington paper. It was drawn by Clifford K. Berryman, a Pulitzer
Prize–winning cartoonist whose influence went back decades to
1902, when one of his cartoons canonized the term "teddy bear,"
naming a friendly ursine after President Theodore Roosevelt.
Now Berryman borrowed lightning-filled storm clouds from the
novel and ironclad weightiness from Karloff's portrayal, mixing
them up with interpretations of his own. His monster was a mus-

From the 1930s on, the Frankenstein myth seemed to be coming to life in world politics. Many saw Hitler as a monster created by man, as in this 1940 image by *Washington Post* cartoonist Clifford K. Berryman.

tachioed war machine who wore a tank with turret guns for a jacket. He toted a smoking gun in one hand and a skull-adorned swastika in the other. The Hitler-monster's facial expression was especially telling. Eyes glazed, eyebrows raised, staring at his makers, this monster—like the one by now known to all through the Universal retellings—marches on a path of destruction without reason or responsibility.

While cartoonists back home made reference to the novel, soldiers on the front were reading it. *Frankenstein* was number 909 of the 1,324 titles published by the nonprofit Council on Books in Wartime, a consortium of publishers, librarians, and other stewards of literature who believed that "books are

weapons in the war of ideas," as one poster put it. More than
three million books were shipped overseas to American soldiers
between 1943 and 1947, some relating directly to history, politics, and warfare, others chosen for inspiration or recreation.
Frankenstein appears to have been chosen for the latter. "How did
Mary Shelley, a twenty-year old girl [*sic*], . . . come to write a tale
of such horror that it has captured the imaginations of countless
writers who have borrowed the 'Frankenstein theme'?" read the
back cover of the Armed Services Edition. "Victor Frankenstein
regretted the creation of his pathetic and frightening monster,
but not we readers, who have shivered with terrified apprecia-
tion of the awful consequences of his experiment."

Four war years after Berryman's Hitler cartoon, Frankenstein
metaphors still loomed on America's editorial pages, but now

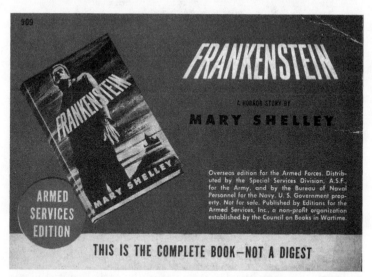

While cartoonists back home borrowed the metaphor to comment on
world politics, soldiers during World War II read Mary Shelley's original
novel, published for distribution by the Council on Books in Wartime.

By 1944 the tables were turned, and political cartoonist Edwin Marcus saw Adolf Hitler as Dr. Frankenstein, under attack by the monster he created—his blitzkrieg tactics.

the roles had reversed. Now Hitler was the monster maker, threatened by his creation. John Masterson in 1943 and Edwin Marcus in 1944 both hopefully envisioned the Allied response to Hitler's blitzkrieg tactics as a monster lashing back. Masterson drew a cannon-nosed bird of prey swooping down on a startled Hitler, its torpedo-size talons out for the kill, and titled the cartoon simply "Frankenstein." Similarly Marcus—like Berryman a mainstay among political cartoonists of the early twentieth century—titled his cartoon "Dr. Frankenstein and His Monster." An angry giant with arched eyebrows and sharp incisors, arms spread out like airplane wings and feet shaped like tanks, over-whelms a tiny Hitler. From monster to monster maker, from puppet to perpetrator: This threesome of cartoons captures key elements in the rise and fall of Adolf Hitler and the dynamics of World War II. Victor Frankenstein may have been a recluse in the novel, working in isolation, but to many living in the 1940s, his story resonated with world events as despots rose, commanded, and then fell victim to their own designs.

THE SONS OF FRANKENSTEIN

Films coming out of Universal Studios in the 1940s also show portrayals of the monster swinging from one extreme to another in a few short years. In 1942 Universal producers summoned the *Ghost of Frankenstein;* in 1943 they arranged it so that *Frankenstein Meets the Wolf Man;* in 1944 the monster fought Boris Karloff, now playing a crazed villain, and ultimately dragged him to death by quicksand near the *House of Frankenstein;* in 1945 the monster and other ghoulish characters gathered in the *House of Dracula;* and by 1948, it was time for peacetime frolics, and the studio had *Abbott and Costello Meet Frankenstein.* Looking at the series as a whole, some psychological truth emerges whereby the comic and the grotesque are two parts of one whole. The myth of the monster, ambiguous at its core, could play to either extreme: horror or humor. Mythic and mercantile forces worked hand in hand, and the challenge faced by those in the monster-making business was to sense just where on the continuum the public would be most thrilled and satisfied. "Universal was always on the verge of col-lapsing," said screenwriter Curt Siodmak, creator of *The Wolf Man* and other Universal horrors of the 1940s. "The studio was kept alive, actually, by the horror films—notably the Frankensteins. They would have been broke without those pictures." Universal

Frankenstein films of the 1940s won little critical acclaim, but
they did make money, and Universal kept cranking out these
soulless spectacles, recycled versions of earlier successes.

A few brave actors took up the challenge to play the monster
in Karloff's wake. First Lon Chaney, Jr., donned the flattop head-
piece and heavy eyelids. The haunted son of one of America's first
horror film stars, Chaney had already won praise for playing
Lennie, the retarded farmhand in the 1939 film of John Stein-
beck's *Of Mice and Men.* Two years later he had donned a stiff synthetic jumpsuit to play the title role in *Man-Made Monster,* a
latter-day *Frankenstein* from Universal.

In *Man-Made Monster* an obsessed scientist—played by Lionel
Atwill, the Frankenstein film veteran who had played Inspector
Krogh in *Son of Frankenstein*—wants to create a race of laborers
"whose only wants are electricity." Atwill's character concedes
that he is mad, but "so was Archimedes, Galileo, Newton, Pas-
teur, Lister, all the others who dared to dream." Such madness,
he says, lies at the heart of all scientific advances. "Fifty years ago,
a man was mad to think of anesthesia. Forty years ago, the idea of
operating on the brain was madness. Today we hold a human heart
in our hands and watch it beat. Who can tell what tomorrow's
madness may be?" The scientist infuses his experimental subject,
played by Lon Chaney, Jr., with electricity. Special effects make
Chaney's character glow on the screen. "There he stands—the
shell of a man, electrically alive," raves the scientist-creator.
"Think of an army of such creatures, doing the work of the world,
fighting its battles." The wartime audience must have cheered at
the thought until the plot unfolded, revealing how easily this character, emptied of conscience, wreaked destruction.

Soon Chaney took on the role of Larry Talbot, the nice guy
who begs to be locked up once a month as the full moon rises,

when the animal inside him takes over and he stalks the neighborhood as the Wolf Man. In hindsight the schizophrenic Wolf
Man character was to become Chaney's chief claim to fame, but
at the time it was another step on his path to becoming Karloff's
successor in *Ghost of Frankenstein,* released by Universal in 1942.

Expanding the house of Frankenstein, Universal writers
dreamed up two new offspring: Ludwig, another son, a brain
surgeon, and Elsa, Ludwig's daughter, a lovely young woman
from whom her family's dark past has been kept secret. The villagers of Frankenstein, convinced that they suffer under "the
curse of Frankenstein," decide to blow up the castle. It is still
inhabited by the mournful Ygor, Bela Lugosi again, who plays his
oboelike horn over his giant pal who—filmgoers may remember—at last sighting had fallen into the boiling mineral pits at
the base of the castle and is now entombed in hardened sulfur.
The villagers' dynamite dislodges the monster, who emerges
weightily, his massive body coated in plaster mud and dust.
Chunks of white stuff fall off with his every step. "The sulfur was
good for you, wasn't it? It preserved you," Ygor says in his raspy
voice. As they escape from the castle, lightning strikes the monster's right neck bolt. He cowers momentarily, then stands tall,
erect and empowered. "The lightning was good for you!" cries
Ygor. "We will go to Ludwig, the second son of Frankenstein.
He has all the secrets of his father. . . . He will give you
strength—strength of a hundred men."

As the melodrama unfolds, a hesitant tipsiness marks the gait
of the monster Chaney portrays. It may have come from the
actor's drinking habits as much as anything else, but it added a
key element to the stereotype of the monster. Karloff created it,
but Chaney clinched it. From the first scene on, this monster
holds up his hands, often straight ahead, feeling his way, reaching

out, balancing his unsteady body. Where Karloff's monster reached for the light, Chaney's monster simply gropes his way around. They are distinctly different interpretations: Karloff's optimistic, evoking compassion; Chaney's darker, less perceptive, and more threatening, evoking little empathy or hope. Trailers for *Ghost of Frankenstein* featured the monster, eyes closed and arms held out, with a promise swashed below: "More weird . . . more terrifying than ever before."

The plot of *Ghost of Frankenstein* swirls around a single conflict. Since a criminal brain has doomed the monster, might Ludwig Frankenstein implant another brain in him instead? Frankenstein wants the monster to receive the brain of Kettering, his brilliant young assistant. The monster wants the brain of a child. He states his preference by kidnapping a naive village girl, who responds with friendly curiosity and strikes the recurring refrain that horror is in the eye of the beholder. Ygor plots to donate his own brain—an act of generosity, perhaps, but also a greedy reach for immortality. His wish is granted through the agency of Dr. Bohmer, Frankenstein's smooth yet evil surgical partner, played by Lionel Atwill, who was getting to be a Frankenstein film regular. The operation succeeds, Frankenstein believing that he has transplanted Kettering's brilliance into the grotesque body. But when the monster speaks, out of those moribund lips comes the voice of Ygor—a sly audio effect accomplished by the ever-more-sophisticated special effects team at Universal.

Ghost of Frankenstein, shot in less than a month, was released on April 3, 1942—just as the Allies were learning of Nazi atrocities in Eastern Europe. Reports counted deaths in the tens of thousands. One *New York Times* correspondent reported Hungarian officers who "had personally seen hundreds of Jewish bodies floating down the Dniester River." Such reports, appearing more frequently through the summer of 1942, added a layer of sub-liminal terror to the film's grand finale, as villagers storm the cas-tle, attacking not Dr. Frankenstein but his evil partner, Bohmer. If Bohmer's Germanic name did not raise associations with the Nazis in the minds of contemporary moviegoers, the career his-tory of the actor playing him might have. Lionel Atwill's crisp mil-itary manner as Inspector Krogh was meant to instill trust in 1935, in *Bride of Frankenstein,* but seven years later, playing another Germanic figure, Atwill embodied treachery and evil.

In an eerie foreshadowing of real-life horrors yet unknown to the world, the movie climaxes as Bohmer throws a switch caus-ing poisonous gas fumes, visible as clouds of white smoke, to spew through the catacombs into which the villagers have charged. "Get back! Get back! You might all be killed!" yells their leader, played by the upright and very American Ralph Bellamy. Villagers cough, panic, and fall to the ground as the monster and Bohmer watch through a window, leering.

In the years between 1935 and 1942, history had turned a cor-ner. It was not a time for moral ambiguity. The monster clearly belonged on the dark side. And, as if to make it perfectly clear, the script for *Ghost of Frankenstein* leaves the monster not only linked with evil but also blind—the result of the misguided brain switch, since Ygor's blood type did not match the monster's. The blinded creature lurches through the laboratory, arms out, crash-ing into electrical equipment and chemical flasks until the entire set goes up in flames. The monster who cannot die meets death another time. We last see him, standing tall, eyes unseeing, arms outreached, engulfed by yet another fire, struck by yet another heavy beam coming down on his superhuman shoulders. His final pose seared itself into the public imagination, creating the iconic gait of a monster who walks stiffly, hands out, groping as if blind.

The groping hands now essential to the monster's image originated in the 1942 film *Ghost of Frankenstein*, during which the monster goes blind after receiving a brain with the wrong blood type. Here Glenn Strange practices the gesture in a publicity still for *House of Frankenstein*, 1944.

THE HORROR

Often horror movies provide a distraction from the real world, but as film historian David Skal has pointed out, in the 1940s they may have helped Americans grasp the physical atrocities facing their friends, sons, and husbands in war. Newsreels wouldn't show the flesh-and-blood reality of bullet wounds and dismemberment by bombs and grenades, but the now-familiar and reliably moralistic Frankenstein melodramas could. "Man-made monsters were the perfect toy soldiers to battle semiconscious fears," proposes Skal. Watching good overwhelm evil, thrilling to combat in which a monster and fellow villains always die, moviegoers could walk back out of the theater and face the horrors of daily life with increased optimism. In this light Skal points out the eerie parallels between Adolf Hitler's lifelong fascination with wolves—his Ukrainian headquarters was even named *Werwolf*—and the popularity of Lon Chaney, Jr.'s Wolf Man, first introduced by Universal in 1941. With Nazi associations already primed by *Ghost of Frankenstein,* the audience was ready for another. It took Universal less than a year to release its next in line, *Frankenstein Meets the Wolf Man.* For the monster to meet the Wolf Man, played by Lon Chaney, Jr., Universal Pictures executives had to find someone else to don flattop, neck bolts, and shoe lifts. Who else but Bela Lugosi?

The Universal formula of one classic monster meeting another snowballed, and by 1944 the studio was bunching as many well-known horror characters and actors up into one story as it could. *House of Frankenstein* contained, "All Together!" as movie posters shouted: the Wolf Man, Dracula, and a hunchback, together with a mad doctor—a part that brought Boris Karloff back into the stream—and Frankenstein's monster—

now played by a relatively unknown though aptly named actor, Glenn Strange.

Acting opposite Strange must have provoked an odd sense of déjà vu in Karloff, who had long since moved on to film roles as professors, doctors, and men of elegance, albeit often tainted with madness or involved in nefarious deeds. He had also distinguished himself as a founding member of the Screen Actors Guild and, in 1941, had returned to the stage in the Broadway production of *Arsenic and Old Lace*. He was by now so famous for the role he had created in 1931 that playwright Joseph Kesselring's script could capitalize on his celebrity. Karloff played Jonathan Brewster, a murderer who escapes from a mental institution and opts for plastic surgery to elude the police. Brewster first appears midplay, shocking his two elderly aunts with his newly constructed face.

"You're nothing like Jonathan, so don't pretend you are!" says one.

"But I've seen that face before," says the other. "Remember when we took the little Schultz boy to the movies and I was so frightened? It was that face!" Brewster's henchman, a plastic surgeon, admits that he saw that movie, too, just before he operated on Jonathan's face. It was a stage gag that could only work because, by 1942, the world knew that face and the monster it stood for.

To turn Glenn Strange into a Karloff monster lookalike, Universal makeup genius Jack Pierce once again applied the outsize flattop, staples, scars, and stitches. Thirty-two years old, six foot four, and athletic, Strange had played cowboys, a robot, and a werewolf. He was fleshy of face and hungry for work when hired to play the monster. With the Universal original at his side as mentor, Strange gave a performance that further enshrined the

Karloff interpretation of Frankenstein's monster. "I told him I needed his help, and he gladly gave it to me," he said of Boris Karloff. "He had finished his scenes and could have gone home, but he stayed on and worked with me. He showed me how to make the monster's moves properly, and how to do the walk that makes the monster so frightening." Critics were not impressed. The *New York Herald-Tribune* called *House of Frankenstein* a "top-heavy attempt to carry on its shoulders too many of yesterday's nightmares." Still, Universal hired Strange to walk that walk through two more films, *House of Dracula* in 1945 and *Abbott and Costello Meet Frankenstein* in 1948. He played the monster for Universal as many times as did Boris Karloff, but his star never rose as high. "He wasn't as lucky as I was," Karloff later said of Glenn Strange. "I got the cream of it, being first."

As version after grotesque version of Frankenstein's creation haunted the silver screen, a mirror world of comic monsters began propagating as well. Boris Karloff had worried that his favorite monster might turn clownish, and indeed the suite of Universal Frankenstein films ended in slapstick, with *Abbott and Costello Meet Frankenstein*. The war was over, spirits were high, and filmgoers would love watching the popular radio comedy duo hold their own against Frankenstein's monster, Dracula, and the Wolf Man all in one film. "The Monsters of Menace vs. the Masters of Mirth!" read the posters. "You'll die . . . laughing." Lon Chaney, Jr., played the Wolf Man, Bela Lugosi played Dracula, and Glenn Strange played the monster, exaggerating the groans, gawky movements, and slow-wittedness now associated with the character. "Frankenstein Monster Acquires a New Look," studio publicity bragged: A mask made of latex and foam rubber brought Strange's makeup session down to an hour a day and allowed him to flex into facial expressions never before seen in a

screen monster. A parade of children visited the set—one-year-
old Chris Costello; eight-year-old Bud Abbott, Jr.; ten-year-old
Bela Lugosi, Jr., home from military school and still in uniform;
and Glenn Strange's daughter, Janine, said to be seeing her father
in monster makeup for the first time. Publicity shots document-
ing each child's visit were broadcast far and wide, as if to assure
the public that this monster was family friendly. In a decade's
time the Universal character had been transformed from an evil
monster without a soul into a laughable dimwit.

SPLIT PERSONALITY

Alternating visions of the story surfaced at the same time in
another medium, the comic book, which saw its golden age, as
cultural historians call it, in the 1930s and 1940s. Some say that
illustrator Dick Briefer came up with the idea for a cartoon version of the monster, unapologetically named Frankenstein from
the start but often nicknamed Franky. From 1940 into the mid-
1950s, Briefer's monster appeared nearly monthly, zigzagging
through transformations that ranged from humble superhero to
awkward buffoon to grotesque avenger. His figure shared proportions with the Karloff monster, and his flattop head sported
the same forehead fringe of stringy black hair. He wore the same
simple jacket, shirt, and trousers, but in primary comic-book col-
ors. Always flat of face, with a stitched scar running down the center of his forehead, this monster's nose had migrated above his
eyes to the point that it was anatomically implausible. Early on,
his strips appeared buried among others in the generically titled
Prize Comics, but by 1945 Dick Briefer's monster had become
popular enough to warrant his own series, Frankenstein Comics.

Briefer's story lines often played on the reputation for horror
already associated with his character. In a 1946 story designed

Comic book artist Dick Briefer adopted the Frankenstein monster as his own and created a character sometimes comic, sometimes grotesque. In this 1946 episode the monster bumbles into membership in the Ghost, Ghoul, and Vampire Union.

strictly for humor, the bolt-necked guy wants to join the G.G. & V.U.—the Ghost, Ghoul, and Vampire Union—but first has to pass the test, proving that he can accomplish three supernatural tasks: change into a mist, pass through a keyhole, and bleed

black. By puffing on a cigar, sawing a six-foot keyhole, and let-
ting a fountain pen leak in his breastpocket, Briefer's Franky
earns his union card. In his adventure-filled life, Franky faced off
with superheroes, met the devil, climbed the Statue of Liberty,
and fought the Nazis. In 1948 the high-nosed character, now
well established, met "Boris Karload, Master of Horror," as they
both attended Karload's new film, *Love That Graveyard*. The cover
illustration, divided into two frames, tells the essence of the
story. On the left, Briefer's Frankenstein dashes out of the
theater, mopping his brow, holding his stomach, and saying "That
Boris Karload scares me!!" On the right, Karload—a caricature
of the familiar actor, who by 1948 had starred in more than
twenty films since *Son of Frankenstein*—strides out the stage
door, mopping his brow, holding his stomach, and exclaims, "I
saw a thing in the audience . . . a horrible, tall creature . . . with
a flat head . . . a high nose . . . oh, how ghastly!!" Karload faints
over and over through pages of comic book antics with the
Briefer monster and ends up clerking at a men's clothing store,
escaping horror by becoming anonymous.

In the 1950s, as war memories faded and comic-book readers
had, like Briefer's monster, escaped into a comfortable middle-
class existence, Dick Briefer's character turned foul. A postwar
comic series titled *The Monster of Frankenstein* introduced a vaguely
familiar character, outlined in Briefer's characteristic strong
brushstrokes, but this time grotesque, with drooping eyelids, rotten teeth, and puckered, corpselike skin. The scar down his forehead had widened, as if it was open and oozing. He did not speak
a word of dialogue. Now Briefer's stories placed him time and
again in the clutches of connivers, who took advantage of him yet
ultimately paid the price. A sculptor who attempts to cast the live
monster in bronze, for instance, draws the revenge of the "seared

During the calm 1950s Dick Briefer's monster turned violent. No longer the lovable simpleton, he had the capacity to respond with animalistic fury—but usually for a justifiable cause, as when a sculptor attempted to cast him live in bronze in this 1954 comic.

and burned and blackened, but very much alive" giant, who retaliates by pouring molten bronze down the sculptor's throat, leaving "his whole digestive tract . . . filled solid with metal!"

The dual identity of the Frankenstein monster, both Jekyll and Hyde coming from the pen of one cartoonist, symbolizes what had happened to this cultural icon midway through the twentieth century. The complex character from the novel, revitalized in Boris Karloff's film portrayals of the 1930s, now split into two extremes: the grotesque and the comic. In some portrayals the monster became an invincible force of evil; in others a lovable oaf. Each alternative tells a tale that is simpler, more approachable, and less disturbing than the ambiguous original, in which the monster contained a bit of both. The Frankenstein story can be turned into a thriller, evoking pure titillating terror, or it can become a fable, leading to some sentimental moral conclusion. When such a split occurs, the story conveys static and limited meaning, if any. This evolution, from myth to fable to caricature, is a process akin to that described by George Orwell in his famous essay, "Politics and the English Language," in which he shows how metaphors die once those who speak them ignore the original elements vital to their meaning. Just as a metaphor can die from overuse, so too, after numerous retellings, a myth can lose vitality. The story becomes an empty shell, an externalization without inner meaning. Complicated moral questions—the kind that cannot be answered simply by saying yes or no, good or evil—drop out altogether. In the middle of the twentieth century the Frankenstein monster was facing such a demise.

TRUE GORE

With film technology offering new opportunities to push horror to its grotesque extremes, a new film production company took up the story of Frankenstein and began to tell it in their own special, living-color way. From 1957 to 1973 Britain's Hammer Films produced seven releases, fashioning a new saga about the creature and his creator. Universal had located the story in a Bavarian village, dimly suggesting the novel's Swiss locale, and in a vaguely contemporary time; Hammer's Frankenstein lives in London—exiting to the English countryside when necessary—in a distinctly Victorian era, complete with horsedrawn carriages. One critic sees the series as an effort to reclaim *Frankenstein* for its author's homeland.

Few other links back to the source influenced the Hammer Frankensteins, though. By the 1950s the story was so familiar it could be retold with little or no reference back to Mary Shelley. James Sangster was a wet-behind-the-ears production manager for Hammer Films when asked to try his hand at writing the script. Hammer "offered me a fee up front, just like a grown-up screenwriter," recalled Sangster in his cheeky autobiography, *Do You Want It Good or Tuesday?* Studio producers laid down "a variety of restrictions," he wrote, most important: "Stay as far away as possible from any of the previous *Frankenstein* movies." "As soon as the project was announced," according to Sangster, "Universal started gnashing their teeth and threatening to beat us to death with their legal cudgels. Never mind that the original Mary Shelley novel was in public domain, they had made the movie, and God forbid we should infringe their 'copyright.'" While the film credits state "Screenplay by Jimmy Sangster / Based on the classic story by Mary W. Shelley," Hammer producers paid more attention to steering clear of the 1931 film than to portraying the original novel. "I didn't want to remake the Universal movie," he wrote. "I wanted to make my own." Sangster defends his Hammer Dracula, saying he read Bram Stoker's novel twice before writing the script—but he mentions no such literary preparation for the Frankenstein films.

Sangster's other restrictions were time and money. Again he

bounced off the Universal model. "Every other *Frankenstein* movie, before or since, has had a bunch of irate villagers descending on the castle," wrote Sangster. "Villagers cost money, so eighty-six the villagers. Talk about them if you like. Threaten to get their help. Hear them baying in the background. But keep them off screen. . . . No special effects please, and not too large a cast. Oh yes, one other thing, design the script so that the director can shoot it in four weeks maximum." Everything was done on a tight budget. One of the actors remembered the 1957 Hammer studio as "a tiny grotto under the office of the producer." Neither Peter Cushing nor Christopher Lee, hired to play Frankenstein and his monster, then had reputations. "I was forty years old and a failure as an actor," Cushing has said of those days. When Lee's agent suggested he play the role of Frankenstein's monster, "it seemed merely like one more indignity" to the thirty-five-year-old. He had played a small part in James Whale's 1939 Universal film, *The Man in the Iron Mask,* and a slightly larger part in Laurence Olivier's 1948 *Hamlet,* but he was better known as a television actor in Britain.

Sangster admitted he was more fascinated with the creator than the creature, and that focus holds throughout the entire suite of Hammer Frankensteins. In Peter Cushing producers found an actor whose gaunt face, crisp elocution, and emotionless demeanor suited their needs. He played the obsessed scientist in all but one of the Hammer films, and if any feature from them entered the general cultural vocabulary, it is Cushing's version of Dr. Frankenstein: cool, calculating, and uncompromisingly evil, ready to risk anything to advance his quest for knowledge. Terence Fisher, director of five of the seven Hammer Frankensteins, described the character's intrigue: "He is either an atheist who doesn't believe in God and believes he can really create man bet-

ter than God ever has, or he is a deep religionist who sold his soul
to the Devil, forsaking the fundamental religious belief that God
creates man." Despite the sensational gore and gruesomeness
central to the Hammer aesthetic, Fisher believed he was creating
morality plays: "If my own films reflect my own personal view of
the world in any way, it is in their showing of the ultimate victory
of good over evil."

To create his character of Frankenstein, Cushing looked not
to Mary Shelley's novel but to a controversial figure from her
era. "I have always based my playing of Frankenstein on Robert
Knox," he commented, referring to a Scottish anatomist at the
heart of a notorious nineteenth-century grave-robbing scandal.
In 1828 Knox was discovered to be teaching with cadavers provided by two scoundrels, William Hare and William Burke, who
had murdered to provide the bodies they sold (a ghoulish
episode in British history that may have heightened public interest in the 1831 reissue of Shelley's novel and that later inspired
an 1884 short story by Robert Louis Stevenson and a 1945 film,
The Body Snatcher, starring Boris Karloff and Bela Lugosi).
Robert Knox never freed himself from associations with the
criminal affair—up to the twentieth century, for Cushing's
Knox-inspired Frankenstein does not hesitate to kill his own
experimental subjects, so single-mindedly dedicated is he to the
quasi-science on which he embarks. To obtain a superior brain
for his creature, he shoves a visiting scholar over a banister. He
kills without conscience, he operates without doubt, and he
begins and ends his career—both in the first film and in the
series as a whole—in a conjured-up Bedlam with dungeonlike
walls of stone and a straw pallet for a bed.

Up against Cushing's Frankenstein, Christopher Lee struck a
ghastly monster in the first Hammer film, *The Curse of Franken-*

stein. Presumably Lee, too—and the makeup artist working on him—were commanded to steer clear of the Karloff look. But Lee had met Karloff, and the Hammer monster did get some valuable advice from his Universal predecessor. "He said to me that an actor must never be faceless, even when that face is obscured by bandages," wrote Christopher Lee in his autobiography, *Tall, Dark and Gruesome.* Lee had to project through more than bandages, as it turned out. "Copyright prevented us from imitating Karloff's robot look," he wrote, "and we made numerous tests on make-ups which didn't work. I wound up looking like a madman's picture of a circus freak." Lee wanted something different—"more like a human being, but a mess"—but Hammer makeup artist Phil Leakey had to create a look that was cheap and fast and that made the most of color film. "There were all sorts of horrid things glued on my face," wrote Lee, "like yellow and white putty, plastic and undertakers' wax." The result was ridged, pimpled, and pockmarked, with livid red scars and eyelids. Early in the film the monster gets shot in the face, after which Lee wears one bulging blind eyeball. In the end, he believed, "we got it more or less human, which after all was what The Creature Mary Shelley invented was, but we overdid the mess in our hurry. Eventually someone wrote, 'Christopher Lee looked like a road accident.'"

From behind that mess of a face, Christopher Lee tried to follow Karloff's advice, creating a monster from the inside out. "It was a case of inventing a being who was neither oneself, nor anybody else, but a composite of pieces of other people, mostly dead," he conceptualized. "I decided that my hands must have an independent life, and that my movements must be spastic and unbalanced." The script did not offer Lee the rich range of emotions expressed by the monster in Shelley's novel or even in the early Universal films. A scholar's brain may have been harvested for him, but that brain falls to the floor during a struggle between Frankenstein and his tutor-turned-accomplice, the voice of social conscience in the film. The glass jar containing the brain shatters, and so the organ implanted into the skull of the creature contains shards of glass, sure to have an effect on any monster's intellectual capacity. "I had a damaged brain, and so I walked slightly lopsidedly," said Lee. "I was limited all the time by the fact that I did not speak, yet I thought that a certain kind of walk and the suggestion that *something* was going through my mind was important, so that the creature would show some depth of character, rather than be just an automaton. . . . Everything I did, I did as if it was forced out of me; as if I was rather unwilling to do it, controlled by a brain that was not my own."

In the Hammer idiom it is not the eyes (as in the novel), not the hand (as in the 1931 film), and not even the heart (as X-rayed in 1939's *Son of Frankenstein*) that symbolizes the life imparted to a body by the work of a human scientist. For Hammer, what mattered was the brain, the organ least amenable to surgery. Surgeons were in fact successfully transplanting other body parts and organs as the Hammer Frankenstein films came out. Corneal transplants dated back to the 1930s, and a kidney transplant between twins had succeeded in 1954. The 1960s, though, were the years when researchers developed immunosuppressive drugs that made surgical transplants practicable. Kidney and lung transplants were attempted early in the decade, and by 1967 those processes had been refined. That same year Christiaan Barnard performed the world's first heart transplant in Cape Town. HEART TRANSPLANT KEEPS MAN ALIVE IN SOUTH AFRICA, read the front page of the *New York Times*. HEART TRANSPLANTED FROM A DEAD WOMAN AND STARTED BY SHOCK. News of the remarkable operation, dependent on electrophysiological technology, sped around the world. In the next year, 1968, more than one hundred heart transplants took place. For centuries regarded as the seat of feeling—and still so, sentimentally and metaphorically—the heart was proving to be a physical entity, simply another body part that could be cut from one body and stitched into another.

To keep audiences thrilled, Frankenstein's ventures had to stay several leaps ahead of contemporary science, and that feat was accomplished through his persistent attempts at brain transplantation. Grim scenes in the 1958 *Revenge of Frankenstein* show Cushing's Frankenstein sawing through the skull of his experimental subjects. The bloody procedure remains just offscreen, but through the rest of the film a livid red scar circles the crown of the monstrous character. Hammer set designers contrived body-size fluid-filled tanks, with oxygen bubbling through them and wires dangling out, as the receptacles where Frankenstein kept bodies and parts of interest. Both visuals—the round-the-head scar and the life-support tank—entered the Frankenstein vocabulary. "The strange thing is that when we first started these films back in 1956, everything that Frankenstein got up to was pretty impossible, but now Dr. Barnard has caught up," Cushing said in the early 1980s. "He hasn't gone quite as far as me," he added slyly, "because I have transplanted brains."

COMIC TRANSFORMATIONS

While Hammer Films was reinventing the screen Frankenstein, others had been reinterpreting the monster's story for the growing comic-book crowd. In the early years of World War II, Albert Lewis Kanter, the American son of Russian Jewish immigrants, came up with a brilliant publishing idea. He had been making a living distributing cheap paperbacks and comics, and he spotted a niche that no one else had filled. Kids loved reading comic books, but parents forbade them, saying they had no social or literary value. Kanter decided to create graphic abridgments of "stories by the world's greatest authors," as the cover of each of his Classic Comics declared. Kanter tested the waters in 1941 with *The Three Musketeers* and *Ivanhoe.* By his third title, *The Count of Monte Cristo,* published in March 1942, his company was thriving. The war years proved profitable, since Kanter swung deals with the Red Cross and the army to sell comics to American servicemen. Unlike other comic-book publishers, he kept a backlist alive. Many Classic Comics—or, as they were renamed in 1947, Classics Illustrated—stayed in print for years. *Frankenstein*, number 26 in the lineup, was reprinted nineteen times between 1945 and 1971. Hundreds of thousands of copies went into the hands of children and adults during that quarter century.

Editor Ruth Roche turned the novel into a story told in about 250 frames. She straightened the novel's circular story line—Walton and the pole-bound ship appear only at the end. She added details where Shelley's prose left questions unanswered. After the death of Elizabeth, for example, Shelley's Frankenstein utters, "What then became of me? I know not." But the omniscient editor Roche did know—and her answer included a padded cell. She chose gently archaic language, addressing her reader directly. "Here is a haunting tale of shame and horror," read the comic's opening page. "Dwell with tolerance, gentle reader, on the incredible life of this nameless monster . . . this creature without a soul!" Dialogue reflected the complex emotions and motivations of both creature and creator. "If I could only find the key to banish disease from the human frame and render man invulnerable to any but a violent death. If . . . if! And I come so close,"Victor thinks, holding a test tube up to the light of a candle.

The creature made by this Frankenstein is manly and muscular, his skin blue-gray. His appearance hints at Karloff's only through his flattop head of straight black hair and his stubby electrodes, which protrude from his neck and knees but play no role in the creation scene pictured in the comic book. At first the monster wears only a knotted loincloth, looking something like an uncorked genie. Later he explains his (and Karloff's) poorly fitting suit: "I remember little of the first day I was created. After you left me I was cold," he tells Frankenstein when they first meet. "I saw your body was clothed, so I took some of your garments and put them on as best they'd fit." Garments he took; shoes he left behind. As if determined to picture this monster in some ways distinctly different from Karloff's, the artist saw to it that he went barefoot through all his adventures.

Robert Hayward Webb illustrated the Classic Comics *Frankenstein;* Ann Brewster inked the final art. Roche, Webb, and Brewster were all veterans of the shop run by comic-book impresario Jerry Iger. Iger had a penchant for wholesome heroines who were buxom, slender of waist, and dressed tightly enough to show it. Earnest risk takers whose escapades always thrust them into suggestive poses, these women earned the nickname "Good Girl art" for Iger's distinctive style. The story of *Frankenstein* offered only a couple of Good Girl opportunities, however. Inside the comic book, Webb dared to silhouette the hanged Justine, her dress slipping down her shoulder, draped over a shapely breast. While James Whale filmed only the outcome of the bridal-bed encounter, Webb honed in on the scene itself, showing an animalistic monster eagerly gripping Elizabeth by the

Countering the Universal Frankensteins, which had wandered further from the original with every new film, comic-book innovator Albert Lewis Kanter returned to Shelley's novel for the story told in his 1945 Classic Comics version of *Frankenstein*.

neck. Her head tilts back, her blond ringlets flying. Red drops of blood spatter her lipsticked mouth.

Cover art for the Classic Comics *Frankenstein* changed over the years, reflecting both the publisher's philosophy and the audience's taste. In 1945 Webb rendered the cover art in the same dark outlines and melodramatics of the interior. We see only the monster, standing on a promontory at the edge of the sea. Dark clouds highlight his figure. His ruddy face grimaces in rage; a telltale bolt protrudes from his neck. He has ripped a tree up by its roots and he holds it shoulder high. Bolts of lightning streak across the frame behind him, positioned as if coming from his body more than from any thundercloud. He is a monster of nature, angry and violent.

Thirteen years later, the publisher commissioned artist Norm

Saunders to paint a new cover for their *Frankenstein*. By 1958, Saunders was a legendary book jacket artist, very much in the school of Good Girl art. His work graced the covers of pulp fiction and popular magazines for twenty years: *Saucy Romances* in the 1930s, *Tom Mix* in the 1940s, *Ellery Queen* and *Marvel Science,* both the British and the American series, in the 1950s. Saunders saw the Classics Illustrated monster in a new light. He set the scene in the Arctic, with little background but a distant horizon of icy peaks. A hooded figure on a dogsled waves from afar. In the foreground the man-made man—fleshy, boltless, looking very human—climbs up an icy ridge. His skin is tawny, with a touch of green that seems reflected off the ice around him. He casts a glance back at the waving figure, his expression more hunted than enraged. The way Saunders has painted him, this monster is more victim than perpetrator.

Eventually other comic-book publishers recognized *Frankenstein* as a winner. With a copyright from Universal Pictures, Dell published a 1963 comic titled *Frankenstein: The Monster Is Back!* In it not only does the monster come back to life, but he also immigrates to the United States. The story begins in "the isolated laboratory of Dr. Frankenstein, somewhere in Eastern Europe," with scenes sketched from the 1931 film: grave plundering, Fritz's blunder and the criminal brain, the platform bed hoisted up to the lightning. A newspaper headline declares, WORLD'S LEADING SCIENTISTS TO MEET IN AMERICA, and the familiar threesome—doctor, assistant, and monster—sneak onto a steamship to cross the Atlantic. When the monster makes a surprise stage appearance at an "International Scientific and Medical Convention," scientists run off screaming and policemen draw their guns. Then, "as if in search for a way back to its native land," reads the narrative, "the monster instinctively heads for the water-

In the 1960s Dell Comics introduced "the New Frankenstein," a superhero of the Superman ilk. While the series
did not last longer than a few issues, it did foretell a
changing attitude toward the monster in the American
consciousness.

front." He boards a ship full of explosives, a fire breaks out, and
the police chief orders the ship towed out to sea. In the next
frame, an explosive blast silhouettes the monster. "A creature

cruelly given life by mankind, and now, about to be destroyed by that same cruelty," reads the narrative. Dr. Frankenstein, babbling to Fritz as the two tread water within sight of the burning ship, predicts that his "super-human" will survive—if only to inhabit more pages of Dell comic books.

And in fact, three years later, Dell Comics did resurrect a Frankenstein, this time "the world's newest, greatest and strangest super hero!" He no longer even resembles the Karloff monster. He is superhero handsome: chiseled features, tough-guy crew cut, muscular physique bulging through his skin-tight suit, cinched with a belt buckle marked *F*. His only odd characteristics are his chartreuse face and snow-white hair. According to this comic's story, a bolt of lightning awakens the creature, who has been lying in "the ruins of a strange and foreboding castle . . . within sight of a great American metropolis" for a hundred years. Like Superman—a familiar figure in comic books and on television at the time—the Frankenstein superhero assumes an everyday identity, moving into the city in the guise of a handsome young heir named Frank Stone. He is strong, nimble, and fearless; he can leap tall buildings in a single bound as well as any other superhero. "Whoever . . . whatever I am, one thing is certain!" he says. "My strength is greater than fifty men and my brain has been endowed with enormous powers . . . so until such time that the world is safe from evil . . . I Frankenstein will utilize my full powers to keep it safe!"

NOT YOUR CLASSIC COMIC

In the world of monster comics, a moralistic superhero did not last very long. It was too simplistic a concept as the nation moved into the latter part of the century. Americans struggled with more complicated questions of good and evil as they viewed horrors from Southeast Asia, then their own city streets and college campuses, broadcast daily on the evening news. Against this tableau of living history, a new comic-book Frankenstein, the Marvel Comics monster—"the most famous, most fearsome monster of all"—took center stage in a series of twenty-eight comic books between 1972 and 1975.

Date: 1898. Location: the Arctic. To use language from the second comic book in the Marvel series: "Robert Walton IV, great-grandson of the last man ever to see the creation of Frankenstein, has found the monster and brought it aboard ship! Now, threatened by a suspicion-riddled, mutinous crew and a killer arctic storm, the monster comes to life . . . posing a far greater threat than any man could manage!" With emotions high and violence erupting on just about every page, the Marvel Comics adaptation of the Frankenstein story roams through the universe of horror, fantasy, and science fiction, plunging the monster into conflicts with enemies ranging far and wide, globally and culturally: an indigenous chieftain of the North, a hunchbacked Gypsy, a seductive female werewolf, a satanic high priest, a gleaming android with a Viking name ("the Berserker"), and a primeval mother figure among forest dwarfs. She ultimately reveals herself to be Baroness Victoria von Frankenstein, "the direct descendent of your creator!"

Three different writers and four different artists created the episodic series, which sometimes doubled back, retold the creation story, and then took off in a new direction. The entire series was overseen by comic-book mastermind Stan Lee, renowned for superheroes with complex personalities such as Spider-Man and the Incredible Hulk. The look of the new character was created by Mike Ploog, who later went on to work with renowned animator Ralph Bakshi and puppeteer Jim Henson. "I related to

that naive monster wandering around a world he had no knowledge of," Ploog said of his Frankenstein. Baby boomer Ploog saw
the Frankenstein creature as "an outsider seeing everything
through the eyes of a child." He associated him not with Geneva
1816 but with the 1950s and his own childhood: "That took me
right back to my childhood, being a farm kid, moving to Burbank,
California, in the middle of the hot rods and the swinging '50s."
After six issues Marvel editors asked Ploog to modernize his
monster. "They wanted to bring Frankenstein up to the 20th century, and have him battle in the streets of New York with Spider-
Man, and I just couldn't do that. To me, I felt it was disrespectful
to the poor monster."

Ploog's Frankenstein monster was extraordinarily tall and
strong, the muscles of his body bulging through the remains of
arm and leg wrappings that bound him when he arose from the
laboratory table. He wore a furry vest, reminiscent of the tunic
from *Son of Frankenstein* and a constant reminder of his primitive
nature. His face borrowed elements from the Boris Karloff portrayal—sunken eyes and cheeks, stringy black hair—and from
Dick Briefer's cartoon character—high pug nose and withered
skin—but his proportions and profile were all his own. A telltale
scar sliced straight across his forehead, along the line that Hammer Films' Frankenstein had sawed.

Both the body and face of this monster moved agilely through
the comic book pages. He could pack a mighty punch, heave and
hurl bodies high above his head, grasp and snap the bones of
attackers, animal or otherwise. His feelings and expressions
ranged from fury to loving concern. When the character spoke,
it was only in childlike, three-word sentences. In many issues he
did not speak at all. "Tell me, poor creature, would you like to
speak?" says a female character to him, soon to identify herself as

Borrowing elements from many of the monsters that came before, Mike Ploog created the Marvel Comics character, at first glance an alien creature but in the long run a sympathetic hero.

Veronica Frankenstein, another imagined daughter of Victor's and a scientist eager to right her father's wrongs. The mute creature cannot voice an answer, but the page contains this empathetic, stream-of-consciousness narrative:

> To speak. To communicate. To share his pain. To avoid further pain. To leave the monster behind and become a man. What a rush of eloquence he would utter in questions and exclamations words pouring forth in an endless stream of searching and joy expression fulfilled and answers broached in a voice his own to command and to shout loudly to the heavens of injustice and horror heaped upon his soul he cannot find nor fulfill with purpose and peace. To speak. . . . Yes, to speak.
>
> He nods, affirmatively . . . and again, emphatically.

Despite the sensationalistic violence portrayed on every comic-book cover—always perpetrated by the monster—a strong element of compassion toward the character runs through these Marvel Comics, which often managed to recapture the essential ambiguity of Mary Shelley's story. The drama is pitched high, but the moral message resounds. The villains who attack the monster threaten human society as well. The angry monster is a misunderstood victim of circumstances; the vengeful monster acts to reestablish the social order. The common man has more kinship with the monster on both counts than he does with the mad scientist who made him. After decades of being portrayed as the outsider and the other, the enemy and the embodiment of all that is ghastly and unhuman, the monster had become a hero. Sympathies had been building since the middle of the twentieth century, in large part thanks to a new entertainment medium over which the monster quickly gained domain: television.

CHAPTER NINE

MONSTERS IN THE LIVING ROOM

He blows his stack when he flips his lid,
Although he's a monster, he's just a big kid.
—THEME SONG, *Milton the Monster,* 1960s

Oh! sweet mystery of life.
—GENE WILDER AND MEL BROOKS,
Young Frankenstein, 1974

It's an iconic image of the 1950s: the American nuclear family, sitting happily together around the television. Beaming right back at them were images of family togetherness: *I Love Lucy, Ozzie and Harriet, Father Knows Best, Leave It to Beaver.* Life was good, and monsters were just a wholesome fictional diversion.

In 1950, 9 percent of American families owned a television set. By 1973, the year of the last Hammer Frankenstein, 96 percent—more than 65 million American households—owned and watched TV. A similar explosion happened in Britain and other European countries. Television quickly became an undeniable cultural force in the second half of the twentieth century, sucking up cheap films for reruns, demanding new material for original shows, and shaping cultural icons, old and new.

Frankenstein's monster got off to an inauspicious television start in January 1952, when the American Broadcasting Company hired Lon Chaney, Jr., to don bald head, putty scars, staples, and stitches and play the monster for its landmark science-fiction series, *Tales of Tomorrow*. "Thrill tonight to the most famous tale of a science-created monster," says the announcer of the episode titled simply "Frankenstein." The drama begins, domestically enough, at the dinner table. Elizabeth and her father, Victor's former science professor, have come to the island where Victor and his little cousin, William, are living in a sixteenth-century castle, chosen by the brilliant scientist as the best place to conduct his experiments. "I think medical science is ready to, uh, to make an artificial human being," Frankenstein mumbles to his guests, clearly hoping to hide his bold intentions. Blond-bobbed Elizabeth finds the concept amusing. Elizabeth's father brushes the topic aside, assuring her that Victor is smart enough to know the limits of human science. Cousin William mimics the idea by waving a creature made of fruit, pineapple body and banana arms, at the television camera.

The visitors depart, leaving Frankenstein to his labors. He strings wires to an unidentified hulk under a sheet atop a laboratory table. "Medical science laughs at the idea of a man being a creator," he says, lifting the sheet and peeking under, "but I have created you. I have made you stronger than ten men. You're indestructible." He turns a few dials and pulls a lever. The set lights flicker and dim. The form under the sheet convulses then rises, fully dressed, eyes full of fear and fury. On occasion the monster stares right at the camera, registering confusion. He stumbles about the castle, emitting grunts of terror, slinging heavy wooden chairs, and killing the castle maid with his bare hands. Frankenstein assigns Elizabeth and William to lure him back into the laboratory, where he gets tangled up in the same equipment that gave him life and dies by electrocution. End of twenty-two-minute story.

Live broadcasting allowed no editing or retakes, to the detriment of this drama. In 1952 Lon Chaney, Jr., was still plagued by drinking problems, and throughout the production of this "tale of tomorrow," he was less than sober. The confusion caught on camera was sincere; the stumbling was not always an act. In the scene that culminates with the maid's murder, he lifts a chair, holds it aloft, then looks right and left, questioning—to those in the know, desperately scanning the crew off set to find out what to do with the thing. Eventually he simply puts it down. His animalistic character absorbed all such vagaries, and the show went on. Several more original *Frankensteins* were aired on American and British television, including a Hammer offering, but none sank deeply into the public consciousness or earned weekly series status—yet.

SHOCK THEATER, COAST TO COAST

Old monsters haunted the black-and-white television screens of the 1950s, though, once Screen Gems began marketing its *Shock!* package of fifty-two Universal horror films to local broadcasting stations and started a coast-to-coast craze in the fall of 1957. "Never Before on TV!" read the promo material, the near-dead face of Glenn Strange's Frankenstein monster looming out of a black background. A color booklet, complete with a 3-D Frankenstein monster pop-up, listed the films and suggested promotional stunts. In major U.S. cities, producers tapped local performers to anchor the broadcasts of these late-night horror shows. In Los Angeles exotic dancer Maila Nurmi pioneered the part, penciling in eyebrow arches, gluing on three-inch fingernails, and cinching her waist to become Vampira. Her ghoulish glamour and highly publicized affair with James Dean made her more sensational than the movies she screened. Every Saturday night in Chicago, kiddy show host Terry Bennett donned thick-lensed horn-rimmed glasses and beatnik black, becoming Mad Marvin at 10 p.m. on WBKB. In Cleveland, Pete Myers became WJW-TV's Mad Daddy, wearing a bat-winged cape and fiddling with miscellaneous laboratory instruments in a haze of dry-ice vapor. In Miami, fresh-faced Charlie Baxter glued on a Nean-derthal unibrow and stuck buck teeth into his mouth to become M. T. Graves, who rose up out of his coffin greeting his viewers as "inmates incarcerated in hospitals, prisons and in your own lit-tle homes!" He appealed to the malcontents in his adolescent audience when he added, "We're all in dungeons of sorts!"

It was the task of these local late-night hosts to bridge between film segments and advertising, to liven up the show when the films were mediocre—and, along the way, to have some fun. Bit actor John Zacherle began his horror-host career in Philadelphia. Wearing an undertaker's frock coat left over from a low-budget Western, Zacherle slithered down a spiral stone staircase, carrying a basket just the right size for a head, imaginary material for some gruesome spectacle. "We would have an experiment with a monkey or a big piece of liver, some-thing like that," he told an interviewer years later. "Chocolate syrup all over the place." (On a black-and-white screen at mid-night, chocolate syrup did fine for blood.) The host's assistant, Igor, stayed chained offstage and was known only by his inarticu-late moans. "Goodnight, whatever you are!" Zacherle groaned at the end of every show. The Philadelphia sensation moved to New York in 1958 and, changing his on-screen name to Zacherley, began hosting WABC's legendary *Creature Features*.

One of many *Shock Theater* hosts across the United States, John Zacherle of WABC-TV in New York introduced the Universal Frankenstein films to a new generation of horror fans in the late 1950s.

Shock Theater, *Creature Features*, *Thrill Theater*, *Chiller Thriller*—it went by many names, but it was the same phenomenon, local yet national, and a smash success. "KRON-TV gave San Francisco the SHOCK treatment," read a Screen Gems ad in *Variety*, claiming that in that market alone, ratings rose 807 percent, audience share rose 267 percent, and television set usage rose 147 percent when the station aired the 1931 *Frankenstein*. By 1958 more than forty cities had their own *Shock Theater* shows. Soon Screen Gems released another package deal, and "Son of Shock!" added more Universal Frankenstein films to those already showing on late-night TV.

While it may have intended for an adult audience, *Shock Theater* attracted the adolescents of the late 1950s. Most baby boomers first met Frankenstein's monster not in the movie theaters but late at night, on the television screen. "September, 1957. I was sitting on the thick brown carpet of our living room watching the old RCA black-and-white TV when my older brother shoved the current issue of *TV Guide* under my nose," recalls Rich Scrivani. He was twelve years old. "This looks like it might be right up your alley," his brother said to him. Scrivani remembers the ad: "Staring out at me was the white pasty face of Boris Karloff from a now-familiar still from *Son of Frankenstein,* and in the lower right corner a profile shot of the Wolf Man, howling at something, the moon or his destiny. . . . And scrawled along the bottom, the magic word, 'SHOCK!'" They had been around much longer than he had, but the Universal monsters were brand-new to Scrivani. He had never heard of Mary Shelley's novel; he had never seen Boris Karloff's monster on the screen. "Part of me winces," he now admits, "at the question I asked my brother, pointing straight to Karloff's famous visage: 'Is that Frankenstein?' To which he answered, 'No, I think that's Dracula.'"

Now an enthusiastic Web-based historian of *Shock Theater,* Scrivani shares such memories with many others who grew up in the 1950s and early 1960s. "It's hard to put into words what it was like being so young and impressionable in those days, the ground floor of baby boomer horror consciousness," he writes. Hundreds of thousands, if not millions, of adolescents either sneaked or connived or begged or bargained in order to stay up after midnight on the weekend to watch their local version of *Shock Theater.* Scrivani told his parents he was staying up late to study his catechism. Then, instead, he would "make my way into the little back room that held the second TV set, turn the dial to WABC channel 7, and out of the dusty tube came my first look at the Franken-

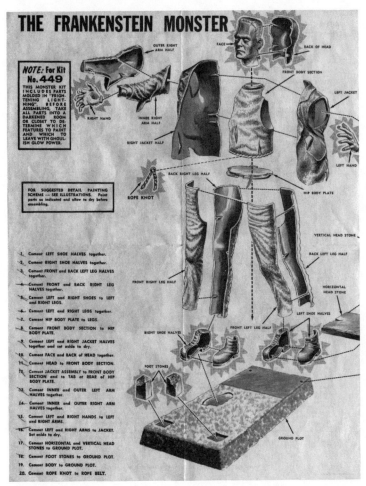

As baby boomers entered adolescence in the 1960s, Aurora models invited them to piece together their own tabletop monsters.

stein Monster." It was almost like pornography, Scrivani says today, so furtive and forbidden. He created scrapbooks, pasting them full of all the horror-film facts, stories, and images he could find. He probably glued together plastic monster models made by Aurora. The first, Frankenstein's monster, came out in 1961, followed by a movable two-foot-tall "Frankie" model in 1964. Scrivani even remembers the order in which he met the Universal Frankensteins—and it was not the order in which they were created. He first saw *Son of Frankenstein,* then *Ghost,* and not until two years later did he view the 1931 original. By then he was a trading-card-carrying member of the cultural phenomenon that now affectionately calls itself the "Monster Boomers."

Somewhere along the way Rich Scrivani decided to read the original *Frankenstein*. He may well have bought the sixty-cent 1963 Airmont Publishing Company paperback edition, which addressed its marketing copy to readers just like him, for whom the monster originated not in Geneva, 1816, but in Hollywood, 1931:

> Many readers, familiar with the Hollywood movies of *Franken-stein,* and opening the book for the first time, may be surprised not to find themselves transported at once to a remote castle, complete with galvanic flashes and the inarticulate grunts of Boris Karloff. Instead, they are bound for the North Pole with an ardent explorer, Robert Walton.
>
> The theme of rejection by society of a man who then turns on society is of course a common one in twentieth century fiction. The appeal of the idea of a man's creating monstrous life is vouched for by the many books and movies on this theme.

Rich Scrivani wrote a book report about Mary Shelley's *Franken-stein* in tenth grade. He recalls that the novel overwhelmed him, but his early-sixties classmates and teacher thought Scrivani was just being weird. "I don't remember who gave that book report on 'Frankenstein,'" one friend wrote in his high school yearbook, "but I sure hope it wasn't you. Please read some better books and you'll do fine."

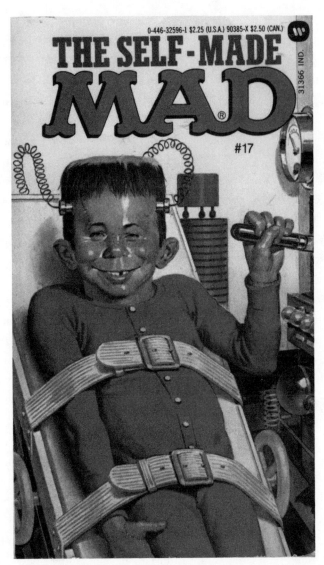

Adolescents in the baby boom generation watched *Shock Theater*, built weird plastic models, and read *Mad* magazine. This 1960 cover reflects their worry-free willingness to identify with the monster within.

As weird as he might have felt in his own neighborhood, there were people everywhere doing what Rich Scrivani was doing. To this day Monster Boomers convene annually at Monster Mania, "3 Days of Sheer Terror" held in May and late October in New Jersey, and at the Monster Bash, held every summer in the Pittsburgh area. Not only a film festival and a "monster memorabilia shopping center," states publicity, the Monster Bash promises a "state of mind," evoking a past "where our imaginations were ignited" with fantasies that "still burn behind our everyday jobs and life." Recent Bash headliners have included Sara Karloff, Boris's daughter; Bert I. Gordon, director of 1950s phantasms including *The Amazing Colossal Man;* and Forrest J. Ackerman, canonized editor of sci-fi and monster magazines, who loyally attends Monster Boomer get-togethers though he is now in his eighties.

Ackerman has been a major force in building the monster cult of the late twentieth and early twenty-first centuries. In February 1958, amid the *Shock Theater* craze, he founded *Famous Monsters of Filmland,* a magazine devoured by kids like Rich Scrivani, with plot summaries, production details, interviews, and photos, the more gruesome the better. Ackerman published *Famous Monsters* for twenty-five years. During that same time, 1962 to 1975, a competing monster-fan magazine, *Castle of Frankenstein,* gave readers the inside scoop on monster movies, old and new, and included a regular "Frankenstein TV Movieguide," alerting horror addicts to every broadcast available. Joining Ackerman in the role of archivist for the Monster Boomer generation, Dennis Druktenis, under pseudonyms including Victor Frankenstein IV, still publishes a family of monster fanzines, including a new rendition of *Castle of Frankenstein.* "Representing the world of the imagination and the macabre," reads one of Druktenis's slogans today. For more than thirty years these magazines have covered the gamut of monsters, horror, and science fiction—from Godzilla to Mr. Spock—but as their titles and logos constantly proclaim, like a beloved mascot, the Frankenstein monster stands for them all.

A PROLIFERATION OF MONSTERS

From the late 1950s on, this new, and younger, generation of monster lovers influenced the direction of horror films about Frankenstein. Film studios large and small swooped in and grabbed what they could of him, first in the United States and Britain and then, through the 1960s, around the world. It was the era of rock and roll and B-grade movies. The number of drive-in theaters in the United States jumped fivefold between 1948 and 1958, and so did the demand for movies that suited them. Lovestruck moviegoers snuggled up in the broad front seats of their Chevy Impalas and watched *I Was a Teenage Frankenstein* (1957)—an LA professor cobbles together a scar-faced monster out of teenage car-wreck victims—and *Frankenstein's Daughter* (1958)—a mysterious professor transforms one high school girl into a monster and kills another for spare body parts. As David Skal points out, a demographic strategy lay behind such spin-offs: In 1958 the first of the baby boom generation entered adolescence, and in that year teenagers represented nearly three-quarters of America's movie-watching public. Even Boris Karloff got pulled back into the swirling vortex of adaptations in *Frankenstein 1970* (1958), a mediocre film about making mediocre films. Karloff plays a broken-down, fourth-generation Frankenstein who rents out his castle to a movie crew making a tawdry horror film, his ulterior motive being to use the crew as subjects in his experiment to create life with a nuclear reactor. "The one . . . the only king of monsters as the new demon of the atomic age!" read the theater posters, leaving it open to interpretation whether the "new demon" was Karloff, his monster, or atomic power.

The spin-offs were spinning out of control, coming out of low-budget film houses not only in the United States but in other countries as well. Between the mid-1960s and the mid-1970s, dozens of cheap Frankensteins thrilled foreign audiences and then found their way to American drive-ins and late-night TV. From France came *Torticola contre Frankensberg* (Twisted Neck Against Frankensberg), in which a monstrous creation with a cork-top skull and hockey gloves saves a Swiss maiden, Lorelei, from laboratory experiments conducted by her uncle. From Mexico came *El Monstruo Resucitado* (The Resuscitated Monster): A deformed experimental scientist, Dr. Ling, transplants a brain into a handsome suicide to attract a pretty reporter. Similarly Egypt's *Haram Alek* (Shame on You), Italy's *Non Perdiamo la Testa* (Don't Lose Your Head), and Mexico's *El Castillo de los Monstruos* (The Castle of the Monsters) all took lighthearted liberties with Frankenstein and his monster. West Germany's *Die Nackte und der Satan*—which translates as "The Naked Woman and the Devil" but was distributed in the United States as *The Head*—portrays a scientist fixated on keeping severed heads alive, only to be outdone in such work by his own assistant. Conceived in Switzerland, published in Britain, made a movie star in the United States, by 1970 the Frankenstein monster was a global property, famous around the world.

Towering over all the international interpretations of Frankenstein was the Japanese film directed by Ishiro Hondu, who had already made film history by creating *Gojira*—Godzilla. Some might call his 1965 film "Frankenstein Meets Godzilla," but it has gone by the names *Frankenstein Tai Baragon* (a transliteration), *Furankenshutain tai chitei kaiju Baragon* (more correct phonetically),

Frankenstein vs. Baragon (a correct interpretation), and *Frankenstein Conquers the World* (an overblown interpretation). The film's story hinges on the hypothesis that the heart of Frankenstein's monster, kept alive in German laboratories, is transferred to Japan during World War II for further study. "The heart is a living thing," says the Japanese doctor receiving the organ, still pulsating in its high-tech valise. "If we can learn from its cellular structure, regardless of wartime or peace . . . illness or injury . . . we [will] be able to help everyone." As he reaches for the heart, the *Enola Gay* streaks across the sky, carrying the bomb about to obliterate Hiroshima.

The film flashes forward fifteen years. Now a vagrant haunts that city's streets, snagging dogs and pet rabbits for food. A pair of radiation scientists—an American man and a Japanese woman—figure out that the monster's heart has regenerated into a savage boy. Inarticulate and confused, gap-toothed and thick of brow, the boy is determined by experts to be Caucasian. Confined in a cell, he grows to be three stories tall. Franken-stein, as he is called, escapes to roam the Japanese countryside. By the time he reaches Mount Fuji, his clothing has devolved to a caveman look: loincloth and shoulder strap. As it happens, he shares this terrain with another monster: a giant reptilian quadruped with an armored body, bat-wing ears, and an ivory proboscis. The two monsters face off. It's an even match. The lizard-monster can breathe flame, but Frankenstein has human instincts and the knowledge of fire. He throws flaming torches at the reptile, then ultimately wrestles him to death. As the giant savage raises his fists, victorious, the mountainside erupts and the earth engulfs both monsters into its shadowy deep.

"Do you think he's dead?" asks the woman scientist.

"No, he's an immortal creature. He'll always survive," answers her American colleague. In a low-budget hour and a half and at many different levels, the film reenacted the past twenty years of world history and its cultural consequences. The secret force of Germany, possessed by the Japanese, then irradiated, takes on the form of a Caucasian giant and grapples with the ancient dragon of the East. While the figurehead of the Western world won, both monsters went down together—and both, every audience member knew, would rise again.

In the spring of 1961, Yuri Gagarin and Alan Shepard made history, becoming the first human beings launched into space. Frankenstein's monster wasn't far behind, according to the 1964 film *Frankenstein Meets the Space Monster*. In this movie American military commanders were perfecting a human for space travel when extraterrestrial beings beat them in the race, bringing their own monster to earth to meet the human one.

For scriptwriter George Garrett the film was a joke from start to finish. Thirty-five at the time, Garrett had published essays, novels, and poems. When he heard about an easy gig writing low-budget horror scripts, he invited a couple of his University of Virginia graduate students along for the ride. The result was one of the worst—and best-loved—Frankenstein rip-offs ever, "a triumph of vulgarity," according to one reviewer; "the pits" according to another.

"They had a title they were sold on, *Frankenstein Meets the Space Monster*. And that's all," wrote Garrett of the film's producers, whom he met only once. "It had to be cheaper than cheap and it had to take place in Florida . . . because they had arranged for some free locations there. Oh, yes, and we also had to find ways in our story to use as much stock footage as possible." Cobbling together free NASA space-launch footage and capitalizing on the recent spate of UFO sightings, Garrett and company projected a

In *Frankenstein Meets the Space Monster* (1964), a man-made astronaut confronts a monster, brought by aliens seeking females to populate their war-torn planet. Scripted on a lark by an English professor and his graduate students, the film has become a camp cult classic.

Frankenstein monster into the world of astronauts and aliens. "Frank, the android American astronaut, was, like Mary Shelley's original, made up of various and sundry body parts," Garrett described. "His legs came off a deceased tap dancer," and, in the original script, "every time somebody hummed or whistled 'Sweet Georgia Brown,' ole Frank's legs would automatically go into his act." That detail, and a lot of other jokes, never made it into the film. "We are in the *horror* film business," Garrett remembers being told by the producers, who critiqued his work by recording their comments on reel-to-reel tapes. "You got your horror and you got your humor and you are not supposed to mix them up. Okay? Stick to the horror."

The resulting film followed the bare thread of a story. Space scientists are readying Frank, a handsome automaton, for his first space launch. Minor programming errors begin to show themselves. A spaceship filled with aliens arrives. They are on a mission: They need to repopulate their planet, recently devastated by nuclear war, and proceed to kidnap American go-go girls for the purpose. Over the course of the movie Frank turns ghoulish, his face tortuously melted during encounters with Mull, the monster stowaway aboard the alien spacecraft. Most of the humor intended by Garrett and his friends got cut out, but secret jokes remain, since the characters' names are often *noms de clef* for people who haunted Virginia's English Department in those days. The robust army general, for example, bears the name of the department chair, Fredson Bowers.

The film made audiences laugh, but not because they got the insider jokes. The times they were a-changin', as Bob Dylan sang that very year, and the kind of horror flick that had gripped a fifties drive-in audience couldn't cut it with the more jaded crowd of the next decade. "The film came to be advertised as the first camp horror film," says Richard H. W. Dillard, one of the graduate students who worked with George Garrett on *Franken-stein Meets the Space Monster*. A decade later Dillard published his book *Horror Films,* written at a time when few scholars took the genre seriously. He devoted an entire chapter to the 1931 *Franken-stein,* finding it "a genuinely vital work of art in which form and content are one."

Born in 1937, Richard Dillard grew up on the Universal films. He remembers first seeing Karloff's *Frankenstein* at the age of nine, even remembers the dreams he had that night. When he read the book, he was disappointed: "I was looking for the movie." With such a passion for the classic horror films, he realized that as much fun as writing the *Space Monster* screenplay might have been, he felt "a sense of total betrayal: I loved the monster." Their knock-off Frank was "a made creature, but no longer made in any Romantic sense at all," Dillard says. "He was made by the government—just a piece of equipment." *Frankenstein Meets the Space Monster* was one step in a long twentieth-century process by which, as Dillard puts it, the monster was "commodified."

THE MONSTER GOES CAMPING

One response to the real-world gore of the Vietnam era was to engage in earnest protest. Another was to rise above it, assuming an attitude of ironic distance and amused detachment. Thus developed the world of high camp, with its own twists on the Frankenstein story. Camp before the concept had even entered the general vocabulary, *Frankenstein Meets the Space Monster* headed up quite a parade.

The first written use of the word "camp" is ascribed to the author Christopher Isherwood, who used it as a verb in 1954: to "camp" about something was not to make fun of it but to make fun out of it. A decade later Susan Sontag published her essay "Notes on 'Camp'" in the *Partisan Review*, defining "camp" as a cult of sensibility, "unmistakably modern, a variant of sophistication but hardly identical with it"; a "way of seeing the world as an aesthetic phenomenon" that "converts the serious into the frivolous." "Alive to the double sense in which some things can be taken," the camp sensibility "turns its back on the good-bad axis of ordinary aesthetic judgment." Style over content, irony not tragedy, "the whole point of Camp is to dethrone the serious," wrote Sontag, and it can be either discovered or intentionally created. King Kong and Flash Gordon were on Sontag's list of unintentional camp; for examples of intentional camp, consider the pair of television shows that premiered the very year she wrote her essay: *The Munsters* and *The Addams Family.*

Ironically it was the producers of the quintessential 1950s family show, *Leave It to Beaver,* who conceived of CBS's Munsters: a family of five—two vampires, male and female; a preadolescent werewolf; a pathetically normal blond; and, as paterfamilias, a Karloff monster lookalike. Nighttime television viewers already knew tall, horse-faced Fred Gwynne as a lovable cop on *Car 54, Where Are You?* He carried that gullible innocence, unburdened joy, and refreshing lack of self-awareness over into his new character, Herman Munster. He donned "forty pounds of padding and ultra-hot makeup," according to fellow cast member Butch Patrick, and put on a costume straight out of the 1931 film: a dark suit jacket with too-short sleeves and thick-soled boots that forced a heavy gait. His temples and wrists bore jagged scars; metallic bolts stuck out of his neck. Makeup made his eyes sink deep and turned his lips into a thin black line. His very appearance terrified people, yet Herman Munster never took their revulsion to heart. Occasionally he was confused, but more often he was oblivious. Feel-good mediator in many a family squabble, Herman Munster was a Frankenstein monster without psychological contradictions—ghoulish on the outside but as problem-free, cheerful, bumbling, and lovable as any sitcom father of his day.

Scriptwriters for the second season of *The Munsters* had some fun linking the program more explicitly to its cultural forebears. In one episode Herman takes a bolt of electricity to the head and wakes up looking, to his family's great distress, like a handsome Fred Gwynne. In another episode Victor Frankenstein IV visits from Germany. Herman notes his visitor's resemblance to the original Victor Frankenstein, who "made me what I am today." The latter-day doctor brings with him Johann, one of his great

Herman Munster, patriarch of television's *The Munsters*, turned the character of Frankenstein's monster—according to one episode, his long-lost brother—into a lovable sitcom buffoon.

grandfather's castoffs, played by Gwynne as well. Johann does not speak, responds to electric lightbulbs with animalistic fury, and wears a faux-fur tunic, just like a Universal monster. The family resemblance is so close, Lily mistakes Johann for her husband and takes him off on a weekend getaway. What was left implicit in the first season became a central plot element in the second: Herman Munster was a bona fide Frankenstein creation.

Also premiering in September 1964, within a week of *The Munsters,* ABC's *The Addams Family* made no claim to such a direct descent, but associations arose anyway. While the Munster characters combined elements from horror movies and family sitcoms, the three generations of Addamses walked off the pages of a magazine. From the mid-1930s on, *The New Yorker* had published the lovable black humor of Charles Addams, whose cartoon world included gargoyles, vultures, and witches; dark basements and dusty attics; turrets and cupolas adorning the quintessential cobweb-filled Gothic house. Addams loved to place ordinary folk in the middle of extraordinary phenomena, like the little girl who, stretching out her string of cut paper dolls, discovers that one in the middle has three legs. From his macabre imagination emerged a family of horror caricatures who peopled the pages of *The New Yorker* for decades without ever being named. The father looked slightly Asian—pencil-thin mustache and hair parted in the middle. The mother looked vampishly witchy—pale skin, bony body, tight black dress with a plunging neckline and a hem that draped like liquid all over the floor. A white-haired crone and a sunken-eyed ghoul represented the older generation; the daughter was a thin, wide-eyed schoolgirl buttoned down in all black; and the brother was a chubby brat in a striped T-shirt. Serving the family was a butler, towering over everyone else, bulky torso, sloping shoulders, and squared-off head topped with sparse, stringy hair.

Many assume that Addams's butler character, named Lurch in the television series, was yet another version of the Frankenstein monster as played by Boris Karloff. Even Karloff believed it to be so, but any resemblance may be merely coincidental. In 1942 Bennett Cerf, founder of Random House, was preparing to publish Charles Addams's first cartoon collection, *Drawn and Quartered*. He prepared a "Note by the Publisher" as an introduction to the book. "When Russel Crouse and Howard Lindsay were confronted with the task of finding somebody who looked like Boris Karloff to play the villain in *Arsenic and Old Lace,* they flew to Hollywood and, by a stroke of genius rarely paralleled in the history of the theatre, cast Boris Karloff himself in the part," wrote Cerf. "We followed the very path that they had blazed when the question of a foreword to *Drawn and Quartered* presented itself."

Karloff was Cerf's neighbor on Manhattan's Upper East Side at the time. "One evening," wrote the actor, "in an unguarded moment, I expressed my whole-souled admiration for the drawings of Charles Addams, and before I was quite aware of the trend of events, that fellow Bennett Cerf had talked me into doing an introduction for this volume." The man who valued his own monster's silence complimented the cartoonist's wordless storytelling as well. Then he laid claim to having influenced Addams. "I hope I will not be accused of undue vanity," wrote Karloff, "if I publicly thank Mr. Addams for immortalizing me in the person of the witch's butler."

Bennett Cerf saw the connection. Boris Karloff saw the connection. But did Charles Addams, creator of the butler character, see it? Not according to his spokesman today. "We think it is important to dispel any misunderstanding . . . concerning the character Mr. Addams created as Lurch, the butler to the Addams Family," says Kevin Miserocchi, executive director of the Tee and Charles Addams Foundation. "Unlike Herman Munster, the character of Lurch, both in print and in theatrical adaptations, was never intended to replicate the Mary Shelley character of Frankenstein, nor the 1931 Hollywood version as

Cartoonist Charles Addams visualized a modern monster maker in this cartoon, included in his first collection, *Drawn and Quartered,* published in 1942.

portrayed by Boris Karloff. Of course, there are similarities,
but that is all." Charles Addams was sketching Lurchlike butlers
in his youth, before Karloff ever donned a monster costume,
says Miserocchi. Indeed, *Drawn and Quartered* contained a cartoon with an oblique reference to the story of Frankenstein. A
shadowy character waits outside a patent attorney's office,
tending a covered shape stretched out on his high-tech gurney.
Frankenstein clearly was a story Addams knew but visualized in
other ways entirely. The cartoonist's own written description
of the butler, part of his September 1963 contract with
Filmways TV Productions, names him "Lurch" for the first time
and specifies only that "one eye is opaque, the scanty hair is
damply clinging to his narrow, flat head." Any resemblance to
literary or film monsters was strictly accidental, but certainly
there. Magnetlike, the powerful icon of Frankenstein's monster
drew anything similar into its sphere.

Our Monsters

Lurch and Herman Munster were bright stars in the evolving constellation of high-camp Frankensteins. The genre multiplied in the 1970s, not only with the appearance of the later Hammer films but also with *Andy Warhol's Flesh for Frankenstein* (1973), a sex and gore fest to be viewed through red-and-blue 3-D glasses; *Blackenstein* (1972), in which the monster is chased by dogs not from a Swiss village but from the Los Angeles Police Department; and *Dracula vs. Frankenstein* (1970), the tacky swan song of Lon Chaney, Jr. For the latter two films, art directors even resurrected Kenneth Strickfaden's laboratory paraphernalia from the Universal prop shop for links back to the glory days of the 1930s.

The camping of Frankenstein reached its peak in *The Rocky Horror Picture Show*. Richard O'Brien, a New Zealand dairyman-turned-London-showman, had written a musical he called *They Came from Denton High*. His title referred to the ingenuous central characters, Brad and Janet, who stumble in on "the Frankenstein place" and enter a rollicking escapade of drag queen quips and horror film in-jokes, sung and danced to rock and roll. Their host for the evening is Frank N. Furter, an alien scientist born on the planet Transsexual in the galaxy Transylvania. Lurid in word and gesture, Frank manages to infuse just about everything he says with sexual innuendo. With his motto, he renovates a link to his literary ancestor, Victor Frankenstein: "Don't dream it—be it!" Lurking about is a humpbacked, sunken-cheeked assistant, a skeletal and cerebral version of Fritz, frequently played by playwright O'Brien himself.

Escaping a rainstorm, Janet and Brad just happen to arrive for the unveiling of the crazed doctor's new creation, a man with physique and libido designed to satisfy Frank N. Furter's wildest desires. The plot twists and turns, giving the cast and chorus girls opportunities aplenty to sing O'Brien's wickedly clever songs. The haunted house set was borrowed from Hammer Films, as was the body-length tank from which the handsome creature arises, newly vivified. Allusions to a dozen or more low-budget horror and science fiction films zing through the script and song lyrics. While all the glitter and glibness, subplots and silliness may hide it, the core story comes from *Frankenstein*.

Retitled *Rocky Horror*—the name Frank gives his creature—O'Brien's musical opened in June 1973 in London's Theatre Upstairs, a new black-box space, the experimental venue of the Royal Court Theatre, traditionally known for cutting-edge drama and for defying the edicts of the Lord Chamberlain, royal theater censor until 1968. To stage a play in the Theatre Upstairs signaled that audiences should expect something unusual, risky, maybe shocking.

"It was only supposed to run for five weeks in a tiny, tiny little theater," says Richard O'Brien. "I thought, along with everybody else, that after the end of the five weeks we would have exhausted our potential audience. Well, here we are, thirty years on, and that obviously isn't true." After six weeks of sell-outs, *Rocky Horror* went mainstream, continuing to sell out all five hundred seats at King's Road Theatre. It was named the best musical of 1973 by London's *Evening Standard*. American pop entrepreneur Lou Adler swiftly purchased U.S. rights, and the musical packed Hollywood's Roxy Theater for nine months more. Out of that success was born the film *The Rocky Horror Picture Show,* released in the fall of 1975 with great expectations—but grudging reviews. The film fizzled. Few saw it during that first run.

Then, on April Fool's Day, 1976, the film showed at the Waverly Theater, a New York landmark that had already made a cult phenomenon of Pittsburgh's low-budget zombie flick, *Night of the Living Dead*. Now the West Village film house did it again with *The Rocky Horror Picture Show*. Midnight crowds swarmed the theater night after night.

"It was a cold snowy night when four friends and I found ourselves outside the Waverly waiting for over an hour before we were allowed to see the show," writes Sal Piro, remembering January 1977. All his friends were talking about the show. One had seen it nineteen times already. "I found the energy and enthusiasm generated in the theater catching," recalls Piro. He names features most vivid in his memory: the lips—blood-red, glistening, disembodied lips that open the film, singing, "Science Fiction / Double Feature / Doctor X will / Build a creature"; the Time Warp—a showgirl dance so inviting that audience members starting doing it in the aisles; and "Frank's fabulous entrance"—all glitter in his gloves, corset, garter belt, stockings, and heels, as he invites Brad and Janet to "come up to the lab and see what's on the slab."

Audience members shouted out gleefully to the characters acting on the screen. It reminded Sal Piro of Zacherle on late-night TV, "who interrupted old 'B' horror films with zany remarks and wisecracks." Back then, Piro remembers, he had always wanted to talk back to the movies, but adults would shush him. Now he could do it all he wanted. He started dressing up like Janet: blond hair, rhinestone ring, wedding hat. Another Waverly regular, Dori Hartley, dressed up like Frank N. Furter. "One night," Piro remembers, "when she was wearing the green surgical robe, she persuaded a blond, Rocky-type regular named John to strip to his underwear. Right on cue, as Frank chased Rocky on the screen, Dori began chasing John around the theater. Audience participation finally had reached the level of true theatrics."The phenomenon swept the country and the world. Fan clubs formed and newsletters were published. Two decades later Sal Piro, president of the International Rocky Horror Picture Show Fan Club, has written books, made guest appearances, played parts in film and television, all in the service of his favorite movie. "What might have been only a passing fad was turning into an important cultural statement," Piro believes.

Amid all the frivolity, the story at the heart of *Rocky Horror* faded from view, and in 2006 Richard O'Brien supported a new British production of his original. "We discovered over the years that lots of things that had been added to the piece had become written in stone, so to speak, and all of the ideas were perhaps not as good as they should have been," says the playwright. For the new production, "we've taken out all the improvements and we've gone back to basics. Let the story tell itself." Why has *Rocky Horror* survived so long? he asks rhetorically. It's "a nice, trashy, camp musical," bouncing with rock and roll, "but it's also a fairy tale." Regarding the mythic origins of his play, O'Brien reaches back in time, past the Shelley novel to its mythic ancestor: "It's a reworking of 'Babes in the Wood,'" he says, "which in itself was a reworking of the fall in Eden, one of the oldest root stories, almost, in our chemical memory, in our DNA."

If Frank is the serpent, Brad and Janet are Adam and Eve, and O'Brien's play is a coming-of-age story. Rocky Horror, the camp-era man-made monster, could be seen as the temptingly delicious apple. He embodies pure sexuality, the cause and consequence of this twentieth-century fall from an ingenue's Eden. This high-camp Frankenstein dared to carry the myth of Frankenstein into radical new directions, soon to be taken up by feminist scholars willing to explore the weird gender dynamics underlying the horrors of birth and death that Mary Shelley had recorded on the page. It was all part of a gradual return to the original novel, powered by a cultural shift during which Shelley's monster made friends with a new and youthful generation.

THE MONSTER GETS CUTE

In 1818, when *Frankenstein* first appeared, the divide between literature for adults and for children was so broad that no one even considered asking whether Shelley's novel was children's fare. Debates over children's literature flared in those years, since early reading material has the power to shape moral character. In fact, as William Godwin was promoting his daughter's novel among London publishers, he was publishing children's books under his own imprint, Juvenile Library. Godwin advocated myths and fairy tales, but he would not countenance horror for children, and he fiercely edited Charles Lamb's manuscript for *The Adventures of Ulysses*. "We live in squeamish days," Godwin wrote Lamb, objecting to a draft that included descriptions of giants "lapping the blood" as they devoured human limbs.

Similar concerns surfaced a century later, as children met monsters at the movies every Saturday. OVEREXCITEMENT SEEN, announced a headline in the *New York Times* on May 28, 1933, reporting on a study sponsored by the Motion Picture Research Council and underwritten by the Payne Fund, a private organization supporting "research into factors in modern life affecting young people." Strapping sensors onto adults and children, researchers measured electrical currents in the audience's bodies as they watched movies. "In the presence of the varying degrees of emotion the body's resistance causes the delicately poised needle of the galvanometer to oscillate," stated the study's spokesman. "So, if you thrill at the feat of Douglas Fairbanks or recoil from the horror of a Mr. Hyde or a Frankenstein monster, the deflection of the needle indicates the intensity of the emotion involved." Through this and other measures, researchers came to the conclusion that children aged six to eleven registered excitement at a level three times higher than that of an adult watching the same motion picture. "The writers of the Payne reports are not averse to occasional moments of excitement for children," the *Times* reported,

> but they believe that such frequent orgies as a large proportion of America's children appear to be having through the movies amount, in the words of Dr. Frederick Peterson, neurologist, quoted in the survey, "to emotional debauch." "Stimulation," he says, "when often repeated is cumulative. Scenes causing terror and fright are sowing the seeds in the system for future nervous disorders."

Researchers conducted a special study of children considered "most frequent moviegoers," and these "movie children" were found to have lower school performances and reputations among teachers and to be less cooperative, less self-controlled, "slightly more deceptive," and "somewhat less emotionally stable" than children who attended fewer movies. These findings resonated with activities afoot in America's religious communities. Roused by a cardinal visiting from the Vatican, who warned that movies were causing the "massacre of innocence of youth," Catholics established the Legion of Decency. Clergy of other denominations soon joined the movement, publicly condemning "indecent and

immoral motion pictures" and encouraging boycotts of theaters
that showed them, all for the sake of children.

At the same time, Hollywood animators were seeing possibilities in the monster as children's entertainment. As early as 1933,
Frankenstein's monster appeared in Walt Disney's "Mickey's Gala
Premiere," a seven-minute animated event. Cartoon versions of
dozens of movie stars—Wallace Beery, Mae West, three Barry-
mores (Ethel, John, and Lionel), Laurel and Hardy, the Marx
Brothers, Maurice Chevalier, Jimmy Durante, Charlie Chaplin—
congregate in a Hollywood theater, avidly awaiting the mouse
who is joining their ranks. Seated among them is a classic monster trio: Bela Lugosi as Count Dracula, Fredric March as Mr.
Hyde, and Boris Karloff as the unnameable creature. The famous
monster's first cartoon appearance went down in history for
another reason. Television viewers across Britain were watching
it on September 1, 1939, when their screens went dead—the
start of the government-imposed wartime blackout. Seven years
later, when the BBC resumed airing, the first thing shown was
"Mickey's Gala Premiere."

The medium suited the monster, and soon he was serving as a
formulaic hair-raiser in the company of one classic cartoon character after another. Porky Pig, Bugs Bunny, Mighty Mouse,
Gandy Goose, Heckle and Jeckle, Woody Woodpecker, and Mis-
ter Magoo all encountered a version of Frankenstein's monster at
one time or another during the 1930s, 1940s, and 1950s. By the
mid-1960s, as Herman Munster grinned out of the television
screen on Thursday evenings, Saturday-morning cartoon shows
likewise beamed out the message that the monster, although
frightening, was really our friend.

At ten o'clock every Saturday kids tuned in to *Milton the Mon-*

ster, a teddy bear of a monster whose family resemblances to Karloff's kind were his massive upper body, his flattop head, and his ragged black chemise. Milton the Monster was the creation of Hal Seeger, a career animator who had worked on Betty Boop and Porky Pig cartoons, among others. The theme song told the familiar story, Milton-style: "On top of old Horror Hill, in a secret laboratory, Professor Weirdo and Count Kook were in their monstrous glory." Their mission: to concoct a being. Adding "six drops of essence of terror" and "five drops of sinister sauce" to the mixture inside a giant body-shaped mold, the professor slipped up and poured in too much tenderness. Up rose Milton, whose name carried literary echoes that meant little to his fondest fans. Steam bubbled up out of Milton's head, as if chemical reactions were still going on as he went on his merry way, escaping the clutches of his creators, who considered his good-hearted nature a fatal flaw in their experiment. Two monster friends, Heebie and Jeebie, joined Milton, and together they sang, "We are three monsters—three ghastly monsters. We may be monsters, but we're all in love with you." Hiram the Fly, who put on superglasses to become Fearless Fly the superhero, was also a regular on the show. The tiny insect with heroic courage and the ghastly giant with a tender heart: together the characters were two halves of a mythic whole that answered vague preadolescent anxieties of being powerless, marginalized, and misunderstood.

As if to lay claim to the legacy, the next year a closer relation to Frankenstein's monster joined the Saturday morning lineup, one of the lesser creations of TV animation gurus William Hanna and Joseph Barbera. A robot with a heart, Hanna-Barbera's Frankenstein Jr. was the invention of brilliant Professor Conroy and his son, Buzz, whose braininess was signified by the contents of his pockets: a slide rule, a pocket periodic table, three transistors, and a hiber-

In the 1960s cartoon series *Milton the Monster*, Professor Weirdo's hand slipped when creating his monster, and too much tenderness went into the mix. The result: a monster with love in his heart, much to his creator's dismay.

nating frog. Frankenstein Jr. was a blue giant towering three stories tall and wearing a superhero's cape, tights, and mask. Bolts hinged his lower jaw, which attached to his face in a perpetual smile. Like the transistor radios that all kids coveted in the mid-1960s, Franky sometimes loses battery power. Then Buzz straps on his personal propellers and flies the portable reenergizer to him. Frankenstein Jr. works as a sentry, protecting the Conroys' laboratory from their nemesis, Dr. Spyclops, and other forces of evil. "He's a monster with a conscience!" Conroy exclaims in one episode.

These cartoons were telling a new story about the famous monster, evoking empathy for the miscreant and asserting categorically that he had more heart and soul than many a human evildoer. The topsy-turvy version of the monster myth resonated with the youthcentric, alternative-culture ideals of the early 1970s. Power mongers like Professor Weirdo, Count Kook, and Dr. Spyklops were the true monsters, while the disenfranchised held the keys to a better future. In *Yellow Submarine*, the 1968 animated movie, a cartoon Ringo Starr walks in on a pigeon-toed giant, identifying him as Frankenstein. The slab-bound monster comes to life, breaks free, downs a test tube of blue bubbles— and turns into John Lennon. All he needs is love.

BELOVED MONSTER

Young Frankenstein—released in 1974, between the stage *Rocky Horror* and the screen *Rocky Horror Picture Show*—sings a love song to the monster. The popular film, considered by many Mel Brooks's finest, blended slapstick, innuendo, and nonstop references to the ghosts of Frankensteins past. "After lunch one afternoon I walked up to my bedroom with a yellow legal pad and a blue felt pen," wrote actor Gene Wilder, who first came up with the idea for the film. "At the top of the page, I wrote, *Young Frankenstein,* and then I wrote two pages of what might happen to me if I were the great grandson of Beaufort von Frankenstein and was called to Transylvania because I had just inherited the Frankenstein estate." The title, he recalls, simply presented itself to his consciousness. Wilder connects it to films in the past, *Young Tom Edison* (1940) and *Young Winston* (1972), but just as likely he was riding the spirit of the times, writing the myth anew for an audience unlikely to trust anyone over thirty (although he was approaching forty at the time). When he called his director pal the next day and told him about the idea, Mel Brooks answered, "That's cute."

In his notes Wilder had also written, "In black & white." Central to the film ultimately created by Brooks and Wilder were its connections to earlier tellings of the tale. At his first appearance Freddy Frankenstein—or, as he insists on pronouncing it, *Frahnkanshteen*—is a latter-day anatomist, lecturing medical students on the structure of the brain. Called to his homeland, now Transylvania—a reference to Dracula that got spliced into the Frankenstein story sometime in the 1940s—the young Frankenstein takes the same train trip to the Old Country that Basil Rathbone's Wolf von Frankenstein took in *Son of Frankenstein*. He is greeted by goggle-eyed Igor, played by Marty Feldman, and lusty Inga, played by Teri Garr, who dons a laboratory robe as Frankenstein's assistant. Tiptoeing through the shadowy castle—the turreted mountaintop edifice to which Frankenstein's home had evolved through the Universal sequence—they discover the elder scientist's private laboratory. Cobwebs festoon familiar equipment: In fact Brooks dusted off Kenneth Strickfaden's 1931 electrical contraptions for another round. Taking possession of an oversize volume—*How I Did It by Victor Frankenstein*—the young monster maker irresistibly follows in his family's footsteps.

"As the minuteness of the parts formed a great hindrance to my speed, I resolved therefore to make the creature of a gigantic stature," reads Freddy Frankenstein, a near-quote from Mary Shelley's original novel.

Inga parses out the meaning in practical terms. "In other words, his veins, his feet, his hands, his organs, would all have to be increased in size. . . . He would have an enormous schwanzstucker!"

A pregnant pause.

"That would go without saying," nods Frankenstein, never losing his composure. To that, Inga can only add an *ooof* of amazement.

"He's going to be very popular," quips Feldman's Igor.

In Peter Boyle, the film's young monster, Brooks created a malleable character, easily lovable. His face was made to look rather neutral—deeply carved bone structure, smooth skin, stitches, staples, and a neck zipper—but his body was, as the doctor ordered, monstrously oversized. As his unanimated body lies on a laboratory gurney, Freddy Frankenstein and Inga respond differently.

"He is hideous," says Inga.

"He is beautiful," says Freddy, "and he is all mine." From the moment the creature moves with new life, this Frankenstein embraces him, reversing the act of abandonment that set the novel's plot off in its ghastly direction. The creature's fingers lift

In Mel Brooks's 1974 film *Young Frankenstein,* the monster (played by Peter Boyle) finally receives the affection from his creator (played by Gene Wilder) that he had been yearning for ever since Mary Shelley wrote her novel.

gently. Wilder's character senses success. The immortal words of his lunatic film predecessor echo through the theater—"It's alive! It's alive!"—and then Freddy Frankenstein approaches his creature with love in his eyes. "Hello, there," he says kindly. "I'm going to set you free." The liberation succeeds so well that the pair soon performs a memorable vaudeville act, tap-dancing in tuxedos with Freddy crooning the verses and the monster grunting out the punch line, his words recognizable only because they are so well known: "Putting on the Ritz!" This monster has been thoroughly civilized.

By the end of *Young Frankenstein,* thanks to an amusing organ transplantation straight out of *Ghost of Frankenstein,* the monster receives his maker's brain, voice, and personality, in exchange for which Freddy Frankenstein receives his creature's "enormous schwanzstucker." Freed by a generation that cheered the downtrodden as hero, flaunted its sexuality, and heralded free love as a guiding ethic, not just Frankenstein but also his monster are young again, ready to continue reproducing their kind.

ROCK-AND-ROLL MONSTERS

By the early 1970s it was safe to identify with—and to liberate —the monster. "They Only Come Out at Night," declared the title of a 1971 album by rock keyboardist Edgar Winter. It might refer to monsters, to the kids who grew up watching them at midnight, or to the weirdos now making rock and roll. The album featured Winter on the synthesizer, an all-electronic instrument still experimental in pop music at the time. The new electrified keyboard sound distinguished an innovative single, included on the album, that soon topped the charts—an honor uncommon for an all-instrumental piece, not to mention one that lasted nearly five minutes. Edgar Winter named his composition "Frankenstein"—a new life, a new sound, electrified, maybe even frightening to those not in the know.

For the generation coming of age in the Vietnam era, the monster was not the other—the monster was us. To be normal was to support the military-industrial complex and to share responsibility for the crimes of napalm, My Lai, pollution, corporate wealth, and presidential arrogance. The only way to be ethical was to be an outsider, a freak, a monster. Damaged by misunderstanding but with more heart and soul than those in power, rising up to overthrow the long-standing pillars of power—the monster character created by Mary Shelley now resonated with hippies and war demonstrators, rock-and-roll singers and their fans, dancing in the aisles along with them. The New York Dolls, protopunk rockers of the early 1970s, promised they were "gonna scream about, gonna shout about," whatever it was that they meant when they uttered the name Frankenstein. For them, it seemed, the monster symbolized the shocking, offbeat, iconoclastic lifestyle that they represented. At the same time, Alice Cooper sang a haunting and nihilistic song, "The Ballad of Dwight Fry [*sic*]." Nothing but the title invites a connection between this song and the Frankenstein legend, but the reference is significant, like a code among the few who understand. Dwight Frye played Fritz in the 1931 *Frankenstein*. A subplot that would have featured him was cut at the last minute from *Bride of Frankenstein*. He was cast as a villager in *Son of Frankenstein,* but most footage showing him was deleted. He got small parts in two more Universal Frankenstein films, but his dwindling acting career forced him into a wartime night job at Douglas Aircraft. With lyrics about loneliness, Alice Cooper shrieked a ballad for this forgotten man of the monster films, culminating in a romanticized exaggeration of suicide and insanity. In fact, Dwight Frye died of a heart attack in 1943. He was forty-four years old. "If God is good I will be able to play comedy," he had said in 1933, just after *Frankenstein*. "And please, God, may it be before I go screwy, playing idiots, half-wits, and lunatics on the talking screen!"

The character called Alice Cooper—born Vincent Damon Furnier in 1948—disappeared from the music scene for more than a decade soon after his 1971 hit record, *Love It to Death,* which included "The Ballad of Dwight Fry." But he blasted back into view in 1986—at the age of thirty-eight—with a new album, *Teenage Frankenstein.* In those fifteen years the image of the horror monster–hero had inspired an entire musical and cultural aesthetic, named variously punk, heavy metal, and—as if to honor its literary roots—Goth. The loud, throbbing music depended on electricity for timbre and volume. Angry singers, their makeup and dress combining the looks of ghoulish *Shock Theater* hosts and camp Rocky Horror showgirls, shouted out lyrics of alienation, insanity, gore, and horror. Taking on the persona of a kid on the block with a "head made of rock," Alice Cooper enshrined his earlier monstrous persona as a symbol of adolescent alienation for a new generation twenty years his junior. He sang the theme song for all "teenage Frankensteins," declaring himself as the neighborhood freak and encouraging his fans to do the same. With his face painted to look like a monster coming back from the dead, Alice Cooper and his teenage Frankenstein image might have turned a few parents' stomachs. But it never hit the heights of scary, for by that time the world had seen it all. Goth was a safe facade. Underneath it all, these monsters were still lovable. We knew that those gruesome faces belonged to friends, siblings, children, loved ones, the girl down the street, or the boy next door. Those monsters were us.

CHAPTER TEN

TAKING THE MONSTER SERIOUSLY

> Monster: . . .*Who is God?*
> Maker: *You never could understand. He's man's God,*
> *not a God of beasts. I made your life with an elixir and*
> *a magnetic spark.* I am your God.

—ADAPTED FROM JOHN BALDERSTON,

Frankenstein (screenplay), 1930

> *The driving impulse of this incoherent*
> *tale is a nameless female dread, the dread*
> *of gestating a monster.*

—GERMAINE GREER, 2007

As offspring of Mary Shelley's monster kick-stepped their way through sci-fi movies, transvestite pageants, kids' cartoons, and rock-and-roll fantasies, scientists around the world were grappling with the real-life implications of developments in biology and genetics. CLUE TO CHEMISTRY OF HEREDITY FOUND, the *New York Times* headline had read on June 13, 1953, and Watson and Crick's description of the double-helical structure of DNA propelled world science in directions foreshadowed yet never foreseen in Mary Shelley's day. A transatlantic scientific partnership had led "to the unraveling of the structural pattern of a substance as important to biologists as uranium is to nuclear physicists," as the *Times* declared. The discovery blasted the world into a new future as irreversibly as the atomic bomb, presenting a chilling set of ethical quandaries that resonated with those posed more than a century before in Shelley's *Frankenstein*.

Deliberate selection and breeding of plants and animals had been practiced for millennia, but techniques now allowed researchers to engineer plant embryos. The search quickly became utilitarian, as scientists sought to create plant strains with resistance to disease. Soon scientists took first steps toward the asexual reproduction of animal species as well. In 1961 Oxford zoologist John B. Gurdon began with adult intestinal cells from *Xenopus laevis,* the African clawed frog, and generated new frogs. British geneticist J. B. S. Haldane gave the procedure a new name: "cloning."

In an optimistic speech delivered in 1963, Haldane explored the role that the science of cloning might play in the future of humankind. He spoke, and his audience—fresh with memories of the Cuban missile crisis—listened. Nuclear war could inflict "grave biological damage," said Haldane. Only a few might survive, those "resistant to high energy quanta and particles." In short, the atom bomb presented huge genetic threats to humankind's future, while positive eugenics, as Haldane called it, offered great promise. He welcomed the prospect of "the production of a clone from cells of persons of attested ability," believing that advances on this scientific frontier "might raise the possibilities of human achievement dramatically."

Nobel Prize–winning biologist Joshua Lederberg came forward as another proponent of the new science of cloning. He used his weekly column in the *Washington Post*, "Science and Man," to wage a campaign in favor of unregulated genetic research. For Lederberg the potential social advantages of cloning far surpassed the risks. He voiced enthusiasm for experimentation and social engineering. "New possibilities of clonal reproduction have arisen as a by-product of experiments on nuclear changes during development of frogs and toads," wrote Lederberg in September 1967:

> Such experiments might eventually be made to work in man, perhaps within a few years, though they are not yet reported even for the laboratory mouse. . . . It is an interesting exercise in social science fiction to contemplate the changes in human affairs that might come about from the generation of a few identical twins of existing personalities. Our reactions to such a fantasy will, of course, depend on just who is immortalized in this way—but if sexual reproduction were less familiar, we might make the same comment about it.

A month later a young biochemist working at the National Institutes of Health wrote a letter to the editor, shocked by Lederberg's "casual and cavalier tone," as he called it. These new genetic advances raised questions not only scientific but also "theological, moral, political," and ethical decisions must guide laboratory experiments, argued twenty-eight-year-old Leon R. Kass. With an MD from the University of Chicago and a PhD in biochemistry from Harvard, Kass had just joined NIH's Laboratory of Molecular Biology. "Biologists today are under strong obligation to raise just such questions publicly so that we may deliberate *before* the new biomedical technology is an accomplished fact," Kass argued. It was the shipboard dialogue of Walton and Frankenstein played out in the twentieth century. "Is the human will sufficient authority to advocate or to attempt to clone a man?" Kass asked. "Who should control the genetic planning?" And, as if raising his head from reading *Frankenstein,* he continued:

> If the attempts to clone a man result in the "production" of a defective "product[,]" who will or should care for "it," and what

rights will "it" have? If the "offspring" is sub-human, are we to consider it *murder* to destroy it? . . . What is the distinction between "human" and "sub-human"? Does not reflection on this question suggest that the programmed reproduction of man will, in fact, de-humanize him?

Six months later Joshua Lederberg sat before a Senate Sub-committee on Government Research in an investigation spear-headed by Walter Mondale, who feared that science was speeding ahead of public policy. The hearings were prompted both by Christiaan Barnard's successful heart transplants and by Stanford biochemist Arthur Kornberg's successful laboratory synthesis of a virus. "Scientists hailed the virus work as a major achievement in genetics research," reported the *New York Times,* "while laymen speculated that the feat might be close to the laboratory produc-tion of life"—an act that the public, despite such advocates as Lederberg, found frightening and repugnant if not outright for-bidden. To create life was to invoke ghosts and monsters, implied the metaphors chosen by the *Times* writer, who commented that "the research raised in some minds the specter of genetic manip-ulation in man."

Barnard, Lederberg, and Kornberg all testified. Barnard asserted that any ethical evaluation or control of organ transplant procedures should come from within the medical profession. "How the human species can foresee and plan its own future is the real subject of these hearings," said Lederberg. "No subject is more important," he asserted, but doubted that government was the appropriate authority in such matters, especially so early in the research. Kornberg, recipient of a 1959 Nobel Prize for syn-thesizing DNA, likewise decried any government oversight or control of genetic research: "There is no legislative way in which you can confine knowledge."

MAKING BABIES

At about the same time, sensational changes were taking place on another biomedical front. In vitro fertilization had become a viable technology during the 1960s. By the time of the first successful fertilization of human oocytes in a petri dish, in 1969, the general public was already abuzz about the prospect of "test-tube babies"—human beings created when scientists unite sperm and egg artificially and grow an embryo outside a mother's womb. Fears and fantasies flew far ahead of laboratory accomplishments, and the idea caused widespread anxiety. "The notion that man might sometime soon be reproduced asexually upsets many people," wrote James D. Watson, one of DNA's discoverers, in the May 1971 *Atlantic*. Watson urged international discussion, both public and legislative, about the implications of new reproductive technologies. "If we do not think about it now, the possibility of our having a free choice will one day suddenly be gone."

On March 5, 1972, the *New York Times Magazine* published an article by Willard Gaylin, Columbia professor of law and psychiatry and president of a three-year-old center founded to investigate "problems that are already here" but that deserve more "time, money and interdisciplinary study." In years to come it would be called the Hastings Institute, after its location in Hastings-on-Hudson, New York. Discussions at that institute, the *Times* explained, formed the underpinnings of Gaylin's commentary on the "ethical and social issues raised by one of the most ominous developments of the 'biological revolution'—cloning." Illustrating the article's opening pages was a checkerboard of alternating portraits, Mozart at the harpsichord and Hitler with fists raised, cued by Gaylin's assertion that a clone of the composer might never write a symphony and a clone of the Führer might turn out saintly. Such uncertainties were among the many reasons why Gaylin felt it necessary to inform the American public about the experiments in life science going on around the world. "The Frankenstein myth becomes a reality," the article opened. "We have the awful knowledge to make exact copies of human beings."

Gaylin's essay referred to Mary Shelley and her novel several times, portraying the book as a fantastical foreshadowing of current reality. "The Frankenstein myth has a viability that transcends its original intentions and a relevance beyond its original time," wrote Gaylin. It was a "ghost story" for Mary Shelley, but now "the inconceivable has become conceivable," what with pacemakers, artificial limbs, and transplanted organs. In the pattern of Victor Frankenstein, scientists of the 1950s had looked back with horror only after the atomic bomb had been loosed on the world. Gaylin hoped that the same was not about to happen in the biosciences. "Some biological scientists, now wary and forewarned, are trying to consider the ethical, social and political implications of their research before its use makes any contemplation merely an expiating exercise. They are even starting to ask whether some research ought to be done at all."

Cloning, Gaylin suggested, could serve as a metaphor for all genetic engineering. Suppose that human beings could be cloned—then what? "The more successful one became at this kind of experimentation," he argued, "the more horrifyingly close to human would be the failures." To the scientist in Mary Shelley's time, experiments were "all promise," and "the only terror was that in his rise he would offend God by assuming too much and reaching too high, by coming too close." By 1900, in Gaylin's history of science and culture, "Man did not have to fear God, he had replaced him. . . . The whole of history seemed to be contrived to serve the purposes and glorify the name of Homo sapiens." Pride preceded the fall, Gaylin implied—and "fall" was the very word he used to describe the last quarter century, when scientists and ethicists had agonized over the moral implications of the atom bomb. "The tragic irony is not that Mary Shelley's 'fantasy' once again has a relevance," Gaylin's article concluded. "The tragedy is that it is no longer a fantasy—and that in its realization we no longer identify with Dr. Frankenstein but with his monster."

In 1972 Paul Berg—a Stanford colleague of Arthur Kornberg and also ultimately a Nobel Prize–winner as well—published his biochemical methods for slicing and splicing into DNA molecules. In 1973 Herbert Boyer and Stanley Cohen successfully introduced genes from the African frog, *Xenopus laevis,* into *Escherichia coli,* a common bacterium. The new organism, constructed by human ingenuity out of two completely different animal species, replicated itself generation after generation, Boyer and Cohen confirmed. When the breakthrough was reported at a microbiology conference, one participant remembers that "someone loudly sounded the excited prediction that 'Now we can combine any DNA.'" Those present, sobered by the implications of the work, drafted a letter to the presidents of the National Academy of Sciences and the Institute of Medicine, alerting them that laboratory techniques might soon reach the capability of creating "new kinds of hybrid plasmids or viruses, with biological activity of unpredictable nature," and that the scientific establishment would be well advised to consider some form of self-regulation. The letter was published in the journal *Science* two months later. In 1974 Berg, Boyer, Cohen, and others active in the field published another warning in *Science,* a paper

titled "Biohazards of Recombinant DNA Molecules." One among
them is reported to have said, "If we had any guts at all, we'd tell
people not to do these experiments," and indeed those involved
announced their voluntary moratorium "until the potential hazards of such recombinant DNA molecules have been better eval-
uated or until adequate methods are developed for preventing
their spread."

In February 1975, close to one hundred researchers from
around the world, together with lawyers, press, and policy makers, gathered for three days at the Asilomar Conference Center
in Monterey, California, hoping to come to consensus on guide-
lines for laboratory research in human genetics. "One aim of the
meeting was to consider whether to lift the voluntary moratorium," wrote Paul Berg, who chaired the conference, "and if so,
under what conditions the research could proceed safely." Tense
debate proceeded. Many questioned whether it was possible to
put limits on science not yet performed. "The new techniques
combining genetic information from very different organisms
place us in an area of biology with many unknowns," stated the
report coming out of the convention. "It is this ignorance that has
compelled us to conclude that it would be wise to exercise the
utmost caution." Undoing the blanket moratorium, conference
attendees concluded that the work should proceed, "but with
appropriate safeguards" and with "standards of protection . . . set
high at the beginning. Each escalation, however small, should be
carefully assessed."

The 1974 moratorium and the 1975 Asilomar conference
were remarkable events, "rare in the history of science," as one
reporter put it. Scientists convened as an international community of concern, willing to place their own ambitions on hold for
the greater good. Laboratory science—a collaborative venture,

nothing like the secret and solitary investigation dramatized in *Frankenstein*—demanded collaborative controls. Soon questions of oversight and regulation would be taken up by government leaders and agencies; soon new biogenetic products would be eyed eagerly by corporations around the world; for the moment, though, the direction of science was still in the hands of those who practiced it. They probed their consciences and, like latter-day Waltons, many wavered over whether to turn their frigates south. Debates raged in the pages of *Science*. One biologist even alluded to the myth of the man-made monster, interpreting it as a warning against hubris. "Are we really that much farther along on the path to comprehensive knowledge that we can forget the over-whelming pride with which Dr. Frankenstein made his monster?" he asked. "It behooves all of us biologists to think very carefully about the conditions of these agreements before we plunge ahead into the darkness."

RETURNING TO THE NOVEL

Scientists may have been ready to look back to Mary Shelley's novel for guidance, but most who practiced the study of English litera-ture professionally would have scoffed at the idea in the early 1970s. For them *Frankenstein* was barely worth reading, let alone studying as a work of art or a moral guidepost. In English depart-ments of the day, on both sides of the Atlantic, neither Mary Shel-ley nor her novel had been admitted into the canon of great literature. She could not possibly compare in caliber or importance, they believed, with writers like William Wordsworth, Samuel Tay-lor Coleridge, John Keats, Lord Byron, or even her husband, Percy Bysshe Shelley. For scholars of the day *Frankenstein* was strictly a pulp novel, and its appearance in contemporary bookstores would take some twists and turns before that opinion changed.

In fact the first cheap American paperback of *Frankenstein* had been published in 1953 by Lion Books, a mass-market publisher that pumped out romances, Westerns, and adventure novels in the 1940s and 1950s. Specializing in cheap editions, Lion Books published novels by pulp-fiction great Jim Thompson, including *The Killer Inside Me* and *A Hell of a Woman;* Thomas Wolfe's posthumous stories and fragments, *The Hills Beyond;* Rex Stout's first novel, *How Like a God;* Erich Maria Remarque's *All Quiet on the Western Front;* and even Voltaire's *Candide.* Adding *Frankenstein* to the list, the company was publishing "the greatest horror story of them all," as the book's front cover declares. "I meddled with the unknown," reads the back cover, ostensibly quoting from the book. "And so was born the monster of Frankenstein, the freak who murdered and pillaged, who thrust naked terror into the lives of half the people in the world." Despite the promise on the copyright page that *"Frankenstein,* like all LION books, is complete and unabridged, not one word cut," the letters from Robert Walton to his sister are missing from the novel's opening. It begins with the voice of Victor Frankenstein—"My dear Captain Walton, I am by birth a Genevese"—yet ends in Walton's. For readers seeking a thrill, perhaps such details of structure and consistency did not matter.

For their twenty-five-cent paperback edition, Lion Books commissioned cover art solidly in the Good Girl style, portraying *Frankenstein* as a contemporary romance thriller. In the foreground of the painting, a hapless victim sprawls across her bed, head down, in the now iconic position. In the background stands a very human perpetrator. Framed by a doorway, he stares at his oversize hands as if shocked to realize what harm they have wrought. This monster and this Elizabeth clearly belong to the 1950s. The redheaded victim wears yellow satin, her disarrayed

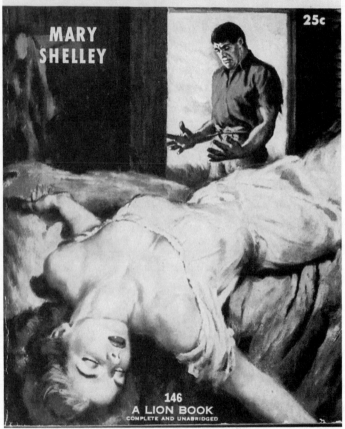

Lion Books published the first twentieth-century paperback edition of
Shelley's novel in 1953. For it they commissioned a cover illustration
in keeping with those of contemporary romance thrillers, modernizing the iconic image of a sprawled Elizabeth and a looming monster.

décolletage showing suggestive cleavage; the attacker wears a tai-
lored, although ragged, red shirt tucked into belted trousers. The
illustration brought the monster up-to-date, implying that, as
archaic as his story might be in some ways, he could be one of us.

Versions of Shelley's novel edited for young readers began to
appear during the Munsters era, when Classics Illustrated comic
books were getting hard to find. In 1965 Wonder Books, a popular children's publisher, issued a fifty-cent large-format paperback—it felt more like a coloring book than a reader—titled
Monsters. From the book's flame-red cover stared a chartreuse-
skinned preadolescent, his black hair cropped close to his flattop
head, his ears nearly pointed, and his cheekbones gauntly
sculpted. From his temples protruded growths shaped like pen-
cil erasers—odd variations on the now classic neck bolts. *Monsters* included, as the title page said, "three famous spine-tingling
tales": "Frankenstein and the Monster," "Dracula the Vampire,"
and "The Strange Case of Dr. Jekyll and Mr. Hyde." Author Walter Gibson told the monster's story in four thousand words. His
language rarely echoed Shelley's; he added his own metaphoric
flourishes instead. When the monster learns that young William
is a Frankenstein, for instance, "his glare turned to venom" and
"his lipless snarl was deadly as a cobra's hiss."

Children's book publishers cautiously introduced pedagogi-
cally sound adaptations of *Frankenstein* for younger and younger
readers. A 1968 Golden Press edition intended for middle
school or high school rearranged story elements but preserved
Shelley's language and imagery. Three-quarters the length of the
original, the 141-page volume began with the creation scene—
"he saw the dull yellow eye of the creature open"—and ended as
the monster leaped from Walton's ship onto an ice raft, "soon
borne away by the waves and lost in darkness and distance." By

1982 the tide had turned in the scholarly world as well. New literary appraisals of Shelley's *Frankenstein* gave publishers the confidence to offer *Frankenstein* as a valuable work for young readers. That year Random House released its easy-reader *Frankenstein*, still in print today, twenty-five years later. Author Larry Weinberg turned the novel into ten short chapters, using a vocabulary matched to second- to fourth-grade reading abilities.

> My name is Victor Frankenstein. I am the one who made the Monster. I am to blame for everything. For all those he has killed. For those who have gone to bed in fear. For his being alive still to this very day.
>
> Yes, I am to blame for what has become of the Monster, too. For all his sadness. And for his hatred of me.
>
> I am sick now and about to die. So I will tell you the story. Perhaps YOU will catch and kill the Monster for me!

Early signs of the shift in assessment appeared in 1974— high-water mark for the monster's pop portrayal, with the release of both *The Rocky Horror Picture Show* and *Young Frankenstein*. In that year editor James Rieger, a professor of English at the University of Rochester, New York, took a risk among colleagues by presenting *Frankenstein* as a novel significant enough to justify bibliographical examination. His was the first step in a long rapprochement between serious students of English literature and Mary Shelley's monster.

For nearly a century and a half the 1831 edition—Shelley's revision, written more than a decade after the novel's first appearance—had been the standard for all English-language editions and translations. Even scholars and professors, the few who paid attention to the novel, studied the 1831 text. Rieger

argued otherwise, deciding to publish the 1818 rather than the
1831 text. "Shelley's eighteen-year-old mistress had become his
remorseful widow," Rieger wrote, and her 1831 revisions produced a novel that had "changed radically as well." Both editions
deserve scholarly attention, to illuminate the book's complicated genesis. Rieger's twenty-five-page introduction included a
thorough overview of Mary Shelley's life, including the writing,
revising, publication, and reception of her novel, and ended with
a brief foray into the novel's twentieth-century adaptations.
Addressing a skeptical audience, Rieger wrote, "Myths are neither validated nor invalidated by the comparative talent, sophistication or honesty of the artists or hacks who transmit them.
The wider a myth's appeal, in fact, the more banal will be its
familiar representation." He mentioned the Universal films, the
Hammer films, and a few other interpretations of the novel. A
modern poem, based on *Bride of Frankenstein,* gave occasion for
Rieger's final rationale: "If the myth has become tawdry and col-
loquial," he paraphrased the poet as saying, "that only proves that
it is very much alive."

Few works of criticism appeared in the selected bibliography
for Rieger's volume: five books, only one of them specifically on
Shelley and her novel, and seven articles, including one whose
title simply named the author "Mrs. Shelley." Rieger cited
Christopher Small, whose little-known book *Ariel Like a Harpy*
had come out in Britain in 1972, then in the United States in
1974, retitled *Mary Shelley's Frankenstein: Tracing the Myth.* New
Zealander Small had begun his book somewhat defensively,
granting up front that it was "not a work of scholarship." In an age
still observant of the great divide between high and low culture,
he clearly stated that he had used no primary materials but had
explored the idea of Frankenstein "in both the 'popular' and the

'literary' imagination." His book now stands as an early example of cultural studies—a respected field today, but when it was published, relegated to the fringe by arbiters of literary criticism. Christopher Small never reentered conversations about the monster, but he later jarred musicologists with two iconoclastic books: his 1987 history of African American music, *Music of the Common Tongue,* and his 1998 interpretation of the symphony experience, *Musicking.*

Among the articles that Rieger cited, Harold Bloom's essay on Frankenstein held the most sway, picked up as it was from *Partisan Review* and printed from 1965 on as an afterword in the broadly distributed Signet Classic paperback *Frankenstein*. "The motion-picture viewer who carries his obscure but still authentic taste for the sublime to the neighborhood theater, there to see the latest in an unending series of *Frankensteins*, becomes a sharer in a romantic terror now nearly one hundred and fifty years old," Bloom began. He urged attention to the novel because of its relation to the finer works of Romantic literature. Quoting passages from William Blake, Percy Bysshe Shelley, and Lord Byron, Bloom concluded that "what makes *Frankenstein* an important book, though it is only a strong, flawed novel with frequent clumsiness in its narrative and characterization, is that it contains one of the most vivid versions we have of the Romantic mythology of the self." The novelist's lack of craft made her work more approachable. "Because it lacks the sophistication and imaginative complexity of such works [as those he cited by Blake, Shelley, and Byron], *Frankenstein* affords a unique introduction to the archetypal world of the Romantics." The novel began appearing occasionally on graduate-level reading lists in English Romantic literature.

At about the same time, editors at *Life* magazine decided that the general public would be interested in meeting the woman behind the monster. In March 1968 they celebrated the novel's sesquicentennial with a cover story on *Frankenstein*. They photographed eighty-year-old Boris Karloff, his naturally heavy-lidded eyes uplit by a swath of red birthday cake candles. "Happy 150th, Dear Frankenstein," read the cover, with a subhead promising within "Strange revelations about how Mrs. Percy Bysshe Shelley created the monster."

Veteran freelancer Samuel Rosenberg started off the article by recalling his own fascination with wee-hours broadcasts of *Bride of Frankenstein*. "I settled back as its pseudodocumentary prologue began to unfold," he wrote. "Had Mary Shelley really been like that, so pretty and wholesome-looking? . . . my intuition told me that there had to be something very strange and remarkable in the story of pretty Mary Shelley and how she came to write about Frankenstein's monster. I decided to search it out." Thus began a seven-thousand-word article detailing Shelley's family heritage, events of the summer of 1816, and the writing, revision, and reception of the novel. Infused with wit and inclined toward psychoanalysis, the article was meant to inspire the average American to go back to the source for the myth of Frankenstein. "After stating his case with remarkable insight for a self-educated pre-Freudian monster," wrote Rosenberg, "the poor nameless son-of-a-botch leaps out of a cabin window onto an ice floe and drifts off. So ends the monster."

Popular and scholarly interest in *Frankenstein* stood miles apart, but slowly through the second half of the twentieth century, they converged. The rise of feminism in the academy shone a new light on the novel. Kate Millett's *Sexual Politics* appeared in 1969; Germaine Greer's *The Female Eunuch*, in 1970; the first issue of *Ms.* magazine appeared in January 1972. In 1970 students could elect

The monster became approachable in the second half of the twentieth century. Here two lucky ladies meet him during a visit to the Visitors' Entertainment Center at Universal Studios, which opened in 1965.

courses in women's studies at only a few universities; a decade later women's studies courses and majors were standard college fare. English professors, especially women, looked on writings by female authors with a newfound respect and curiosity. Few women had been allowed into the grand parade of authors in the academically sanctioned literary canon, and yet, since 1750 on, if not earlier, they had produced plenty of the books and poems published in the English language. Feminist scholars made a concerted effort to right that wrong, including Barnard College professor Ellen Moers, who in 1976 published *Literary Women: The Great Writers*. "If ever there was a time which teaches that one must know the history of women to understand the history of literature, it is now," wrote Moers.

In an influential chapter of her book, titled "Female Gothic," Moers tackled two topics not highly regarded in traditional scholarly circles: the woman writer and the Gothic novel. She opened the chapter with a quotation from Dr. Spock, the influential child psychologist of the 1950s sometimes blamed for the antiauthoritarianism that erupted among the baby boomers. "A baby at birth is usually disappointing-looking to a parent who hasn't seen one before," begins the passage, followed by blunt, unsavory descriptions of a newborn's skin tones, hairiness, and head shape. This is woman's experience, Moers implied. Birth, bleeding, nursing—and with them, the immediacy of death—are central to women's lives, and these bodily realities inform women's writing. Moers proposed a new feminist definition of the Gothic as literature whose purpose is "to scare" by reaching "down into the depths of the soul" and by getting "to the body itself, . . . quickly arousing and quickly allaying the physiological reactions to fear." As an example she cited Mary Shelley's *Frankenstein*.

Weaving Mary Shelley's life story into her reading of the novel, Moers adopted a technique verboten among her senior colleagues. Shelley's "early and chaotic experience, at the very time she became an author, with motherhood" mattered tremendously, stated Moers. Shelley was "pregnant at sixteen, and almost constantly pregnant throughout the following five years; yet not a secure mother, for she lost most of her babies soon after they were born; and not a lawful mother, for she was not married—not at least when, at the age of eighteen, Mary Godwin began to write *Frankenstein*. So are monsters born." Further, her own mother had died giving birth to her. "No outside influence need be sought to explain Mary Shelley's fantasy of the newborn as at once monstrous agent of destruction and piteous victim of parent abandonment." For the feminist critic Mary Shelley presented rich material: a single woman who supported her young son with her writing, a woman who had experienced the pain of childbirth in many ways, and the early-nineteenth-century author of a novel with lasting influence on world culture.

One can only imagine the scintillating small talk going on at the party in 1974 when English professors George Levine and Uli Knoepflmacher got onto the subject of *Frankenstein*. The conversation took a turn that oddly mirrored the ghost-story contest of 1816. "When several of us discovered that we were all closet aficionados of Mary Shelley's novel, we suggested, half-jokingly, that a book might be written in which each contributor-contestant might try to account for the persistent hold that *Frankenstein* continues to exercise on the popular imagination," wrote Levine and Knoepflmacher. In the next few months four new adaptations of the Frankenstein story appeared on film or TV, and the two scholars "took these manifestations as an auspicious sign." They recognized that such a project might taint their reputations; like Shelley's novel, it might evoke "amusement and disbelief." The compulsively self-referential academic community might judge a critical work on *Frankenstein* as high camp, a kind of scholarly *Rocky Horror Picture Show,* "a self-parody of the solemnity of academic criticism." The novel's "stunning ambivalences" might make a many-authored work seem a body made of mismatched parts.

Levine and Knoepflmacher embarked on the project never-theless, reprinting Moers's landmark "Female Gothic" with essays by eleven others, including Knoepflmacher on Mary Shelley's relationship with her father, Judith Wilt on comparions between the novel and medieval mystery plays, Albert J. LaValley on stage and film interpretations, and Peter Brooks on language as a theme in the novel. George Levine wrote the book's first essay, "The Ambiguous Heritage of *Frankenstein*," which confronted head-on the schizophrenia of American culture, which had embraced the myth in the vernacular but ignored it in the ivory tower. "Every-body talks about *Frankenstein,* but nobody reads it," Levine began. The novel deserved attention, he stated, because of its powerful grip on the social imagination. "It has tapped into the center of Western feeling and imagination," Levine argued, and "has become a metaphor for our own cultural crises."

The soil was plowed, the seeds sown for ready acceptance of *The Endurance of Frankenstein: Essays on Mary Shelley's Novel*, pub-lished in 1979. Not only was this collection of essays swiftly embraced by academics, becoming essential reading for Roman-tic scholars; it also crossed the line into popular culture, scoring a two-page review in *Time* magazine. "Of all the imaginary mon-sters that have lurched forth in the past two centuries," wrote critic Paul Gray, "none has frightened more people more often than the one sparked into life by the idealistic scientist Victor Frankenstein." Mentioning Karloff, *The Munsters,* and *Young Frankenstein,* Gray called the novel "a surprisingly open-ended source of disturbing, even terrifying implications" whose "awk-wardness and philosophical uncertainties" make it "the first and most powerful modern myth, not a pure Jungian river flowing through the collective unconscious but a polluted industrial spillway." Although Gray complained of the essay collection's scholarly inclinations—its "preening citations of the obvious" and "the fancy notion among professors that authors and characters 'articulate' rather than speak"—he congratulated Mary Shelley and her novel for surviving through such "fussy attention" and fascinating readers for almost two hundred years.

That same year, 1979, another milestone of feminist criticism anchored its claims in the work of Mary Shelley. In *The Madwoman in the Attic: The Woman Writer and the Nineteenth-Century Literary Imagination,* Sandra M. Gilbert and Susan Gubar, like Moers, singled her out as a central player in the Romantic tradition, highlighting *Frankenstein* as a key period response to Milton. They argued that if *Frankenstein* retells the myth of the Garden of Eden, then both Victor Frankenstein and his creation play the part of Eve. Frankenstein ventures beyond stated limits and eats the apple, figuratively; he also generates offspring, no matter how monstrous the birth process or product might be. But the creature sees Frankenstein as Adam, having "come forth from the hands of God a perfect creature, . . . allowed to converse with, and acquire knowledge from beings of a superior nature," while he is consigned to a lesser existence. "I ought to be thy Adam," the creature says to Frankenstein, but instead he remains "wretched, helpless, and alone"—a moral and physical underling, more akin to Milton's Eve.

As others joined Gilbert and Gubar in considering Mary Shelley's a noteworthy voice in the ongoing dialogue of great English literature, *Frankenstein* began appearing as required reading in freshman English composition courses—often taught by graduate students, who could slide a favorite work into the syllabus without offending the keepers of the canon—or in such interdepartmental electives as Science Fiction, Literature and Technology, or

History of Revolutionary Thought. Standard survey courses and literary anthologies through the 1970s taught that English Romantic literature meant the "Big Six"—Blake, Wordsworth, and Coleridge; Byron, Shelley, and Keats. Even the 1974 *Norton Anthology of English Literature*, a mainstay in college English survey courses, included a special section on the Romantic response to Milton's Satan, with passages from Blake, Coleridge, Byron, P. B. Shelley, and the Gothic novelist Ann Radcliffe—and nowhere in the section's ten pages was Mary Shelley's *Frankenstein* mentioned. By 1979, though, the *Norton Anthology*'s Romantic landscape had changed. Now alongside the Big Six appeared Mary Wollstonecraft, Dorothy Wordsworth, and Mary Wollstonecraft Shelley, represented by her 1831 introduction to *Frankenstein* and by the 1830 short story "Transformation." An introduction called *Frankenstein* an "artfully structured" work that "transcends in literary interest both its antecedents and successors." Editors noted that *"Frankenstein* is not only a major Romantic achievement," but it had become "a modern myth which recurs persistently in fiction, melodrama, and film, and haunts the popular consciousness."

Stephen C. Behrendt, distinguished professor of English at the University of Nebraska, remembers that after he had presented a paper on *Frankenstein* at the 1988 Modern Language Association (MLA) meeting, "one of the comments from the floor was to the effect that it was now clear that Mary Shelley needed to be included among the canonical writers of Romanticism." Shortly thereafter Behrendt was recruited by the MLA to edit *Approaches to Teaching Frankenstein,* a sure sign that many were now teaching the novel. Chelsea House Publishers had by that time asked Harold Bloom to collect essays on *Frankenstein* for its Modern Critical Interpretations series. A 1991 statistical study of courses in English Romantic literature at American universities confirmed "the slow infiltration of women writers into our standard teaching canon." Fully half of the courses surveyed, from undergraduate overviews to graduate seminars, included *Frankenstein* on the syllabus. The researcher concluded that "the canon in British Romanticism now includes seven writers rather than the former standard six." Mary Wollstonecraft Godwin Shelley and her monster had made it into the ivory tower.

MAKING MONSTERS

As scholars began deepening their understanding of Mary Shelley's monster, genetics laboratories around the world were developing new techniques soon to make a greater impact than ever on daily lives. Ethical debates once waged only in closed sessions among the scientific elite filled the pages of newspapers and magazines and spilled out in sound bites on radio and television. Since the 1975 Asilomar conference, landmark accomplishments in genetic science and engineering had made what once was predicted seem now all too real. In 1980 a closely split U.S. Supreme Court decision granted patent rights to microbiologist Ananda Chakrabarty for a new strain of bacteria designed to break down oil molecules and clean up the environment. "A live, human-made microorganism is patentable," read the Court's decision. Chakrabarty's "discovery is not nature's handiwork, but his own."

Commissioner of Patents Sidney A. Diamond had submitted briefs that, according to Chief Justice Warren Burger, "present a gruesome parade of horribles," arguing that the Court should protect the nation against the hazards of genetic invention by denying patent rights to Chakrabarty. "These arguments," wrote Burger, "remind us that, at times, human ingenuity seems unable to control fully the forces it creates." But history has suggested that "legislative or judicial fiat as to patentability will not deter the scientific mind from probing into the unknown." The Court quoted Thomas Jefferson, commenting on the U.S. Patent Act of 1793: "Ingenuity should receive a liberal encouragement." Unless Congress decided to amend the patent statute to exclude organisms produced by genetic engineering—as it had for products used solely to produce nuclear weapons—Chakrabarty and others like him deserved patent protection. In 1988, Harvard scientists received the first U.S. patent on a genetically engineered mammal. Nicknamed Oncomouse, this little monster's genetic design made it especially susceptible to cancer, hence a boon in researching the nature, causes, and cures of the disease.

By the mid-1990s genetically engineered agricultural products were on the market worldwide. By altering corn seed with genes from a common bacterium, *Bacillus thuringesis,* genetic engineers succeeded in foiling the corn borer, a crop-destroying worm, so farmers did not have to apply insecticides to their corn crops. Soybeans were designed to resist a specific herbicide, so farmers would buy that product to kill off the weeds and still leave the cash crop flourishing. Around the world, genetic engineers sought ways to increase vitamin A in rice, to develop tomatoes with longer shelf life. Not long into this sweep of new science, however, familiar comments began surfacing. "Would a specific type of genetic alteration create new weeds, growing where they weren't wanted or invading neighboring ecosystems?" asked ecologist Rob Colwell, insinuating that the new products might be monsters unleashed on the world.

Nowhere did this skepticism and fear grip so tightly or evoke such strong rhetoric as in Great Britain, where tabloids shouted out the hazards of genetically modified foods, amplifying public sentiment. Concerns came from on high when an article written by Charles, Prince of Wales, appeared in the *Daily Mail* on June 1, 1999, encouraging "wider public debate about what I see as a fundamental issue and one which affects each and every one of us, and future generations." Neither he nor most of the British public could understand the science involved, he admitted, but "instinctively we are nervous about tampering with Nature when we can't be sure that we know enough about all the consequences." The situation reverberated with so many similarities to a British novel of the nineteenth century that genetically modified agricultural products took on a nickname, uttered with a derisive sneer: "Frankenfoods."

It's a coinage with a known origin, just like the myth from which it derives. In June 1992 Paul Lewis, a Boston College professor known for public pronouncements against technology, wrote a letter to the *New York Times,* adding his voice to others who wanted the FDA to show more vigilance in considering genetically modified agricultural products. "Ever since Mary Shelley's baron rolled his improved human out of the lab, scientists have been bringing just such good things to life," wrote Lewis, echoing the corporate slogan of General Electric. "If they want to sell us Frankenfood, perhaps it's time to gather the villagers, light some torches and head to the castle." Clearly he knew the movie better than the book, but his coinage worked.

A lengthy roundup of genetics developments published in the *Times* at the end of that same month cited Lewis's letter as proof that the public is "uneasy." GENETICISTS' LATEST DISCOVERY: PUBLIC FEAR OF "FRANKENFOOD," declared the headline. British tabloid writers grabbed the moniker in a flash. To this day, linguistic offspring continue to multiply: "Frankencorn," "Frankenwheat," "Frankencotton," even "Frankentrees." Every utterance instantly evokes a cluster of ethical judgments: This is a product created by humans; this product threatens not only the human race but the entire biosphere; its very existence defies the laws of nature; it is the result of modern hubris and corporate greed and a symbol of the triumph of intellect, technology, and the profit motive over heart and soul, love and compassion, common sense and dedication to humankind.

Recently the coinage has jumped the boundary from plant to animal studies, and now we read about "Frankenpigs." Animal biologists, particularly those involved with farm animals, have also been conducting experiments since the 1980s, exploring the many facets of controlled reproduction—freezing sperm, freezing eggs, and developing techniques to grow entire animals from single embryonic cells. CLONING BRINGS FACTORY PRECISION TO THE FARM, read a February 1988 headline in the *New York Times*. The technique was to begin with a five-day-old, thirty-two-cell embryo. Nuclei from those embryonic cells would be put into the cells of unfertilized eggs, thus presenting the possibility of creating thirty-two identical animals. In the experiment that made the news, seven genetically identical bulls were born. "Advances in animal reproduction technology have frequently presaged similar developments in human reproduction," stated the article somewhat matter-of-factly. One week later a *Times* editorial reflected on the announcement, together with the patent office's willingness to grant life forms the status of intellectual property and the National Academy of Science's recent proposal to develop a three-billion-dollar database of the human genetic code. "Lawmakers must be vigilant," for "science fiction has prepared everyone for the worst." The comment may have alluded to recent films, such as Ridley Scott's 1982 *Blade Runner,* which projected concepts from *Frankenstein* into a sleet-filled

By 2000 the Frankenstein monster was an international symbol for the health and environmental threats associated with genetically modified (GM) agricultural products. In Buenos Aires in July 2000, a Greenpeace demonstrator dressed like the monster and ladled out green soup as part of a protest against GM foods.

metropolis of the future where clones called replicants—soulless human lookalikes—threaten to take over the world.

"Do Androids Dream of Electric Sheep?" asked Philip K. Dick in the title of the story that inspired *Blade Runner*. The phrase seemed an absurdist fiction in 1968 when it was written, but in 1996 a different sort of sheep came into the world, and science fact moved one step closer to science fiction. On July 5, 1996, a Finn Dorset sheep was born in Scotland from a Black Welsh Mountain sheep, an entirely different breed. The newborn sheep had been created by humans, who removed a cell from the udder of an adult Finn Dorset, set it growing by cloning techniques, then inserted the embryo into a surrogate Black Welsh Mountain mother. Unlike procedures past, this cloning technique had the potential of creating a genetic replica of a living adult animal, an accomplishment far more revolutionary than the manipulation of sperm-and-egg combinations. Of 834 cells from three different cell donors, researchers Ian Wilmut and Keith Campbell successfully midwifed one into the world as a healthy, normal animal. In whimsical celebration of her anatomical origins, Wilmut and Campbell named her after Dolly Parton.

Dolly's arrival was not publicly announced for months, although news circulated through the scientific rumor mill. According to *New York Times* science reporter Gina Kolata, Princeton geneticist Lee Silver had just drafted a chapter for a book, declaring that cloning from adult cells could not be done, when he read the paper published in the top English science periodical, *Nature,* on March 13, 1997. "Now there are no boundaries," Silver told Kolata. "Now all of science fiction is true." Soon the whole world knew about Dolly, and the commotion took Wilmut and Campbell by surprise. After all, they had already brought two sheep to life the year before, conceived by introducing DNA material into undifferentiated sheep embryo cells that were then transferred into surrogate mothers. But neither the scientific community nor the general public had paid much heed in 1995 when that happened, or in 1996 when that work was reported in *Nature.* Now, all of a sudden, Dolly moved into the empyrean of cultural icons, transspecies cousin to Frankenstein's monster.

Despite a press embargo, newspapers jumped the gun and wrote about the experiment days before Wilmut and Campbell's article appeared in *Nature.* SCIENTISTS SOUND WARNING ON

"HUMAN CLONES," read *The Times*'s headline on February 24, 1997, leaping from laboratory fact to fantasy in six words. Dolly's birth "opened up the theoretical prospect of a world populated by identical clones of human beings," *Times* writers warned, or even of "creating an army of identical drones or duplicate copies of a dictator." Journalism historian Iina Hellsten tracked all the articles about Dolly and cloning published in *Nature* and *The Times* of London during 1997 and found that "the debate was metaphorical through and through." While scientists conveyed the potential benefits implied in the cloning success, reporters and editorialists tinted the news with fear and skepticism. The metaphor of mass-produced copies, applied to the human realm, permeated pieces on cloning in the London *Times* that year and struck an alarmist tone. Articles referred to "carbon-copy people" and "extra organ factories." In a lengthy opinion piece in the *Sunday Times* on March 2, editors exhorted, "Science marches on, trampling over ethical frontiers." Observers quickly criticized the tone of such reporting, calling the newspaper's editors "Frankenstein's alarmists" and complaining of associations constantly imputed among "Dolly, Adolf Hitler and Frankenstein." But not only *The Times* of London was raising the specter of Frankenstein's monster in its response to the news about Dolly. "The most immediate medical consequence of cloning the Scottish sheep Dolly has been a major outbreak of the Frankenstein Syndrome," wrote a *Washington Post* correspondent two weeks after Dolly went public. "In this recurring epidemic, many people from all walks of life are seized with grandiose fantasies that a supernatural force of evil is about to be unleashed on an unsuspecting world."

The myth of Frankenstein glimmered in the minds of thinking individuals everywhere as they grappled with the implications of Dolly's birth. And by the late twentieth century, to think of

The monster metaphor is irresistible in political cartoons regarding debates over human genetic engineering.

Frankenstein in such a context was almost invariably to think of it as a cautionary tale, whether or not that was what the author originally wrote. Summaries of the novel in the science news context by and large tilted the interpretation toward the negative. Fears about cloning "mirror those of Mary Shelley," read one typical commentary. "Her Dr. Frankenstein created life—and created a being without a soul." To evoke the myth of Frankenstein in the popular media was to remember a morality play that clearly warned against the progress of science beyond boundaries, whether those boundaries were decreed by God, sensed by man's higher nature, or legislated by society. "Western culture is replete with myths and legends alluding to human cloning, most of which have stressed its dark side," wrote a distinguished professor and his students in a law review in 2001. They showed that

Frankenstein played a seminal role in the formation of law and public policy regarding cloning. The novel clustered with other legends and religious dicta in the consciousness of "a skeptical public [that] has greeted cloning with disbelief and delighted amazement, as well as repulsion, fear, and distrust."

A few observers noticed the gap between the public view of Frankenstein and the original story. As early as 1987 popular science writer Stephen Jay Gould assailed the validity of Frankenstein references in arguments over science and technology, not because he questioned the value of literature in ethical debate but because he believed that many people were misinterpreting the story. He blamed the film industry. "Hollywood knows only one theme in making monster movies," he wrote, "from the archetypal *Frankenstein* of 1931 to the recent mega-hit *Jurassic Park*." He summarized that theme: "Human technology must not go beyond an intended order decreed by God or set by nature's laws." But then he explored the very language of Mary Shelley's novel, pointing out its complexities, and concluded:

> Frankenstein's creature becomes a monster because he is cruelly ensnared by one of the deepest predispositions of our biological inheritance—our instinctive aversion toward seriously malformed individuals. . . . We are now appalled by the injustice of such a predisposition, but this proper moral feeling is an evolutionary latecomer, imposed by human consciousness upon a much older mammalian pattern.

To Gould, the novel was less about runaway science and more about the power of society to create monsters through repulsion and exclusion. But his essay did not stanch the flow of rhetoric using the monster and his maker to represent skepticism over scientific progress.

While Frankenstein and his monster stood front and center in the public debate over genetic engineering, few scientists paid much attention. No scientist can be expected to view the book or the myth it propagated as a moral guide to research ethics, comments one professional who has made a career of writing about advances in biomedical science. "In the forums that count—the Food and Drug Administration, the recombinant DNA advisory committees, Congress, etc.—I don't think anyone would take seriously a reference to Frankenstein," she says. "People with a political motive can play on the public's ignorance and whip up irrational fear by summoning up a popular myth or suggesting analogies to historic disasters and thereby engender reactions that are completely out of proportion to the risks."

Just When We Need Him Most

Scientists live and operate within a larger world of culture, and the myths that shape that world exert an influence on their beliefs, fears, and aspirations. Such a revelation came to Donald A. B. Lindberg—a pathologist, an expert in the application of computer technology to the medical sciences, and the director of the National Library of Medicine—as he was visiting Minneapolis's Bakken Museum of Electricity and Life. Established by the man who invented the pacemaker, the Bakken Museum exhibits represent Mary Shelley's imaginative vision as a precursor to the modern life-prolonging electrical device. Curators have reconstructed a laboratory complete with eighteenth-century scientific equipment, including a battery of Leyden jars, an electrostatic generator, and a universal discharger (attached to a replica frog) to evoke the setting in which Victor Frankenstein's monster might have received the spark of life.

"I was hooked," recalls Lindberg after he saw the exhibit, and he went home determined to develop something similar.

"Frankenstein: Penetrating the Secrets of Nature" opened at the
National Library of Medicine in Bethesda, Maryland, on Halloween 1997. Combining art and artifacts from collections near
and far, curator Susan E. Lederer and her team wove together
strands of cultural, political, scientific, and medical history.
Visual displays explored the myth back to its source and traced
its many manifestations in the coming twenty-first century,
focusing especially on the connections between *Frankenstein* and
cutting-edge science. The exhibit began traveling to schools and
libraries around the country in 2002, sponsored by the American
Library Association. Twenty-three towns displayed it in 2005.
Many host communities celebrate its visit with lectures, film
screenings, and special events, broadcasting the myth, the history, and the relevance of the monster ever further.

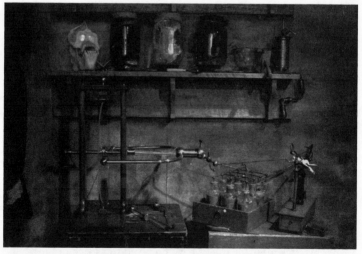

At Minneapolis's Bakken Museum, showcasing the history of electricity and
electrical devices, a collection of late-eighteenth-century instruments represents what the laboratory of Victor Frankenstein might have contained.

"Why would the National Institutes of Health mount a major exhibition on *Frankenstein?*" asked Elizabeth Fee, chief of the library's history of medicine division, in the exhibition catalog. "Our mission at the Library is to make the latest and most accurate scientific information about health and disease readily available to the widest possible public," she answered.

> We felt that by addressing head-on the public's fears about xeno-transplantation [cross-species organ transplants], cloning, and genetic engineering, . . . we could simultaneously educate and inform, while creating an exhibition that would present difficult scientific issues in a manner engaging to children, their parents, and the many scientific and medical visitors to the Library.

First mounted in the bicentennial year of Mary Wollstonecraft Godwin Shelley's birth, 1997, the exhibit saw to it that her story and its many strands of meaning, historic and contemporary, were reaching more people than ever before.

Meanwhile those entrusted with the job of advising the president on bioethical issues turned in a different direction. As much as National Library of Medicine officials considered it central to the international dialogue, Mary Shelley's novel did not appear on the reading list of the President's Council on Bioethics, formed in 2001 by George W. Bush. In its charter the president charged the council with advising him "on bioethical issues that may emerge as a consequence of advances in biomedical science and technology." The executive order specified that the council should "undertake fundamental inquiry into the human and moral significance" of advances and trends in biomedical science and technology, explore related "ethical and policy issues," and provide a "forum for national discussion of bioethical issues." To head the council, Bush appointed a man who had made a career of questioning the ethics of science for the past thirty years: Leon R. Kass.

In the years since writing his letter to the editor of the *Washington Post,* doubting the promise of human genetic engineering, Kass had become one of the nation's most persistent voices bringing traditional values into the discussion of science's new frontiers. In 1998, soon after Dolly arrived, Kass's influential article, "Making Babies: The New Biology and the 'Old' Morality," appeared in the *Public Interest.* "New biomedical technologies are challenging many of the formulations which have served since ancient times to define the specifically human—to demarcate human beings from the beasts on the one hand, and from the gods on the other," Kass began, plunging right into the theological dimensions of the argument. "The advent of these new powers for human engineering means that some men may be destined to play God, to re-create other men in their own image." Kass gathered evidence and arguments to show that human beings do not "have sufficient wisdom to embark upon new ways for making babies," and that "in the absence of such wisdom, we can be wise enough to know that we are not wise enough." He urged discussion, review and monitoring procedures, and international controls on the new biomedical technologies.

That same year Kass contributed an essay to a little volume on the ethics of cloning published by the American Enterprise Institute, an influential nonprofit that promotes discourse, primarily conservative, on public policy. To this day that essay, "The Wisdom of Repugnance," is considered the classic argument against cloning. Kass argued against substituting any human reproductive technology for sexual procreation: The resulting child will have no unique identity, no traditional family bonds, no place in society—the very deprivations of which the monster complained when he met his maker in the Alps. Even more deeply, Kass argued, a "prearticulate human moral sense" exists, and if people pay attention, they will notice their own visceral responses to the concept of a human artificially made by a human. Those gut-level feelings of repugnance offer reliable grounds for momentous ethical decisions, Kass proposed.

"People are repelled by many aspects of human cloning," wrote Kass, infusing his language with the metaphor of the monster:

> They recoil from the prospect of mass production of human beings, with large clones of look-alikes, compromised in their individuality; the idea of father-son or mother-daughter twins; the bizarre prospects of a woman's giving birth to and rearing a genetic copy of herself, her spouse, or even her deceased father or mother; . . . the narcissism of those who would clone themselves and the arrogance of others who think they know who deserves to be cloned or which genotype any child-to-be should be thrilled to receive; the Frankensteinian hubris to create human life and increasingly to control its destiny; man playing God.

Certain forces inside an individual and a community halt the momentum of pressing beyond scientific frontiers, and Kass regards that hesitation not as fear but as wisdom. "We are repelled by the prospect of cloning human beings not because of the strangeness or novelty of the undertaking, but because we intuit and feel, immediately and without argument, the violation of things that we rightfully hold dear." Where Stephen Jay Gould congratulated scientists for defying their instinctive aversion on the path to new discoveries, Leon Kass urged them to heed such instincts. "Repugnance, here as elsewhere," Kass argued, "revolts against the excesses of human willfulness, warning us not to transgress what is unspeakably profound." For him the laboratory genesis of human beings—whether by in vitro fertilization, cloning, or other techniques—irreparably dehumanized God's intended creation.

A respectful student of cultural history—who has written a lengthy volume on the Book of Genesis and coedited an anthology on courtship and marriage—Leon Kass understands that literature plays an important role in the formation and expression of ethical ideas, even when the subject under debate is highly technical. So as he convened the President's Council, he asked its seventeen august members—by and large distinguished university professors in science, medicine, law, ethics, and government—to plan on discussing works of literature as part of their shared intellectual inquiry. All came to the first meeting, in Washington in January 2002, having read "The Birthmark," the 1843 short story by Nathaniel Hawthorne with echoes of *Frankenstein*.

As the story goes, an eminent scientist falls in love with a beautiful woman, whose only flaw is a red hand-shaped birthmark on her left cheek. After they marry Aylmer, the scientist, becomes obsessed with removing that birthmark. Finally his wife agrees to undergo an intricate medical procedure, and, in Hawthorne's words, "as the last crimson tint of the birthmark— that sole token of human imperfection—faded from her cheek, the parting breath of the now perfect woman passed into the atmosphere, and her soul, lingering a moment near her husband, took its heavenward flight." Here the story ends, demonstrating how Aylmer failed "to find the perfect future in the present."

Kass opened the conversation by pointing out Hawthorne's interest in "our human aspiration . . . to pursue some kind of perfection." He cited this story as symbolic of the many works of literature pertinent to the topics at hand and hoped that by beginning their talks with a story, the council members could "start conversing at this table not as scientists or humanists but as fellow human beings." Council members spoke of the shudder that the story caused in them. They asked whether the protagonist could truly represent the scientist, and if modern practitioners ever enacted the same drive toward perfection in their scientific or medical practice. William B. Hurlbut, a biology professor from Stanford, said the story raised "the question of the meaning of suffering and imperfection in life and the role of science in relationship to that." Some view life as evolutionary, he said, and some as "initiated and produced by a benevolent force." The interpretation of Hawthorne's "Birthmark" would depend on worldview, "but either way we are caught in this strange middle space between desperation and aspiration." He could have said the same thing of *Frankenstein,* but Shelley's novel was not included on the list of books to be read by council members.

In 2005 Kass explained its absence. "The council, under my chairmanship, was already under suspicion of being anti-science," he wrote in an e-mail, "and any trafficking in *Frankenstein* would have only given ammunition to our critics." Shelley's book, in other words, carried too much baggage. Rarely, in fact, did council members even refer to the myth or the novel, noted Kass. The council pointedly decided to discuss the *perfection* and not the *creation* of human life, for one thing, but Kass and others may also have felt, as he put it, that "casual recourse to Frankenstein would only be misunderstood, both in substance and as to our motive. One should not just make public reference to this very complex work without careful textual treatment, and we were not really in the business of extensive literary analysis." On the one hand the stereotype of Frankenstein was too simplistic, too burdened with interpretations, attributed meanings, and connotations; on the

other, the authentic novel was too complex and dangerously mul-
tivalent. Amid a culture drowning in references to the monster,
those truly grappling with the issue of making monsters looked
the other way.

And yet the monster made a surprise guest appearance before
the council nonetheless. The readings shared by that first council—including, along with the "The Birthmark," excerpts from
War and Peace and a poem by Emily Dickinson—were collected
and bound into a book, *Being Human: Core Readings in the Humanities.* "We may have at one point discussed using a selection from
Frankenstein in the *Being Human* reader that we produced,"
recalled Kass, the volume's editor. "Whether we did or not, I
would have argued against doing so." Yet in celebration of the
book's publication, early in 2003, Kass invited an old acquain-
tance, English professor Paul A. Cantor, to speak on the intersec-
tion of science and literature. Cantor, a chaired professor at the
University of Virginia and specialist in the Romantics, had published *Creature and Creator: Myth-making and English Romanticism* in
1984, one of the early scholarly works portraying *Frankenstein* as
a central expression of its time.

"The Romantics were the first poets to confront science in its
fully modern sense," Cantor told Council members, dignitaries,
and guests convened at the gala event. He countered the stereotype of the Romantics as fuzzy-minded naysayers of science and
technology by quoting the opinions and accomplishments of
Goethe, Blake, Wordsworth, Coleridge, and P. B. Shelley to
show otherwise. He ended his talk with a lengthy comment on
Mrs. Shelley.

"If there is one imaginative work of the Romantic era that scientists should pay attention to, it is undoubtedly Mary Shelley's
Frankenstein," Cantor told the group. "Very much rooted in the

science of its day, *Frankenstein* embodies a profound awareness of the larger context of scientific endeavor." He granted that popular culture had thrown up a smokescreen of misinterpretation and thrills, but "if we go back to the original story in Mary Shelley's novel . . . we will get our fullest sense of what literature might have to say to science." Suggesting that *Frankenstein* might be called "one of the most prophetic books ever written," Cantor summarized its message this way:

> The basic lesson *Frankenstein* can teach us is this: science can tell us *how* to do something, but it cannot tell us whether we *should* do it. To explore that question, we must step outside the narrow range of science's purely technical questions, and look at the full human context and consequences of what we are doing. To fill in our sense of that context and those consequences, literature can come to the aid of science. No matter how imaginative science itself can be—and recall that Shelley does see Frankenstein as fired up by his imagination—literature is better at imagining the human things.

As Cantor says today, Leon Kass may have been squirming as his invited guest turned the spotlight on the one cultural reference that he had hoped to avoid. Cantor knew nothing of Kass's deliberate avoidance of the novel—but Kass should have known that by the twenty-first century, no romanticist would consider talking about science and literature without invoking *Frankenstein*.

THE MONSTER AND
HIS MYTH TODAY

The ideal being was man created by man.
And so was the supreme monster.

——D. H. LAWRENCE, essay on
Benjamin Franklin, 1923

At the turn of the twenty-first century, Frankenstein's monster was a myth, a legend, an icon—and a hot property. The character had such universal appeal (or repugnance) that just one or two physical features could evoke the character and his entire story. He had starred on stage, screen, and television. He had ascended from comic books to newsmagazines and scholarly journals. In 1996 alone, the monster appeared four times in cartoons in *The New Yorker*. He made it onto the cover of the magazine for Valentine's Day 1997, as cartoonist Edward Sorel depicted the bolt-necked romantic bringing flowers and a box of candy to a gauze-wrapped female, supine on a laboratory slab. The name, the image, and the story of Frankenstein's monster bridged all differences. It carried

meaning to old and young, rich and poor, simple and sophisticated, around the world.

His name could be uttered without apology by political commentators, news reporters, and intellectual powerhouses.
"How can we keep the government we create from becoming a
Frankenstein that will destroy the very freedom we establish it
to protect?" asked revered economist Milton Friedman, echoing
those who saw the monstrous implications of new corporation
laws in the 1930s. Al Qaeda was a Frankenstein monster created
by the United States in Afghanistan, argued a blogger, "and now
we are creating for it a twin in Iraq." "China is the Frankenstein
created by American businessmen," stated a legislator. Paramili-
tary groups in Colombia were publicly termed "a Frankenstein's
monster, killing anyone even suspected of supporting FARC, the
Marxist rebels." In Britain investigations into local government
misconduct, taking too long and costing too much, were termed
"a Frankenstein's monster which is completely out of control."
Outraged that the Bulgarian parliament supported a minority
ethnic Turk administration, the opposing party leader called it "a
political Frankenstein." A reader of *Greater Kashmir Online* in Sri-
nagar, India, called nuclear capability "a Frankenstein monster
that devours the one who creates it." The metaphor circles the
globe, wobbling in meaning yet always prompting some vague
sense that human enterprise, detached from its moral mooring,
has gone monstrously awry.

With so many allusions, each utterance emphasizes a slightly
different aspect of the multifaceted story. When Hardee's introduced a 1,420-calorie sandwich, "the Monster Thickburger,"
USA Today dubbed it "fast food's first edible Frankenstein." Legal
documents filed in a suit against McDonald's for its unhealthful
fare—and featured in the 2005 film, *Super Size Me*—dubbed

one product of the fast-food chain "a McFrankenstein creation." Both references highlight the dangers a monster meal might pose to health and livelihood. FRANKEN-SWINE! FARMER USES LIGHTNING TO SHOCK PRIZE PIG BACK TO LIFE! read the head-lines of *Weekly World News*, finding the electrical implications apt. A nine-year-old boy in Virginia nicknamed his malignant brain tumor Frankenstein: unhuman and invasive. His mother sold bumper stickers saying Frank Must Die. Her broadly publicized campaign caught the eye and the sympathy of the American public, and she successfully raised the funds needed to pay for her son's struggle, via chemotherapy, radiation, and surgery, against the menacing intruder. A year and a half later, Frank had been driven to extinction, the boy was declared cancer-free, and all involved could congratulate themselves for overwhelming a malignant monster.

Frankenstein imagery tumbles through political cartoons, as it has since the novel first appeared. The monster was called up to satirize presidential candidates of both major parties in the 2004 U.S. elections, with bolt-necked caricatures of "Frankenbush" and "John Scary." Cartoonist Sandy Huffaker mocked the nomination process itself by drawing a bespectacled consultant, dressed in a white lab coat and aided by his gap-toothed, humpbacked assistant. Laboring in a dungeonlike laboratory, the two conspirators have sewn on hands marked "Left" and "Right" and dressed their candidate in a sweater labeled "Warm and Fuzzy." "I think that does it, Igor!" says the consultant, topping his creation with a well-coiffed toupee. Into the trash can they have tossed an organ-shaped entity labeled "Soul."

Power, presence, recognizability, strength of character: The monster has what it takes to serve the almighty dollar, pound, and yen. General Mills produced a matched pair of supersweet-

References to Frankenstein and the making of monsters ricochet through public discourse during presidential elections, as in this 2003 cartoon by Sandy Huffaker.

ened breakfast cereals with names and mascots designed to win the loyalty of American children, and soon Count Chocula and Frankenberry haunted many a morning meal. A fast-food franchise selling hot dogs and beer trademarked the name "Frank 'n' Stein." The Frankenstein Pub in Aberdeen, Scotland—its logo reading "The World Famous Frankenstein 1818"—served a supersize burger dubbed "The Monster," shot drinks called "The Spark of Life" and "Dr. Victor," and a pitcher of vodka, Cointreau, and juices called the "Electric Storm." The dance floor looked like *The Rocky Horror Picture Show* performed on the set of *Titanic*.

In short, the Frankenstein monster sells. Going back to the 1950s, manufacturers of items ranging from Bic pens to Smirnoff vodka have borrowed his familiar figure for their advertising campaigns. "I used to be known as a big stiff," read one full-page magazine ad. A green-complected, bolt-necked, black-suited character grins out from a comfy leather armchair, casually gesturing toward a movie poster showing the familiar stiff-armed pose. "Now Osteo Bi-Flex has put new life in my joints," reads the copy, part of a multimedia campaign to sell an over-the-counter arthritis remedy. Corresponding television ads grabbed the viewer with brief black-and-white clips from the 1931 movie, then cut to the friendly face of the now-flexible monster, sitting in his living room. "That was me," he says sincerely to the camera. "So stiff, my achey joints made it hard for me to get around." Now, thanks to the new remedy, he dons lily white tai chi togs and gracefully salutes the sun. You too, he promises, can "put some life back into your joints."

Frankenstein's monster roams the cultural landscape freely, not only among members of the increasingly arthritic baby boomer generation. The monster is such a familiar figure among children that authors now write scripts and books that only hint back at their monstrous predecessor, fully confident that the character and his story are common knowledge. The genre goes back to 1984, when fledgling filmmaker Tim Burton directed a short for Disney Studios called *Frankenweenie*, the story of a boy who revivifies his dog by stitching its body back together and electrifying it with canine neck bolts. Since then, more and more monstrous spin-off children's products have come onto the market. When the Bailey School Kids, characters in a popular early reader series from Scholastic, visit the Shelley Museum of Science, it doesn't take them long to guess the identity of the tall guy who meets them at the door. But they are puzzled when he shows them the greenhouse—because everyone knows, as the title says, *Frankenstein Doesn't Plant Petunias.* In 1993, when the book came out, series editors could assume that their young readers not only knew the monster but considered him a friend who could instruct, delight, and terrify.

These days many children's book authors use the monster just for the fun of it. Jan Wahl wrote a book about *Frankenstein's Dog,* who teaches a grunting, oafish monster how to fetch and dig for bones. Curtis Jobling took that idea in another direction in *Frankenstein's Cat.* "Now, we all know the story of Frankenstein and his monster," the book begins. "Frank was a misunderstood, some would say mad, doctor, who made a man out of body parts. Monster goes mad, lots of tears, end of story." With those few words Jobling flies by the original and introduces a cat created by "Frank" before he dabbled in human parts.

Colin McNaughton wrote a book of "monstrous poems and pictures," titled *Making Friends with Frankenstein*, including this jingle that gives the book its title:

> When I am feeling lonely,
> For Igor I will send.
> We'll go to my laboratory
> And we will make a friend!

An illustration shows a frizzy-haired doctor, arm and arm with his hunchback assistant, surrounded by goofy body parts. In Keith Graves's 1999 picture book, *Frank Was a Monster Who Wanted to Dance,* a screwball stitched-up monster dreams of dancing onstage. His act becomes a slapstick scene of disembodiment. His head unzips, his brain falls out, one eye comes unplugged, and then his head falls off his body. In the last line of the cheerfully rhyming text, Frank grins and says, "I might be a monster, but man can I dance!" Kids coming to this book need not know anything about its literary origins. Indeed Graves's picture book could mean a first step toward a years-long fascination, leading to Sharon Darrow's *Through the Tempests Dark and Wild* (2003)—a picture book about Mary Shelley as a girl born to tell stories.

By the twenty-first century, the monster was a central player in the mythic cast of characters parading through children's imaginations. When a California after-school art teacher invited her students to create their own comic characters, one kindergartener created "The House of Doom," where resided, among others, a "girl Frankenstein" whose monstrous intentions were enacted thanks to her "retractable, poison-tipped bellybutton." Rumors of a Disney version of *Frankenstein* have long circulated, and if that ever happens, the mythic character will assume another shape and body, backed by such corporate wherewithal, marketing power, and commodification potential that it may indeed rival Karloff's as a new look for the monster.

OWNING THE IMAGE

Amid this chaotic proliferation of monsters, many mirroring the look created by Boris Karloff in 1931, it was just a matter of time before someone laid claim to the monster as intellectual property, worthy of copyright protection. The idea started forming in 1993. Seven thousand monster fans descended on Crystal City, Virginia, over Memorial Day, for the Famous Monsters of Filmland World Convention, billed as "the fantasy film fan event of a lifetime." All eagerly paid homage to Forrest Ackerman, Ray

Bradbury, and dozens of less familiar horror greats. Among those featured were the adult offspring of four Universal horror stars. Ron Chaney, Dwight Frye, Jr., Sara Karloff, and Bela Lugosi, Jr., met for the first time in a Northern Virginia hotel and got to talking about their shared heritage.

Lugosi, a Los Angeles attorney, had spent years in the courtroom and the boardroom, fighting on behalf of celebrity heirs to control the profits coming from the work of their famous forebears. As a young man he had brought suit against Universal Pictures, maintaining that he deserved legal ownership of the Dracula character created by his father. Some monsters may have been thought up by Universal, but Bela Lugosi had played Dracula onstage and had then brought the character to the company, he argued. He lost the court battle but won the law war. In 1979 a California supreme court judge ruled that rights to a famous name and likeness do not outlive the individual, but nearly a decade later California enacted a civil code granting a celebrity's heirs the right to inherit, and therefore control, ownership of a "deceased personality's name, voice, signature, photograph, or likeness in advertising or soliciting." Lugosi went on to become a recognized expert in the field of celebrity intellectual property rights, defending the Three Stooges in a famous case against a merchandiser and establishing his own firm, Lugosi Enterprises, to create, market, and protect his father's vampire look.

Sara Karloff remembers that she listened eagerly to Lugosi and, inspired by what she learned, began working with lawyers to reclaim her own father's heritage. It was a tall order, reining in control of an image that so permeated world culture. The Frankenstein myth had such staying power, and the image of the monster from the 1931 film so dominated popular portrayals, that in 1993 to say "Frankenstein" was to see Boris Karloff in makeup and costume: gray-green skin, heavy eyelids, flattop head, sunken cheeks, neck bolts, too-small suit, weighted shoes, the whole bit. After a long and private negotiation, Sara Karloff reached a settlement with Universal, by no means the only entity profiting from Karloff's monster portrayal, but a key starting point in her quest. The other heirs were doing the same, and a final joint licensing agreement among Karloff, Lugosi, Chaney, and Universal meant that in the late 1990s the whole cast of 1930s classic horror characters burst back onto the scene.

Universal had already been marketing monster products for years—cheap plastic toys and gadgets decorated with imagery of the classic monsters—but now iconic, realistic portraits of five movie-star icons were commissioned. The paintings established the trademark look of Karloff's Monster, Karloff's Mummy, Lugosi's Dracula, Chaney Sr.'s Phantom of the Opera, and Chaney Jr.'s Wolf Man. Soon Universal's brand-named Classic Monsters were every-where—T-shirts, hats, trading cards, candy wrappers, toy cars, plastic figurines, Halloween costumes, Valentine's Day cards. Lengthy copyright language on every product hinted at the complex relationship established between family-run corporations—Chaney, Lugosi, or Karloff Enterprises—and Universal Studios. According to Sara Karloff, her arrangement was that Universal would be the licensing agent, sharing approval rights and profits with Karloff Enterprises. It was a licensing bonanza. "Scare up some fun," called out posters at Burger King franchises across the nation, where kids received a Universal Monster figure with their burgers and fries. The Teenage Mutant Ninja Turtles all donned Universal Monster identities. Michelangelo became the Frankenstein monster, and his action figure had a flattop head, neck bolts, wrist stitches, and accessories that included nunchakus with bolts for handles and a beastly beaker containing monster ooze.

To top it off, the band of heirs presented a petition with seventeen thousand signatures to the U.S. Postal Service. They
wanted their fathers' monsters nationally recognized for their
place in American entertainment history. Their request was
timely, coming amid concerns over a floundering postal system.
USPS marketers had been looking for a way to sell more stamps
and to interest younger Americans in stamp collecting. Monster
stamps might be the answer.

So in 1997 the U.S. Postal Service issued a stamp series featuring the Universal monsters, and Karloff's representation of
Frankenstein's monster assumed a position of honor among presidents and heroes. The creature conceived by Mary Shelley in
1818, embodied by Karloff and made up by Jack Pierce in 1931,
trademarked by Karloff Enterprises in 1993, and copyrighted by
Universal City Studios in 1996, was licensed to the United States
Postal Service. The monster-stamp enterprise developed an an
entire marketing campaign, rolled out for Halloween season. The
Postal Service distributed "124,000 educational and entertaining
'Get the Creeps' kits to educators, postmaster, librarians, and
community groups," according to its press release, predicting
that "millions of Monster stamps will be scaring up interest in
stamp collecting among our nation's youth." Post offices around
the country sold a sheet of twenty stamps, framed with the
actors' portraits and signatures and titled "Classic Movie Monsters." Products spun off like crazy, merchandise with the stamp
imagery printed on it: magnets, mouse pads, pencils, lapel pins.
The imagery propagated onto other products. A copyrighted
monster seemed to be appearing everywhere.

The same year, the United Kingdom released its own stamps
commemorating "Classic Tales of Horror" with images of a
British foursome, printed in ink that glowed under ultraviolet

light. Their chosen monsters included the Hound of the Baskervilles and Dr. Jekyll and Mr. Hyde along with the world-renowned horror duo, Dracula and Frankenstein. Artist Ian Pollock's portrayal of the monster on the thirty-one-penny stamp took on an expressionistic look all its own, but the first-day-cover cancellation mark, reading "Shelley—Frankenstein" in Gothic script, did not match the stamp at all. Instead it clearly copied the universally recognized face of Karloff's monster.

The licensing relationship between Karloff Enterprises and Universal Studios stayed on an even keel for a few years, says Sara Karloff. She funneled any inquiries about the use of her father's image, either as Frankenstein's monster or as the Mummy, over to Universal. "They promised that they would buy a lot of products and sell them at their Universal theme parks," she says, an added incentive to go with Universal's plan, "and then they didn't do it. They used a classic bait and switch." Products came out with images of the monster, skin hue and costume like those of Karloff's character but facial features just different enough to be someone else. "They screwed the families," Sara Karloff says bluntly. "They made the line between the classic and the generic so gray that the public didn't care—and kids didn't know. They priced the classic right out of the marketplace."

In 2000 Karloff filed a new suit in Los Angeles Superior Court, claiming more than ten million dollars in lost royalties. She brought with her a long list of inquiries she had received and directed to Universal, all of which had resulted in licenses, yet none of which had ultimately used her father's version of the monster. Monster Valentines had come out every February, Halloween candies every October labeled "Universal Monsters." Scholastic Books published a paperback series of modern versions of the monster tales. *Frankenstein* by Larry Mike Garmon

Through a partnership among Universal Studios, the U.S.
Postal Service, and the heirs of Hollywood's most famous horror stars, stunning portraits of five classic movie monsters,
including Frankenstein's, graced a special commemorative
sheet of stamps in 1997.

appeared in 2001, with licensing indicators that "the Universal
Studio Monsters are trademarks and copyrights of Universal Studios" and that Frankenstein was a "trademark and copyright of
Universal Studios," all rights reserved. Gracing each item was a
greenish face, sunken eyes and cheeks, black lips and neck bolts,

adapted just enough that it no longer looked like Boris Karloff. Sara Karloff accused Universal of fraud, breach of contract, and violation of rights of publicity. The judge ruled in Karloff's favor. Settlement terms were reached out of court, and details of the case were muffled. After a brief period of agreement over what Frankenstein's monster looked like, the parties went their separate ways—and the monster broke free again.

FRANKENSTEIN REBOUNDS

While in Mary Shelley's novel, the monster disappears, "lost in darkness and distance," he is never far away from us today. Many adaptations call the monster immortal; that claim might just as likely apply to the myth itself. Frankenstein's monster is in our bookstores, on our film and television screens, from morning cartoons to wee-hours rerun movies. He plays roles in advertising and political debate, he appears at public library story hours and on graduate-level reading lists. He is both a joke and a profound ethical dilemma. Known around the world by name and appearance, he is an emanation of the current human condition—a bundle of contradictions and a universal meaning all in one.

More than one hundred editions of the novel are scattered on bookstore shelves today. The best-selling versions sell tens of thousands of copies every year. At least one hundred films are available on VHS or DVD retelling some version of the monster's tale. As pop novelist Dean Koontz shot out two volumes of a modern-day Frankenstein saga in 2005, with a third promised for 2007, the books instantly leaped up onto the mass-market paperback bestseller list. A search for "Frankenstein" on Amazon or eBay brings more than fifteen hundred entries each, from Halloween bobbleheads to collectible comics, from stuffed figurines costing a dollar to rare books costing a thousand. References to Frankenstein crop up in newspapers and magazines every day. He—the monster and the man who made him—is everywhere.

Such omnipresence does not mean that we pay close attention—quite the contrary. Through all these years and all these thousands of retellings of the myth of the man-made monster, some stand out, deserving special recognition. As much as it has been worked over and over, *Frankenstein* continues to inspire. Occasionally an author or an artist, propelled by Mary Shelley's original, creates a response so thought-provoking that it stands out among the parade. Many of these have been lost in the shadows; all deserve to come back into the light.

An early book of poems by Margaret Atwood, *Speeches for Dr. Frankenstein,* was produced in a limited edition in 1966, illustrated and printed by Charles Pachter. "You sliced me loose / and said it was / Creation," reads the final poem of the collection. "Now you would like to heal / that chasm in your side, / but I recede. I prowl. / I will not come when you call." The haunting possibilities of creating life continue to interest Atwood, as shown in her 2003 novel *Oryx and Crake,* compared by some to *Frankenstein* for its portrayal of a future in which well-meaning efforts to create new life forms lead to the end of human society.

The Spirit of the Beehive, a haunting Spanish film directed by Víctor Erice, was created in 1973. In a quiet, childlike way it evokes life in the early days of the Franco regime, around 1940. Whale's *Frankenstein* has just come to the dust-colored village, and the clamor of children rushing to see the monster on the screen begins the film. With actual clips from the 1931 film and dreamy visual scenes in which the monster enters the rural landscape, the film conjures up the inner life of a young girl as she glimpses adulthood and begins to reckon with sex and death. The monster looms, seen only by the film's young heroine, at first terrorizing her but eventually offering her silent, secret comfort as she moves into a bleak and unknown future.

Minneapolis's Guthrie Theatre commissioned a stage version of *Frankenstein* from playwright Barbara Field in the late 1980s. She agreed, then read the book. "I thought the idea was gigantic, but the writing was not very good," she recalls as her response to the novel. She tried to finagle her way out of the assignment, but Guthrie director Garland Wright encouraged her. Forget trying to retell the story, he told Field; simply respond to it. The image that loomed in the playwright's imagination was a Regency-era chair sitting on an Arctic ice floe. What fascinated her was the character interplay between creator and creation.

"Why do you hate me?" the Creature asks Frankenstein in Field's version.

"Because you're hideous," Frankenstein replies. "Why did you destroy my life?"

"Because you hate me," says the Creature.

Field's play, *Playing with Fire,* juxtaposes two pairs of characters. An aging Frankenstein and his aging creature observe key scenes from their past—the creation scene, their alpine encounter, the destruction of the creature's mate, the murder of Elizabeth— enacted onstage by the other pair of characters, their earlier selves, named Victor and Adam. "There is no good and evil," Frankenstein says near the end. "Just you and I are left rattling around on this planet, all alone. A parody of God chasing a parody of the Ideal Man."

Hollywood refreshed the myth in 1994 when director Kenneth Branagh and actor Robert De Niro created the TriStar spectacular, *Mary Shelley's Frankenstein.* Explaining the film's title, Branagh wrote, "Our intent was always to arrive at an interpre-

Barbara Field's theatrical response to *Frankenstein* dramatizes two parallel
worlds: young Victor and his creature named Adam, shown here, and a
nihilistic elderly Frankenstein and his monster. The staging mingled mini-
malist electrical and mechanical contraptions with the symbolism of sym-
metry, balance, and wholeness.

tation that's more faithful than earlier versions to the spirit of her
book," yet he had consciously ricocheted off his iconic 1931
predecessor. "It was critical to conceive of a look for this Creature . . . that would be very different from Boris Karloff's," wrote
Branagh. The look began with actor Robert De Niro, naturally
subtle and somewhat corpulent in his middle age. De Niro
received a distinctively new makeup approach, fleshy and wrinkled. His face, body, and hands were crisscrossed with realistic
scars and stitching, his skin turned singed and ruddy. The creation scene became a momentous technological birthing, De
Niro's naked body emerging out of a vat of primordial slime,
physically midwifed by Frankenstein, played by a sweat-soaked,
bare-chested Branagh. "Frankenstein in the Age of Prozac," literary critic A. C. Goodson called it, pointing out that in the hands

of Branagh, the myth becomes a "collective depression narrative" suiting end-of-century malaise.

Theodore Roszak published a response to *Frankenstein* in 1995 and shifted the balance of Mary Shelley's male-dominated novel by telling the story from Elizabeth's point of view. In *The Memoirs of Elizabeth Frankenstein,* Roszak hypothesized that it was from his mother that Victor Frankenstein gained such a deep fascination and familiarity with the secrets of death and life. According to Roszak's fiction, Mrs. Frankenstein was a leader of a mystical coven, and she had selected Elizabeth, the orphan brought into the Frankenstein home, as Victor's spiritual mate. One scene in the novel depicts a pagan ceremony, in which young Victor and Elizabeth perform a ritual reenactment of the alchemical union, mercury and lead, that culminates in gold, spirit and body in one.

French composer Francis Dhomont, a pioneer in the field of electronic music, created a symphony-length sound collage in 1997, splicing together bits of recorded performances of works by himself and other composers, together with found sounds and electric noises. The result is a musical work that is alluring, mechanical, mysterious, and unearthly. "Armed with a scalpel and a splicing (operational) block, I sample several morphological organs from the works of 22 composers and friends," wrote Dhomont, delighting in all the parallels he could find between his composition and Mary Shelley's. The result he calls "a hybrid thing in four movements, made of cut-up pieces, pasted, assembled, sowed [*sic*] parts that are alike and contrasted, and that I have named, for obvious reasons, the Frankenstein Symphony: an unusual electroacoustic adventure."

Musicals, operas, and ballets have reinterpreted the Franken-stein story. Local theaters stage their own renditions, playwrights re-creating new versions of the monster myth year after year. Pop musicians continue to get mileage from references to the name: George Clinton has long called himself Dr. Funkenstein, while popular punk bands have taken names such as Electric Frankenstein and Frankenstein Drag Queens from Planet 13. Films and television documentaries have retold the story of the summer of 1816 as well as the myth itself. Science fiction writers galore have created their own sequels, set in the past, the present, the future, or a time-warp combination of them all, as in Brian Aldiss's interesting *Frankenstein Unbound,* a 1973 novel made into a 1990 film starring John Hurt. The monster haunts all media. Fascination with his story seems never to end.

In the early 1970s Christopher Isherwood and his partner, Don Bachardy, worked together on a new version of *Frankenstein,* coproduced by Universal Studios and NBC to be shown as one of NBC's World Premiere Movies in 1973. The scriptwriters took liberties with the plot, molding it to highlight psychologies that interested them. The creature arises, a beautiful and naive young man, nearly a mirror image of his creator. Through a glitch in the scientific process, his beauty slowly disintegrates. His skin develops pockmarks; his features become disfigured; in short, he becomes a monster, and his creator responds with horror and disgust. Victor Frankenstein abandons his creature, inflicting psychological and physical damage. The two reunite in the end, their voices and faces mirroring each other's, and they die together, smothered under an Arctic avalanche.

When the script was filmed for television, without Isherwood and Bachardy's participation, the resulting product differed from the story they had intended. Distressed, they made sure that Avon Books published their original script intact. They could not persuade Avon to remove the TV title, however: *Frankenstein: The True Story.* "Neither Don Bachardy nor I are in favor of the subtitle," Isherwood wrote his Avon editor. "It wasn't our idea. How can one claim that one version is 'truer' than another; unless, of course, one had written a screenplay which followed Mary Shelley's novel in every particular. We haven't done this; and neither has anybody else, so far."

Neither will anyone else—for any response to a work of literature will carry the myth one step farther from its source, yet one step closer to explication and understanding. That Mary Shelley's *Frankenstein* has spawned so many new versions is a sign of its undying interest the world around. Endlessly interpretable, or so it seems, the story of Frankenstein continues to offer meaning to new generations, again and again. Some new interpretations harmonize with precursors; others present mutually exclusive contradictions. The emanations of the novel are now so abundant that no interpretation can begin afresh. The original novel shimmers with ambiguities nigh unto self-contradictions—the monster is to be loved and feared, his maker is both champion and transgressor. And, as postmodern literary critics will affirm, perhaps the very thought that there is one, solitary, real, and only text even for Mary Shelley's *Frankenstein* is a false assumption. The very "plasticity" of the novel, as more than one critic has mentioned, goes far in explaining *Frankenstein*'s longevity.

There's something more here, though, than simply a story that can morph to match the times. At its heart *Frankenstein* speaks of an eternal conflict in the human condition. It is the tension between what we have and what we desire, between that which is firmly within our grasp and that which we can dream but not materialize. The story summons the universal dialogue between what our culture now calls red and blue, conservative and liberal, traditional and progressive, authoritarian and libertarian, conservative and radical. It projects in a relatively simple plot line an earthly version of the biblical paradox at the center of the Garden of Eden: There's the tree, but you can't eat from it. As Leon Kass observes in *The Beginning of Wisdom,* his book on Genesis, "the simple, primordial human being, because he is primordially *human,*" contains "something disquieting in his original nature. Some innate capacities or potentialities in the human soul dangerously threaten to upset the tranquillity of man's simple and innocent life." Those threats to tranquillity are symbolized, Kass suggests, by the two special trees in the garden: the Tree of Life and the Tree of the Knowledge of Good and Evil. It's the second tree whose fruit was explicitly forbidden to the first two humans by their maker. The first was never forbidden because, according to Kass, until Adam and Eve ate of the second, they knew no death, hence had no interest in life or immortality.

It was inevitable. Someone was going to slip back into the garden and pick fruit from the other tree. That is the story told in Mary Shelley's *Frankenstein.* Surrounded by talk of poetry, atheism, and science, the imagination of this unmarried teenage mother in the early nineteenth century tapped into a mythic realm where a story had been standing, unplucked, for centuries. She dared to approach the forbidden, ignoring conventional laws of good and evil; she went to the heart of the matter, to the secret of life. She wrote the story humankind had been waiting to hear and, having written it, sent it out into the world—her "hideous progeny," as she called it—to be heard, read, enacted, viewed, analyzed, interpreted, remembered, rebuffed, and, yet again, retold.

———————

When Victor Frankenstein encounters his creation on the icy slopes of Mont Blanc, he responds with anger and disgust, shouting at the creature, "Begone! relieve me from the sight of your detested form!"

In response, the monster simply places his hands over Frankenstein's eyes. "Thus I relieve thee, my creator," he says. "Thus I take from thee a sight which you abhor. Still thou canst listen to me, and grant me thy compassion. Hear my tale; it is long and strange."

We are still listening.

ACKNOWLEDGMENTS

It all began in the years when I was teaching literature, writing, and the humanities to undergraduates in the University of Virginia's School of Engineering and Applied Sciences. One fall it so happened that my class was discussing *Frankenstein* on the afternoon of October 31—the season when the monster reappears most vigorously, at least in the United States. On a lark I wore a lurid green face mask to class that day, and we spent the entire hour contrasting the assumptions my students already held about the monster and his myth, having never read the novel. From that Halloween forward, I began collecting what I have come to call Frankensteiniana—dolls and tea towels, cards and costumes, boxer shorts and potholders, not to mention dozens of books for audiences ranging from preschoolers to lascivious adults.

My interest in the original *Frankenstein* dates back to the years when I studied the Shelley circle in graduate school. Christopher Small's *Ariel Like a Harpy* helped me begin to tune in to the harmonics of the novel and its creation. Stephen Forry's *Hideous Progenies* convinced me that it wasn't just my generation who took to the story. Steven Jones's *Frankenstein Scrapbook* showed me how broadly the myth had propagated among the masses, not just the literary elite. Richard Holmes's *Shelley: The Pursuit* inspired in me the belief that scholarship can infuse lively narrative. More recently Charles Robinson, in his two-volume manuscript reproduction of *Frankenstein,* and William St. Clair, in his eloquent volume about publishing and reading books in the Romantic era, led me down the path of fascinating details in the conception, birth, and evolution of the monster and his novel. Jon Turney's *Frankenstein's Footsteps* pointed the way to some fascinating scientific successors. These and many others preceded me with careful reading, broad-reaching research, and thoughtful writing, without which I could never have accomplished my own.

When the time came to write about this evolving myth and its meaning, my research unearthed more than I could ever have imagined. I have discarded more references here than I have been able to use. The myth of Frankenstein and the monster he made permeates world culture, and not just in the way of Halloween ephemera. It has a deep and lasting meaning that continues to matter. To all those friends, teachers, and students who were willing to take the monster seriously along with me, I give thanks.

A number of people made important contributions to my research effort, and I wish to single them out for thanks here. For their generosity in conversation, correspondence, and ideas, I thank Michael Rodemeyer, Charles Robinson, Richard Dillard, George Garrett, Richard Scrivani, Keith Miserocchi, Celia Hooper, Terry Belanger, and my brother, Hugh Hitchcock.

For help on specific points of fact, I thank Gerry Mandel, Jim Miller, Leonard de Graaf, Frederick C. Wiebel, Jr., and Nina Carbe. Important help in my search for images came from the staff at Photofest and from Judy Ladendorf at the Permissions Group. Jeanne and Nic Siler helped capture elusive monster imagery in digital form. Sara Karloff was particularly supportive all along, beginning with our breakfast meeting at Monster Bash in 2005. Barbara Field graciously shared her memories of writing *Playing with Fire*. Several people were kind and patient enough to respond to early drafts of the book, namely Ashton Nichols, Dorrit Green, Rachel Mann, Paul Cantor, and my father, H. Wiley Hitchcock. From them I learned a lot, and I hope I made use of those lessons well. Bella Stander was there to cheer me on.

My agents, Miriam Goderich and Jane Dystel, supported me tremendously, as always. At W. W. Norton, Jill Bialosky expressed enthusiasm from the start, and Evan Carver hewed this book into something more graceful than I could create by myself. My children, Alison and John, kept me well supplied with a continuing flow of new Frankenstein gewgaws and sightings, and my husband, David, loved me through it all. Thank you, everyone, for believing in me and my monster.

NOTES

A FEW COMMENTS ON CITATIONS

All quotations from Mary Shelley's *Frankenstein; or, The Modern Prometheus,* are taken from J. Paul Hunter's 1996 Norton Critical Edition, which uses as its source the 1818 edition of the novel. When important to distinguish, quotations from the 1831 edition of Mary Shelley's *Frankenstein* come from the 1965 Signet Classic edition, edited by Harold Bloom. Since Hunter includes the Introduction written by Mary Shelley for the 1831 edition as an appendix, I quote from that text.

These primary sources will be referred to by the following abbreviations:

Shelley, *Frankenstein*: Shelley's *Frankenstein* (1818 edition), ed. Hunter (Norton, 1996)

Shelley, *Frankenstein* (1831): Shelley's *Frankenstein* (1831 edition), ed. Bloom (Signet, 1965)

Shelley, 1831 Introduction: Shelley's Introduction to *Frankenstein* (1831 edition), ed. Hunter (Norton, 1996)

I also refer to the landmark University of Chicago 1974 publication of the 1818 text of the novel, edited by James Rieger. This and other editions of the novel will be clearly identified by publisher and year.

Several other primary sources used frequently in the Notes—volumes of letters, journals, and such—will be referred to by abbreviated citations as well:

Byron's Poetry: *Byron's Poetry,* ed. Frank D. McConnell (Norton, 1978)

Clairmont Correspondence: *The Clairmont Correspondence: Letters of Claire Clairmont, Charles Clairmont, and Fanny Imlay Godwin,* vol. I, ed. Marion Kingston Stocking (Johns Hopkins University Press, 1995)

Clairmont Journals: *The Journals of Claire Clairmont,* ed. Marion Kingston Stocking (Harvard University Press, 1968)

Milton, *Paradise Lost*: John Milton, *Paradise Lost,* ed. Gordon Teskey (Norton, 2005)

MS Journals: *The Journals of Mary Shelley, 1814–1844,* ed. Paula R. Feldman and Diana Scott-Kilvert (Johns Hopkins University Press, 1987)

MS Letters: *The Letters of Mary Wollstonecraft Shelley,* 2 volumes, ed. Betty T. Bennett (Johns Hopkins University Press, 1980)

PBS Letters: *The Letters of Percy Bysshe Shelley,* 2 volumes, ed. Frederick L. Jones (Oxford University Press, 1964)

PBS Poetical Works: *Shelley: Poetical Works,* ed. Thomas Hutchinson (Oxford University Press, 1967)

Polidori, *The Vampyre*: John W. Polidori, *The Vampyre and Ernestus Berchtold; or, The Modern Oedipus. A Tale,* ed. D. L. Macdonald and Kathleen Scherf (University of Toronto Press, 1994)

INTRODUCTION

Information on the many editions of Shelley's *Frankenstein* comes from the *National Union Catalog,* from a Web site in progress under the leadership of Stuart Curran at the University of Pennsylvania, and from commentary in *Eyre Apparent,* a Book Arts Press exhibit curated by John Buchtel and Barbara Heritage at the University of Virginia in 2006.

7   *More than five hundred editions:* According to *Eyre Apparent,* in October 2005 *Bowker's Global Books in Print* cited 548 editions of *Frankenstein,* the highest number of any novel in the world. *Jane Eyre* was second, with 541.

11 *a tally of the words Mary Shelley gave:* Baldick, *In Frankenstein's Shadow,* 10n1.

CHAPTER ONE: CONCEPTION

Iwan Rhys Morus's book *Frankenstein's Children* helps to flesh out the scientific backdrop to Shelley's *Frankenstein* both during its writing and its reception.

16 *"An almost perpetual rain . . .":* MS to [Fanny Imlay?], 1 June 1816, *MS Letters,* I, 20.

16 *"We watch them . . .":* Ibid.

18 *"unexpectedly alive . . .":* Probably Wednesday, 22 February 1815. *MS Journals,* 65.

19   *"A bustle of moving"*: Ibid., 67.

19   *"find my baby dead . . ."*: Ibid., 68.

19   *"It was perfectly well . . ."*: To Thomas Jefferson Hogg, [6 March 1815], *MS Letters*, I, 10.

19   *"Mrs. Godwin will probably be glad . . ."*: To William Godwin, 25 January 1816 (Letter 315), *PBS Letters*, I, 447.

21   *"An utter stranger . . ."*: Letter no. 9 (Presumed from Claire Clairmont to Lord Byron, March or April 1816), *Clairmont Correspondence*, 24–25.

21   *"He is completely lost . . ."*: As cited in *Clairmont Correspondence*, 27.

22   *"A man is a man . . ."*: As quoted in editor's commentary, *MS Journals*, 108, citing as source Leslie Marchand, *Byron: A Biography*.

23   *"Getting out [of a boat]. . ."*: [Polidori], *The Diary of Dr. John William Polidori, 1816*, 99, 101.

27   *he signed on with literary aspirations*: D. L. MacDonald, *Poor Polidori*, 56.

27   *"for years a favorite Plan . . ."*: *Clairmont Journals*, 40.

27   *"It is not singular that . . ."*: Shelley, 1831 Introduction, 169.

28   *"very anxious that I should prove myself . . ."*: Ibid.

28   *"Ah, me! in sooth he was . . ."*: *Childe Harold's Pilgrimage*, Canto I, verse ii, *Byron's Poetry*, 26.

29   Queen Mab *"must not be published . . ."*: To Catherine Nugent, 21 May [1813], in *PBS Letters*, I, 367n2.

29   *"This book is sacred . . ."*: Sunstein, *Mary Shelley: Romance and Reality*, 76.

29   *"smallest light that twinkles . . ."*: *Queen Mab*, I, 251, 253, 254, in *PBS Poetical Works*.

29   *"Where Athens, Rome, and Sparta stood . . ."*: Ibid., II, 162–63.

29   *"It is impossible to believe . . ."*: Notes on *Queen Mab*, I, 252–53.

30   *"I was an infant when . . ."*: *Queen Mab*, VII, 1–2, 12–13.

30   *"There is no God! . . ."*: *Queen Mab*, VII, 13–16, 21–26.

30   *He ordered the printing himself*: Holmes, *Shelley: The Pursuit*, 308–09.

31   *"allegorical of one of the most interesting . . ."*: Preface to *Alastor, or the Spirit of Solitude*, in *PBS Poetical Works*, 14.

31   *"He lay breathing there . . ."*: *Alastor*, 644–45, 654.

31   *"none of Shelley's poems . . ."*: A Note on *Alastor*, by Mrs. Shelley, in *PBS Poetical Works*, 30.

32   *"Organic life beneath the shoreless waves . . ."*: Darwin, *The Temple of Nature*, V, 295–96, 300–302, in *Romantic Natural Histories*, ed. Nichols, 131.

32 *"In paste composed of flour and water . . .":* Darwin, "Note I. Spontaneous Vitality of Microscopic Animals," *The Temple of Nature,* 194–95, 192.

33 *"the production of the galvanic fluid . . .":* Quoted in Morus, *Frankenstein's Children,* 127.

33 *"On the first application of the process . . .":* From *Philosophical Magazine* 14 (1802), quoted in ibid., 128.

33 *"Galvanism had given token . . .":* Shelley, 1831 Introduction, 172.

35 *an English edition:* Namely *Tales of the Dead principally Translated from the French,* ed. Sarah Elizabeth Utterson (London: Printed for White, Cochrane, and Co., Fleet-Street, 1813).

35 *"There was the History of the Inconstant Lover":* Shelley, 1831 Introduction, 170.

35 *"'We will each write a ghost story'":* Ibid.

35 *"some peculiar circumstances . . .":* "Lord Byron, 'A Fragment,' Appendix C: The Ghost-Story Contest," in Shelley, *Frankenstein; or, The Modern Prometheus: The 1818 Text,* ed. Rieger, 260–65.

36 *"A noble author having determined . . .":* Polidori, *The Vampyre,* 51–52.

37 *"more remarkable for his singularities . . .":* Ibid., 33.

37 *"marks of teeth having opened . . .":* Ibid., 41.

37 *"Lord Strongmore had disappeared . . .":* Ibid., 47–49.

37 *"I busied myself . . .":* Shelley, 1831 Introduction, 171.

38 *"My imagination, unbidden . . .":* Shelley, 1831 Introduction, 172.

39 *"The idea so possessed my mind . . .":* Ibid.

39 *"On the morrow I announced . . .":* Ibid.

CHAPTER TWO: BIRTH AND LINEAGE

Tim Marshall's *Murdering to Dissect,* while focusing especially on the years after the publication of *Frankenstein,* presents the fascinating work—and crimes—going on in the fields of anatomy and physiology at the time. Thorough and useful information about the composition and publishing history of *Frankenstein* comes in the form of a detailed introductory time-line in Charles Robinson's edition of Mary Shelley's *The Frankenstein Notebooks.* William St. Clair devotes an entire chapter to the publication of *Frankenstein* in his book *The Reading Nation in the Romantic Period.* Thank you to Terry Belanger for pointing me in the direction of that book.

41 *"His limbs were in proportion . . .":* Shelley, *Frankenstein,* 34.

41 *"With an anxiety that almost amounted . . .":* Ibid.

42 *"I am by birth a Genevese . . .":* Ibid., 17.

42 *"sad trash":* Ibid., 21

43 *"my utmost wonder was engaged . . .":* Ibid., 22. This passage was removed from the 1831 edition.

44 *"The thunder burst at once . . .":* Ibid., 22–23.

45 *He replies, "electricity," and then . . . :* Ibid., 23.

45 *"completed the overthrow":* Ibid.

46 *"Anatomical knowledge is the only foundation . . .":* In his Hunterian Oration, 1819, as quoted in Marshall, *Murdering to Dissect,* 17.

46 *"To examine the causes of life . . .":* Shelley, *Frankenstein,* 30.

46 *"A church-yard," he says:* Ibid.

46 *"I paused, examining and analysing . . .":* Ibid.

47 *"the minuteness of the parts":* Ibid., 31.

47 *"The beauty of the dream vanished . . .":* Ibid., 34.

47 *"By the dim and yellow light . . .":* Ibid., 35.

48 *"confused and indistinct":* Ibid., 69.

48 *"happy to have found . . .":* Ibid., 71.

48 *"The gentle manners and beauty . . .":* Ibid., 75.

48 "It is not God who hath made man . . .": Volney, *A New Translation of Volney's Ruins,* I, 15, 101. Emphasis in original.

49 *two of the "treasures . . .":* Shelley, *Frankenstein,* 86.

49 *"I learned from Werter's* [sic] *imaginations . . .":* Ibid.

49 "Paradise Lost *excited different . . .":* Ibid., 87.

50 *"I was created apparently united . . .":* Ibid.

50 *"for often, like him, when I viewed . . .":* Ibid.

50 *"of the Devil's party . . .":* Blake, *The Marriage of Heaven and Hell,* plates 5–6, in *Blake: Complete Writings,* ed. Geoffry Keynes, 150.

50 *"At first I thought that liberty . . .":* Milton, *Paradise Lost,* Book Six, 164–65, 166.

50 *"Knowledge forbidden? . . .":* Ibid., Book Four, 515, 516–17.

51 *"the earth outstretched immense . . .":* Ibid., 88–89.

51 *"gods or angels, demigods":* Ibid., Book Nine, 937.

51 *"lowly wise," "dream not . . .":* Ibid., Book Eight, 173, 175.

51 *"O fleeting joys . . .":* Ibid., Book Ten, 741–46.

51   *"I submit,"Adam tells himself:* Ibid., 769–70.

52   *"for they stretched their power . . .":* Hesiod, *Theogony,* 127, 149, 155–56, 209–10.

52   *"the far-seen glory . . .":* Ibid., 565–67, 569.

53   *"Titan!"he wrote:* "Prometheus," *Byron's Poetry,* 1, 35, 38.

53   *"the immortal prototype . . .":* Kerenyí, *Prometheus: Archetypal Image of Human Existence,* 17.

53   *Sociobiologist Edward O.Wilson:* See Lumsden and Wilson, *Promethean Fire.*

53   *"livid and motionless . . .":* Shelley, *Frankenstein,* 45.

54   *"A flash of lightning . . .":* Ibid., 48.

54   *as if "belonging to another earth . . .":* Ibid., 62.

54   *The first word out of Frankenstein's mouth:* Ibid., 65.

55   *"I could have torn him . . .":* Ibid., 91.

55   *"rage and revenge":* Ibid., 92.

56   *"Remember, that I am thy creature . . .":* Ibid., 66.

56   *"Everyone carries a shadow . . .":* Jung, *Psychology and Religion,* 94.

56   *"consisting not just of . . .":* Jung, *Psychology and Religion:West and East,* 131.

56   *"there emerges a raging monster":* Jung, "On the Psychology of the Unconscious," in *Two Essays on Analytical Psychology,* 35.

56   *"the invisible saurian tail . . .":* Jung, *The Integration of the Personality.*

57   *"a foaming cataract";"pyramids & stalactites":* MS *Journals,* 114–15.

57   *"I never knew I never imagined . . .":* To Thomas Love Peacock, 22 July 1816, *PBS Letters,* I, 497.

57   *"The trees in many places . . .":* MS *Journals,* I, 117–18.

58   *"so that I narrowly escaped . . .":* To Thomas Love Peacock, 22 July 1816, *PBS Letters,* I, 497.

58   *"Iced mountains surround it . . .":* MS *Journals,* 119.

58   *"In these regions . . .":* To Thomas Love Peacock, 22 July 1816, *PBS Letters,* I, 497.

58   *"We arrived wet to the skin . . .":* MS *Journals,* 118.

59   "une vie de libertinage . . .": To the Countess Guiccioli, ?9 August 1821, *PBS Letters,* II, 326–28.

60   *"I have long determined . . .":* MS *Journals,* 139n2.

60   *these brief journal entries:* Ibid., 146–47.

61   *"Sweet Elf,"Mary wrote . . . :* To Percy Bysshe Shelley, 5 December 1816, MS *Letters,* I, 22.

61   *"While I was yet endeavouring . . .":* Thomas Hookham to Shelley, 13 December 1816, *PBS Letters,* I, 519n1.

61   *a message to "my dear Bysshe . . .":* Also quoted in ibid.

63   *"All your fears and sorrows . . .":* To Leigh Hunt, 18 March 1817, *MS Letters,* I, 35.

64   *"I thought I saw Elizabeth . . .":* Shelley, *Frankenstein,* 34.

64   *"She might become ten thousand times . . .":* Ibid., 114.

65   *"I shall be with you . . .":* Ibid., 116.

65   *"Suddenly I heard a shrill and dreadful scream. . . .":* Ibid., 135.

65   *"the purest creature of earth . . .":* Ibid.

66   *"to seek new adventures . . .":* Quoted in Fulford, Lee, and Kitson, *Literature, Science and Exploration in the Romantic Era,* 160.

67   *"I may there discover . . .":* Shelley, *Frankenstein,* 7.

67   *"We perceived a low carriage . . .":* Ibid., 13.

67   *"You seek for knowledge . . .":* Ibid., 17.

68   *"Are you then so easily turned . . .":* Ibid., 149–50.

68   *"You may give up . . .":* Ibid., 151.

68   *"Farewell, Walton! Seek happiness . . .":* Ibid., 152.

68   *"The tale which I have recorded . . .":* Ibid.

68   *"the lifeless form of his creator . . .":* Ibid., 153.

68   *"gigantic in stature . . .":* Ibid., 152.

69   *"The fallen angel becomes . . .":* Ibid., 154.

69   *"Am I to be thought . . .":* Ibid., 220–21.

69   *"I give you carte blanche . . .":* To Shelley, 24 October 1817 (b), *MS Letters,* I, 42.

70   *"was entirely written by him":* Shelley, 1831 Introduction, 173.

70   *"The season was cold and rainy . . .":* Shelley, *Frankenstein,* 6.

70   *a "courtly publisher":* To Shelley, 29 May 1817, *MS Letters,* I, 36.

70   *"I hope Frankenstein did not give you bad dreams":* To Charles Ollier, 8 August 1817, *PBS Letters,* I, 552.

70   *"Cheapest Bookseller in the World":* St. Clair, *The Reading Nation in the Romantic Period,* 197.

71   *specialized in books on magic:* Shelley, *The Frankenstein Notebooks,* ed. Robinson, I, lxxxviii.

71   *"I ought to have mentioned . . .":* To Lackington, Allen & Co., 22 August 1817, *PBS Letters,* I, 553.

71   *Lackington agreed to a royalty:* St. Clair, *The Reading Nation in the Romantic Period,* 359; Shelley, *The Frankenstein Notebooks,* ed. Robinson, I, xci.

71   *"I am confined . . .":* *MS Journals,* 179.

71   *"On Monday, Dec. 29, 1817, will be published . . .":* Quoted in Shelley, *The Frankenstein Notebooks,* ed. Robinson, I, xcii.

71   *"Frankenstein sold for . . .":* Ibid.; St. Clair, *The Reading Nation in the Romantic Period,* 196.

73   *"The Author has requested me . . .":* To [Sir Walter Scott], 2 January 1818, *PBS Letters,* I, 590.

73   *"Fran^tein comes":* MS Journals, 189.

CHAPTER THREE: RECEPTION AND REVISION

Essential background material, reviews, and scripts of plays proceeding from Shelley's *Frankenstein* appear in Steven Earl Forry's *Hideous Progenies.* After each initial citation, only the play's author and title will be listed. A collection of chapbook adaptations, including *The Monster Made by Man,* and introduced with a thoughtful overview, comes from The Zittaw Press as *The Monster Made by Man: A Compendium of Gothic Adaptations,* ed. Franz J. Potter.

74   *"This Tale is evidently . . .":* Anonymous review in *Gentleman's Magazine,* April 1818, 334–35.

74   *"Waking dreams of horror . . .":* "Frankenstein; or the Modern Prometheus," in *The British Critic,* April 1818, 432–38.

74   *"an uncouth story . . .":* Monthly Review, April 1818, 439.

74   *"a tissue of horrible . . .":* "Frankenstein, or the Modern Prometheus," in *The Quarterly Review,* 383.

74   *"nonsense decked out . . .":* Ibid., 385.

75   *"extraordinary tale . . .":* "Remarks on Frankenstein, or the Modern Prometheus; a Novel," in *Blackwood's Edinburgh Magazine,* 619.

75   *"This is, perhaps, the foulest . . .":* Quoted in Baldick, *In Frankenstein's Shadow,* 56.

75   *"This is a very* bold *fiction . . .":* "Frankenstein; or, The Modern Prometheus," in *La Belle Assemblée; being Bell's Court and Fashionable Magazine,* 139.

75   *"we have some idea . . .":* "Frankenstein; or, the Modern Prometheus," in *Literary Panorama and National Register,* 414.

76   *"If our authoress can forget . . .":* "Frankenstein; or the Modern Prometheus," in *The British Critic,* 438.

76 *"It is not health but life . . .":* To William Godwin, 7 December 1817, *PBS Letters,* I, 573.

77 *"It seems to be universally known . . .":* 30 August 1818; quoted in Shelley, *The Frankenstein Notebooks,* ed. Robinson, I, xcvii.

77 *of the £208 net profit:* St. Clair, *The Reading Nation in the Romantic Period,* 360.

77 *"Shelley and Clare are gone . . .":* To Maria Gisborne, 17 August 1818, *MS Letters,* I, 77.

77 *"We went from England comparatively prosperous . . .":* To Marianne Hunt, 29 June 1819, *MS Letters,* I, 101.

78 *"The Vampyre made considerable noise . . .":* "The Anniversary" [review], in *Knight's Quarterly Magazine,* 196.

79 *an editor's note, identifying:* Appendix B, "Preliminaries for *The Vampyre,*" in Polidori, *The Vampyre,* 177–83.

79 *Four more English editions: The Vampyre's* complicated publication history is detailed in Viets, "The London Editions of Polidori's *The Vampyre,*" *Papers of the Bibliographical Society of America.*

79 *an outline "of Miss Godwin":* Polidori, *The Vampyre,* 183.

79 *"Vampyre crew / Who hate the virtues . . .":* Quoted in Shelley, *The Frankenstein Notebooks,* ed. Robinson, I, xcviii.

81 *"Frankenstein is universally known . . .":* *MS Journals,* 456–57n3.

81 *"Lo & behold! . . .":* To Leigh Hunt, 9 September [1823], *MS Letters,* I, 378.

81 *"bursts on to the stage . . .":* "English Opera-House" [review], *The Times,* 29 July 1823, 3.

81 *"dark black flowing hair . . .":* Peake, *Presumption; or, The Fate of Frankenstein,* in Forry, *Hideous Progenies,* 135–36.

83 *"the devil's own flame . . .":* Ibid., 143.

83 *"amazed and pleased . . .":* Ibid., 147.

83 *"Wild Border of the Lake":* Ibid., 160.

84 "Avalanche *(the Stage Elephant) . . .":* *Birmingham Spectator,* 3 July 1824, quoted in Forry, *Hideous Progenies,* 7.

84 *"the Master Carpenter being . . .":* Quoted in Forry, *Hideous Progenies,* 7.

84 *"full of hope & expectation":* To Leigh Hunt, 9 September [1823], *MS Letters,* I, 378.

84 *"The play bill amused me . . .":* Ibid.

84 *"Cooke played _____'s part . . .":* Ibid.

86   *"it appeared to excite . . .":* Ibid.

86   *"The piece upon the whole . . .":* "English Opera-House," *The Times,* 29 July
      1823, 3.

86   *"the moderns may do no more . . .":* "The Drama," *The Sunday Times,* 3
      August 1823.

86   *stay away from "the monstrous Drama . . .":* Quoted in Forry, *Hideous Prog-
      enies,* 5.

86   *"As if the impious description . . .":* "Caution to Playhouse Frequenters,"
      Birmingham, 1824 (London, British Museum), reproduced in Forry,
      Hideous Progenies, 8.

87   *"This evening . . .":* "Royalty Theatre" [performance notice], *The Times,*
      22 September 1823, 2.

87   *"an entirely new outlandish . . .":* "Adelphi Theatre" [performance notice],
      The Times, 20 October 1823, 2.

87   *"Prometheus of old . . .":* Peake, *Another Piece of Presumption,* in Forry,
      Hideous Progenies, 161–76.

88   *"THIS PRESENT EVENING . . .":* Quoted in Forry, *Hideous Progenies,*
      29.

89   *"has not been inattentive . . .":* "House of Lords, Tuesday, March 16: Ame-
      lioration of the Condition of the Slave Population in the West Indies,"
      ed. Hansard, *The Parliamentary Debates,* vol. X, 1103.

89   *"To turn him loose . . .":* Ibid.

89   *"Canning paid a compliment . . .":* To Edward Trelawny, 22 March [1824],
      MS Letters, I, 417.

89   *she was still bragging:* To Teresa Guiccioli, 10 August 1827, *MS Letters,* I,
      564.

90   *"unbounded applause":* Quoted in Forry, *Hideous Progenies,* 11.

90   *"crucibles, alembecks [sic], and devil's kitchen utensils":* Ibid.

90   *"Le succès du* Monstre *. . .":* Ibid.

90   *"Oh! presumption, and is this . . .":* Milner, *Frankenstein; or, the Man and the
      Monster,* in Forry, *Hideous Progenies,* 198.

90   *"Now I think the best thing . . .":* Ibid., 202–3.

91   *"sometimes thought his master . . .":* "The Monster Made by Man; or, The
      Punishment of Presumption," in *The Monster Made by Man,* ed. Potter, 17.

91   *"As it gradually arose . . .":* Ibid.

93   *"whole frame appeared convulsed . . .":* Ibid., 18.

93   *"Thou art a sensible monster . . .":* Ibid., 27.

93 *"of being in uncertainties . . ."*: To George and Tom Keats, 21, 27(?) December 1817, *Letters of John Keats,* ed. Gittings, 43.

96 *"betook myself to the mathematics"*: Shelley, *Frankenstein* (1831), 33.

96 *"When I look back . . ."*: Ibid.

97 *"There is something at work in my soul . . ."*: Ibid., 11.

97 *"Unhappy man! . . ."*: Ibid., 19.

97 *"Awake, fairest, thy lover . . ."*: Ibid., 151–52.

99 *"the living monument of presumption . . ."*: Ibid., 178.

99 *"poor Polidori"*: Shelley, 1831 Introduction, 171.

99 *"blank incapability of invention"*: Ibid.

99 *"the pale student . . ."*: Ibid., 172.

99 *"yellow, watery, but speculative eyes"*: Ibid.

CHAPTER FOUR: THE MONSTER LIVES ON

Quotations from later stage adaptations of *Frankenstein* continue to come from the scripts included in Steven Earl Forry's *Hideous Progenies*. A fascinating study of mid-nineteenth-century electrical science, used in this chapter, comes in Iwan Rhys Morus's *Frankenstein's Children*. Peter Haining's collection of derivative short fiction, *The Frankenstein Omnibus,* offered the text of many of the mid- to late-nineteenth-century Frankenstein responses quoted here. As with the plays from the Forry volume, repeated citations will name the story's author and title only.

101 *A good seven thousand copies:* St. Clair, *The Reading Nation in the Romantic Period,* 364.

101 *One actor, T. P. Cooke:* Forry, *Hideous Progenies,* ix, 11.

102 *the title of Thomas Gray's:* Briggs, *The Power of Steam,* 92.

102 *"A mechanical man . . ."*: Brough, *Frankenstein; or, The Model Man,* reprinted in Forry, *Hideous Progenies,* 231.

102 *"Macassar oil . . ."*: Ibid., 233.

103 *newspapers were filled with:* All product names and quotation from "Supplement" to *The Times* on a single day, 16 July 1849.

103 *"You may with this Elixer . . ."*: Brough, *Frankenstein; or, The Model Man,* 233.

104 *"full, nay, laborious breathing . . ."*: As quoted in Morus, *Frankenstein's Children,* 128.

104 *In fourteen days he observed:* Ibid., 139–40.

104 *"I am neither an 'Atheist,' nor . . ."*: Ibid., 140.

105 *"to my infinite regret . . ."*: Maginn, "The New Frankenstein," in Haining, ed., *Frankenstein Omnibus,* 40–54.

106 *"After I had made this monster . . ."*: Dickens, *Great Expectations,* 169.

106 *"The imaginary student . . ."*: Ibid., 254–55.

111 *The worker "was apparently better off . . ."*: Webb, "The Disintegration of the Old Synthesis," in *Fabian Essays on Socialism,* ed. Shaw, 54–55.

112 *"a sensible treatise . . ."*: *New York Daily Times,* 14 December 1842. This and most subsequent references to newspaper articles researched through ProQuest Historical Newspapers.

112 *"the soulless monster . . ."*: Reported in E. Cobham Brewer, *Dictionary of Phrase and Fable, 1898,* as listed on http://www.bartleby.com/.

114 *"a sort of* Frankenstein *. . ."*: *New York Times,* 19 May 1879, 4.

114 *"Schwab was not . . ."*: Ibid., 20 May 1885, 3.

114 *a writer imagined what might happen*: Ibid., 6 March 1887, 12.

114 *"We deem it wise to pursue . . ."*: Ibid., 3 September 1896, 3.

115 *"The mistake is frequently made . . ."*: Ibid., 22 October 1902, 8.

115 *"Frankenstein at last became accessible . . ."*: St. Clair, *The Reading Nation in the Romantic Period,* 365.

115 *"The number of writers who should have read . . ."*: *New York Times,* 28 September 1901, BR4.

CHAPTER FIVE: MAKING MORE MONSTERS

As in the last chapter, quotations from short-fiction adaptations of *Frankenstein* come from Peter Haining's *Frankenstein Omnibus*. Information and quotations on the history of the Edison Film Company and their production of *Frankenstein* come from material in the Museum of Modern Art Film Archives, including copies of the "Synopsis" and "Schematic" production notes for the film. Further background information on Thomas Edison and his role in film history comes from conversations with archivist Leonard de Graaf and from a Library of Congress Web site, "Inventing Entertainment: The Motion Pictures and Sound Recordings of the Edison Companies," http://rs6.loc.gov/ammem/edhtml/edhome.html/. Frederick C. Wiebel, Jr., was generous with his time and knowledge about the history and reception of Edison's *Frankenstein*.

119 *"And what was I? . . ."*: Shelley, *Frankenstein,* 80–81.

120 *In* La recherche: These and other literary echoes are discussed in Baldick, *In Frankenstein's Shadow*.

121 *"a man of science ..."*: Hawthorne, "The Birthmark," *Mosses from an Old Manse,* 28.

121 *"a triumph of civilisation ..."*: Kellett, "The New Frankenstein," in Haining, *Frankenstein Omnibus,* 241.

121 *"There was a whirr ..."*: Ibid., 261.

122 *"department of Synthetic Chemistry ..."*: Cummins, "The Man Who Made a Man," in Haining, *Frankenstein Omnibus,* 263.

122 *"only the contents ..."*: Ibid., 265.

122 *"The man who had made ..."*: Ibid., 266.

125 *Titles included:* Wiebel, *Edison's Frankenstein,* n.p.

125 *The producer's dramatic synopsis:* Dramatic Synopsis #287, *Frankenstein,* 14 February 1910.

125 *"the mystery of life ..."*: Titles transcribed from *Edison's Frankenstein,* DVD.

125 *"Flesh begins to creep ..."*: Schematic #287, *Frankenstein,* 14 February 1910.

125 *"probably the most weird ..."*: "'Frankenstein': A Liberal Adaptation of the Classic Novel by Mary Shelley," in *The Edison Kinetogram.*

128 *"shrinks away ..."*: Schematic #287, *Frankenstein,* 14 February 1910.

128 *"Monster enters ..."*: Ibid.

129 *"In making the film ..."*: "'Frankenstein': A Liberal Adaptation of the Classic Novel by Mary Shelley," in *The Edison Kinetogram.*

130 *"The actually repulsive situations . . ."*: As quoted in Wiebel, *Edison's Frankenstein.*

130 *"The entire film ..."*: Ibid.

131 *"It was in bad shape ..."*: Wiebel, personal conversation and *Edison's Frankenstein.*

132 *"SAYS HE CAN CREATE LIFE ..."*: *New York Times,* 30 June 1904, 9.

133 *"ideas may do more ..."*: Duffus, "High Place for Loeb in Science Pantheon," *New York Times,* 24 February 1924, 24.

133 *"all living things ..."*: Paul H. de Kruif, quoted in ibid.

133 *"Nothing indicates ..."*: "Jacques Loeb Dies in Bermuda," *New York Times,* 13 February 1924; Duffus, "High Place for Loeb," op. cit.

134 *"HEART TISSUE BEATS ..."*: *New York Times,* 2 May 1912, 8.

134 *"modern Frankenstein"*: Huber, "An Incredible Miracle of Surgery," *Washington Post,* 17 January 1915, MS8.

134 *"CLOSE TO MYSTERY ..."*: *New York Times,* 21 July 1912, C4.

135 *"Cheap Labor...."*: Čapek, *R.U.R.,* 1.

135 *"It was in the year ..."*: Čapek, *R.U.R.,* 10–11.

1 3 5 *"If you can't make him quicker . . .":* Čapek, *R.U.R.,* 14.

1 3 6 *"The author cannot be blamed . . .":* Čapek, "The Author of the Robots Defends Himself," trans. Simsa, *Science Fiction Studies,* March 1996, http://www.depauw.edu/sfs/documents/capek68.htm/.

1 3 7 *"protest against the mechanical superstition . . .":* Ibid.

1 3 7 *"The world needed mechanical . . .":* Ibid.

CHAPTER SIX: A MONSTER FOR MODERN TIMES

Information on the history behind the Universal Frankenstein films, significant to this and later chapters, comes from David J. Skal's *The Monster Show* and Gregory William Mank's *It's Alive!* I got to know Peggy Webling's *Frankenstein* by reading her typescript on microfilm, part of the Library of Congress's Manuscripts Collection, and I was able to find a rich collection of publicity, clippings, and production notes from the Universal films in the Museum of Modern Art Film Archives. Sara Karloff, daughter of Boris, was generous with her time, knowledge, and memories of her father. Details about the life and work of Kenneth Strickfaden come from Harry Goldman's book *Kenneth Strickfaden: Dr. Frankenstein's Electrician.* Dialogue from the Universal *Frankenstein* is transcribed from the 2004 Universal Studios Legacy Collection DVD and cross-checked against *Frankenstein,* Richard J. Anobile's frame-by-frame volume of the Universal production.

1 3 9 *"a gentle little gray-haired lady":* Ivan Butler, quoted in Skal, *Monster Show,* 102.

1 3 9 *"I warn you, solemnly . . .":* Webling, *Frankenstein,* Act I, 16.

1 3 9 *"slowly clenches and unclenches . . .":* Ibid., Act I, 22.

1 4 0 *"I call him . . .":* Ibid.

1 4 0 *"stand facing . . .":* Ibid., Act I, 14, 22.

1 4 0 *"a strange mixture . . .":* Ivan Butler, quoted in Skal, *Monster Show,* 104.

1 4 0 *"Except for the final . . .":* Ibid.

1 4 1 *"What is the courage . . .":* Webling, *Frankenstein,* Act I, 11.

1 4 2 *"leaps at Henry's . . .":* Ibid., Act III, 13.

1 4 2 *"People like the tragic . . .":* Quoted in Skal, *Monster Show,* 139.

1 4 3 *"this disquieting and startling . . .":* Bell, "Thoughts on Horror Era Renaissance and Miss Ulric," *Washington Post,* 21 February 1932, A1.

1 4 3 *"monopolize the 'law business' . . .":* Dawson, "Frankenstein, Inc."

144 *"Perhaps they knew . . .":* Ibid., 275.

144 *"We are all familiar . . .":* Wormser, *Frankenstein, Incorporated,* vi, footnote.

144 *"a few all-powerful corporate . . .":* Ibid., 229.

146 *an image, Florey later recounted:* Mank, *It's Alive!,* 14.

146 *Universal paid $20,100:* Ibid., 13.

146 *"It was the strongest meat . . .":* "James Whale and 'Frankenstein,'" *New York Times,* 20 December 1931, X4.

147 *"I see Frankenstein as . . .":* "'Frankenstein' Finished," *New York Telegraph,* 11 October 1931.

147 *more like a doll:* As quoted in Mank, *It's Alive!,* 15.

147 *"I was a star . . .":* Ibid.

148 *"It does not walk like . . .":* Quoted from the filmscript in Skal, *Monster Show,* 130.

148 *"Boris Karloff's face . . .":* "James Whale and 'Frankenstein.'"

148 *A January 1931 casting directory:* Reproduced in Lindsay, *Dear Boris,* 41.

148 *"Suddenly he caught my eye . . .":* Quoted in ibid., 54.

148 *"studio executive . . .":* Karloff, "My Life as a Monster," *Films and Filming,* November 1957, 34.

149 *"I donned black tights . . .":* Eisenberg and Eisenberg, "Memoirs of a Monster," *The Saturday Evening Post,* 3 November 1962, 79.

149 *"Karloff came from relatives . . .":* Ibid., 77.

149 *"an obscure actor . . .":* Ibid., 79.

149 *"For the first time in my life . . .":* Lindsay, *Dear Boris,* 54.

149 *"sharp, bony ridges . . .":* "James Whale and 'Frankenstein.'"

150 *"I made him the way . . .":* Quoted in "Oh, You Beautiful Monster," *New York Times,* 29 January 1939, X4.

151 *He removed a dental . . .:* Sara Karloff, personal conversation, June 2005.

151 *lifted a good three inches . . .:* Sara Karloff, e-mail communication, March 2007.

152 *"full horrifying armor . . .":* Boris Karloff, "Houses I Have Haunted," *Liberty,* 4 October 1941, 16, 17.

152 *"a sudden inspiration . . .":* Quoted in Skal, *Monster Show,* 133.

153 *It grossed $53,100:* Mank, *It's Alive!,* 36–37.

156 *"My conception of the scene . . .":* Quoted in Kanfer, "Frankenstein at Sixty," *Connoisseur,* January 1991, 44.

157 *Some state film censors:* See Skal, *Monster Show,* 136ff.

157 *"Frankenstein's own sweetheart . . .":* Reel, "Boris Karloff, Colin Clive Deliver Fine Acting in State-Lake Thriller," *Chicago American,* 4 December 1931.

160 *"It has no theme . . .":* Quoted in Gifford, *Karloff:The Man, the Monster, the Movies,* 37.

160 *The Kansas State Board of Censors:* Mank, *It's Alive!,* 36.

160 *"eliminate [the] scene . . .":* Quoted in Skal, *Monster Show,* 138.

161 *"Chicagoans must be a pretty brave lot . . .":* Reel, "Boris Karloff, Colin Clive Deliver."

161 *"We needed a weird . . .":* Thirer, "'Frankenstein' Weird Chiller," *New York Daily News,* 5 December 1931.

161 *"As a concession . . .":* Hall, "A Man-Made Monster in Grand Guignol Film Story," *New York Times,* 5 December 1931.

161 *on his list of the ten best:* Hall, "Blue-Ribbon Pictures of 1931," *New York Times,* 3 January 1932, X5.

162 *"WEIRD THEME PICTURED . . .":* "Weird Theme Pictured in Rialto Film," *Washington Post,* 22 November 1931, A1.

162 *"great, gangling automaton . . .":* "Rialto," *Washington Post,* 28 November 1931, 14.

162 *"one of the best features . . .":* Richard Watts, Jr., "'Frankenstein'—Mayfair," *New York Herald Tribune,* 12 December 1931.

CHAPTER SEVEN: THE BRAVE NEW WORLD OF MONSTERS

David J. Skal's *The Monster Show* and Gregory William Mank's *It's Alive!* were important sources for this chapter on the continuing saga of Universal Frankenstein films. Background on the George Macy Companies was found on the Web site of the Harry Ransom Humanities Research Center at the University of Texas at Austin, http://www.hrc.utexas.edu/research/fa/macy.html/. Production notes from several Universal Frankenstein films were provided to me by archivists at the Film Collection of the Library of Congress. Titles and dialogue from *Bride of Frankenstein* and *Son of Frankenstein* were transcribed from the 2004 Universal Studios Legacy Collection DVD.

164 *a thirteen-part radio serial: Frankenstein: Original 1932 Radio Broadcast.*

165 *"Hold him! Hold him! . . .":* Shelley, *Frankenstein* (Grosset & Dunlap, n.d. [1932]), opposite p. 154.

169 *"In 1931 there appeared . . .":* Pearson, Introduction, in Shelley, *Franken-stein,* The Limited Editions Club edition, xii, xiii.

171 *"Readers can be relied upon . . .":* Ibid., xiv–xv.

171 *including Edmund Pearson:* Production notes, *Return of Frankenstein.*

172 *"They've had a script . . .":* Quoted in Jensen, *The Men Who Made the Monsters,* 41.

172 *"He knew it was never going to . . .":* Ibid., 52.

172 *"they'd made a dreadful mistake . . .":* Eisenberg and Eisenberg, "Memoirs of a Monster," 80.

172 *the new costume weighed . . . :* Ruddy, "The Dulwich Horror," in Ackerman, ed., *The Frankenscience Monster,* 34.

172 *"I am genuinely glad . . .":* Ibid., 36.

173 *"Time and time again . . .":* Quoted in Ron Haydock, "Boris Karloff—The King of Horror Films," in Haining, ed., *The Frankenstein File,* 59–60.

173 *"When the monster did speak . . .":* Karloff, "My Life as a Monster," 34.

174 *gauze-and-sequin gown:* Quoted in Mank, *It's Alive!,* 58.

177 *An early version of the screenplay:* Ibid., 63n.

178 *"Can you imagine the advertising . . .":* Advance publicity piece reproduced in ibid., 50.

178 *"elfish Bohemian":* Ibid., 54.

178 *"James's feeling was that . . .":* Ibid., 54–55.

179 *"For a whole hour . . .":* Ibid., 59.

181 *"I was just an unimportant free-lance actor . . .":* Eisenberg and Eisenberg, "Memoirs of a Monster," 79.

182 *"After having scared . . .":* "Revival of the Undead," *New York Times,* 16 October 1938, 160.

182 *Universal obeyed stringent:* Skal, *Monster Show,* 137.

182 *"Four thousand frenzied Mormons . . .":* "Revival of the Undead."

183 *In Cincinnati, Indianapolis . . . :* Skal, *Monster Show,* 204.

184 *"called for the horror . . .":* "Revival of the Undead."

184 *"Throw away the book! . . .":* Trade advertisement reprinted in Skal, *Monster Show,* 204.

184 *"The public came, shrieked . . .":* "Revival of the Undead."

184 *Even some stateside observers:* See Skal, *Monster Show,* 205.

184 *"'Nightmares for everybody'":* Quoted in Skal, *Monster Show,* 209, from an article in *Look,* 28 February 1939.

185 *"clear the stigma . . .":* "Production Data from Universal Studios: 'Son of Frankenstein,'" 2.

185 *"A horrible creature . . .":* Teaser line from *Son of Frankenstein* publicity, quoted in Mank, *It's Alive!, 77.*

185 *"furs and muck":* Quoted in Mank, *It's Alive!, 78.*

188 *It opened in Hollywood:* Ibid., 83.

188 *Record crowds lined up:* Vieira, *Hollywood Horror from Gothic to Cosmic,* 93.

188 *"For its type . . .":* Quoted in Bojarski and Beale, *The Films of Boris Karloff,* 137.

188 *"masterpiece" of "literary melodrama":* Mank, *It's Alive!, 83.*

188 *"He was going downhill . . .":* Quoted by Ken Beale, "Boris Karloff, Master of Horror," *Castle of Frankenstein Monster Annual* (Gothic Publishing Co., 1966), 58, cited by Mank, *It's Alive!,* 119.

188 *"My dear old Monster . . .":* Quoted in Gifford, *Karloff: The Man, the Monster, the Movies,* 37.

189 *"Whale and I both saw . . .":* Ibid., 45.

189 *"The most heartrending . . .":* Ibid.

CHAPTER EIGHT: THE HORROR AND THE HUMOR

Background information on cartoonist Clifford Berryman came from the Web site of the Gelman Library, George Washington University, http:// www.gwu.edu/gelman/spec/collections/manuscript/berryman.html/. Information on the Council on Books in Wartime came from the Princeton University Libraries online archive at http://infoshare1.princeton.edu/ libraries/firestone/rbsc/finding_aids/cbw.html#series26/. Dialogue from all films is transcribed from DVDs, which are listed in full in the bibliography. On twentieth-century science that mirrored Mary Shelley's visions, Jon Turney's book *Frankenstein's Footsteps* offered much information and analysis and many leads to further research materials. William B. Jones's book *Classics Illustrated: A Cultural History* provided me with an overview of the series history as well as some details on the place of *Frankenstein* in it. Information on illustrator Norm Saunders came through correspondence with his daughter, Zina Saunders, and from an interview with her on the Web site, "Zelda's Mars Attacks!," http://www.marsattacksfan .com/zina.htm/.

195 *"How did Mary Shelley . . .":* Cover copy, *Frankenstein,* Armed Services Edition [1945?].

197 *"Universal was always . . .":* Quoted in Mank, *It's Alive!,* 112.

200 *Hungarian officers who:* "Terror of Nazism in Balkans Told," *New York Times,* 14 March 1942, 7.

203 *"Man-made monsters . . .":* Skal, *Monster Show,* 213.

204 *"You're nothing like Jonathan . . .":* Kesselring, *Arsenic and Old Lace,* 43.

205 *"I told him I needed his help . . .":* [Strange], "My Life as a Monster," *Mad Monsters,* November 1962, 14.

205 *"top-heavy attempt . . .":* Quoted by Mank, *It's Alive!,* 138.

205 *"He wasn't as lucky . . .":* Interview with Karloff by Mike Parry and Harry Nadler in *Castle of Frankenstein* 9, quoted in Mank, *It's Alive!,* 139.

205 *"The Monsters of Menace . . .":* Gregory William Mank, "Production Background," in Riley, ed., *Abbott and Costello Meet Frankenstein,* 26.

206 *In a 1946 story:* Briefer, "Frankenstein," *Prize Comics* 59 (May–June 1946).

208 *In his adventure-filled life:* For more on Dick Briefer's Frankenstein comics, see Glut, *The Frankenstein Archive,* 306–13.

208 *In 1948 the high-nosed character:* Briefer, "Frankenstein meets Boris Karload, Master of Horror," *Frankenstein* 11 (January–February 1948), reprinted in *The Journal of Frankenstein* #5, October 2001, 54–58.

208 *A sculptor who attempts:* Briefer, "The Monster of Frankenstein," *The Monster of Frankenstein* 30 (April–May 1954), 9.

211 *One critic sees the series:* Hutchings, *Hammer and Beyond,* 102–03.

211 *"offered me a fee up front . . .":* Sangster, *Do You Want It Good or Tuesday?,* 35.

211 *he read Bram Stoker's novel twice:* Ibid., 51.

212 *"Every other* Frankenstein *movie . . .":* Ibid.

212 *"a tiny grotto . . .":* Lee, *Tall, Dark and Gruesome,* 196.

212 *"I was forty years old . . .":* Cushing, "Dr. Frankenstein and I," in Haining, ed., *The Frankenstein File,* 82.

212 *"it seemed merely like . . .":* Lee, *Tall, Dark and Gruesome,* 195.

212 *"He is either an atheist . . .":* Quoted in "The Fisher King," in Jones, *Frankenstein Scrapbook,* 71.

213 *"I have always based my playing . . .":* Cushing, "Dr. Frankenstein and I," 82.

214 *"He said to me that an actor . . .":* Lee, *Tall, Dark and Gruesome,* 195.

214 *"Copyright prevented us . . .":* Ibid., 196.

214 *"There were all sorts of horrid things . . .":* Christopher Lee, "Frankenstein, Dracula and Me," in Haining, ed., *Frankenstein File,* 86.

214 *"we got it more or less human . . ."*: Lee, *Tall, Dark and Gruesome*, 196.

214 *"It was a case of inventing . . ."*: Ibid., 197.

215 *"I had a damaged brain . . ."*: Lee, "Frankenstein, Dracula and Me," 86.

215 *"HEART TRANSPLANT KEEPS . . ."*: *New York Times*, 4 December 1967, 1.

216 *In the next year, 1968:* Turney, *Frankenstein's Footsteps*, 154.

216 *"The strange thing . . ."*: Cushing, "Dr. Frankenstein and I," 82.

217 *"What then became of me? . . ."*: Shelley, *Frankenstein*, 137.

217 *"Here is a haunting tale . . ."*: Shelley, *Frankenstein* (Classics Illustrated edition), n.d., n.p.

220 *"the isolated laboratory . . ."*: *Frankenstein*, no. 1 (Dell Comics), 1963, reprinted August-October 1964, n.p.

222 *"the world's newest, greatest and strangest . . ."*: *Frankenstein*, no. 2 (Dell Comics), 1966, n.p.

223 *"the most famous, most fearsome . . ."*: *The Monster of Frankenstein*, vol. 1, no. 1 (January 1972).

223 *"Robert Walton IV, great-grandson . . ."*: "Bride of the Monster," *The Monster of Frankenstein*, vol. 1, no. 2 (March 1972), reprinted in Friedrich and Moench, *The Essential Monster of Frankenstein*, vol. 1, n.p.

223 *"the direct descendent . . ."*: "Lady of the House," *The Frankenstein Monster!*, no. 18 (September 1975), reprinted in Friedrich and Moench, *The Essential Monster of Frankenstein*, vol. 1, n.p.

223 *"I related to that naive monster . . ."*: Quoted in Cooke, "The Man Called Ploog," *Comic Book Artist* #2 (Summer 1998).

224 *"They wanted to bring Frankenstein . . ."*: Ibid.

224 *"Tell me, poor creature . . ."*: "Code Name: Berserker!," *The Frankenstein Monster* 16 (May 1975), reprinted in Friedrich and Moench, *The Essential Monster of Frankenstein*, vol. 1, n.p.

226 *"To speak. To communicate. . . ."*: Ibid.

CHAPTER NINE: MONSTERS IN THE LIVING ROOM

Statistics on television history come from the Web site "Television History—The First 75 Years," http://www.tvhistory.tv/. Dialogue from the Lon Chaney, Jr., television performance on *Tales from Tomorrow*, from *Frankenstein Tai Baragon*, from *The Rocky Horror Picture Show*, and from *Young Frankenstein* is transcribed from the DVDs cited in the bibliography. Details on the on-screen antics of John Zacherle come in large part from a radio interview of him conducted by Bruce Underwood, originally aired on 27 April 1968, and now online at *Broadcast Pioneers of Philadelphia,* http:// www.angelfire.com/tv2/philapioneers/roland.html/. Richard Scrivani posts his "'Shock Theater' Memories" online at http://www.scrabo.com/ scrivani4.htm/, but he was also kind enough to answer further questions by e-mail and telephone. The history of drive-in theaters is outlined on "The Drive-In Theater History Page," http://www.driveintheater.com/ history/1950.htm/. Generous information on the many Frankenstein spin-off films and television shows can be found in Stephen Jones's *The Frankenstein Scrapbook.* George Garrett and Richard Dillard kindly shared their memories and thoughts on the monster with me. Kevin Miserocchi provided thoughts and information on Charles Addams's connection (or lack thereof) to the Frankenstein monster. Lyrics from the theme song of *Milton the Monster* are transcribed from an online recording on the Toon Tracker Web site, http://www.toontracker.com/, and used with permission from the family and counsel of Hal Seeger.

229 *Several more original* Frankensteins: Glut, *Frankenstein Legend,* 266–70.

229 *In Los Angeles exotic dancer:* Skal, *Monster Show,* 237–45.

230 *Every Saturday night in Chicago:* "TV Horror Hosts," http://myweb .wvnet.edu/e-gor/tvhorrorhosts/fmshock.html/.

230 *In Cleveland, Pete Myers:* Weldon, "The Hosts That Ate Cleveland," *Fangoria* 24 (1982), reprinted at http://www.psychotronicvideo.com/ wow/ghoulardi/fangoria.shtml/.

230 *"inmates incarcerated in hospitals ...":* Castain, "A Ghoulorious Tribute," http://myweb.wvnet.edu/e-gor/mtgraves/.

230 *"We would have an experiment ...":* Underwood interview with Zacherle, http://www.angelfire.com/tv2/philapioneers/roland.html/.

231 *"KRON-TV gave San Francisco ...":* Advertisements online at http://www .milwaukee-horror-hosts.com/Variety.html/.

231 *By 1958 more than forty cities ...:* "TV Horror Hosts."

232 *"September, 1957. I was sitting ...":* Scrivani, " 'Shock Theater' Memories," The Scrivani Pages, http://www.scrabo.com/scrivani4.htm/.

234 *"Many readers, familiar with ...":* Jacket copy, Shelley, *Frankenstein* (Airmont Publishing, 1963).

234 *Rich Scrivani wrote a book report:* Scrivani, e-mail and conversation, May 2006.

236 *Not only a film festival* Promotional material online at "What is the Monster Bash?," http://www.creepyclassics.com/.

236 *"Representing the world of the imagination . . .":* As printed on the masthead of the October 2001 issue.

237 *As David Skal points out:* Skal, *Monster Show,* 255.

237 *"The one . . . the only king of monsters . . .":* As reprinted on the box containing the VHS of *Frankenstein 1970.*

238 *dozens of cheap Frankensteins:* This list only begins to represent the Frankenstein films of the 1960s and 1970s worldwide. For a more thorough listing, see Jones, *Frankenstein Notebook,* from which most of these titles and summaries were culled.

240 *For scriptwriter George Garrett:* Sussman, "The Dramatic Writings of George Garrett," *The Southern Quarterly,* Winter-Spring 1995, 200.

240 *"a triumph of vulgarity";"the pits":* Quoted in Garrett, "The Crossover Beard; or, the True Story of Frankenstein Meets the Space Monster (Among Other Things)," *Virginia Quarterly Review,* Winter 2005, 27.

240 *"They had a title . . .":* Ibid., 26.

241 *"Frank, the android American astronaut . . .":* Ibid., 33.

241 *"We are in the* horror *film business . . .":* Ibid., 9.

242 *"The film came to be advertised . . .":* Dillard, personal conversation, May 2005.

242 *"a genuinely vital . . .":* Dillard, *Horror Films,* 32.

242 *"I was looking for the movie. . . .":* Dillard, personal conversation, May 2005.

243 *defining "camp" as a cult of sensibility:* Sontag, "Notes on 'Camp,'" *Partisan Review* (Fall 1964).

244 *"forty pounds of padding . . .":* According to Butch Patrick on The Munsters Web site, http://www.munsters.com/.

244 *Herman takes a bolt of electricity:* "Just Another Pretty Face," *The Munsters,* Season 2, first aired January 13, 1966.

244 *Victor Frankenstein IV visits:* "A Visit from Johann," *The Munsters,* Season 2, first aired March 17, 1966.

247 *"When Russel Crouse . . .":* Cerf, "A Note by the Publisher" in Addams, *Drawn and Quartered,* n.p.

247 *"One evening . . .":* Karloff, "Foreword," in ibid.

247 *"We think it is important to dispel . . .":* Miserocchi, e-mail, September 2005.

248 *"one eye is opaque . . .":* Excerpted from the 1 September 1963 contract between Charles Addams and Filmways TV Productions, Inc., reprinted courtesy of the Tee and Charles Addams Foundation.

250 *The haunted house set was borrowed:* "Trivia for *The Rocky Horror Picture Show* (1975)," The Internet Movie Database, http://www.imdb .com/.

250 *"It was only supposed to run . . .":* "A message from Richard O'Brien," video presentation on the Rocky Horror Show Web site, http://www .rockyhorror.co.uk/.

251 *"It was a cold snowy night . . .":* Sal Piro, "It Was Great When It All Began," from *Creatures of the Night,* reprinted on The Rocky Horror Picture Show official fan site, http://www.rockyhorror.com/.

251 *"One night . . .":* Ibid.

252 *"We discovered over the years . . .":* "A message from Richard O'Brien," http://www.rockyhorror.co.uk/.

253 *"We live in squeamish days . . .":* William Godwin to Charles Lamb, 10 March 1808, quoted in Marrs, *The Letters of Charles and Mary Anne Lamb,* vol. 2, 278.

253 *"OVEREXCITEMENT SEEN":* "Child's Reactions to Movies Shown," *New York Times,* 28 May 1933, B7.

254 *"The writers of the Payne reports . . .":* Ibid.

254 *Roused by a cardinal:* Heins, "*The Miracle:* Film Censorship and the Entanglement of Church and State," University of Virginia Forum for Contemporary Thought, 28 October 2002, online at http://www .fepproject.org/.

255 *As early as 1933:* As described by Jackson King on the Monsters in Animation Web site, http://www.jimhillmedia.com/.

256 *"On top of old Horror Hill . . .":* "Milton the Monster," Toon Tracker Web site, http://www.toontracker.com/.

257 *"He's a monster with a conscience!":* Fallberg, *Frankenstein, Jr.: The Menace of the Heartless Monster,* 62.

258 *"After lunch one afternoon . . .":* Wilder, *Kiss Me Like a Stranger,* 139.

258 *When he called his director pal:* Ibid., 140.

258 *"In black & white":* Ibid., 142.

262 *"gonna scream about . . .":* "Frankenstein," New York Dolls.

263 *"If God is good . . .":* Quoted in Mank, *It's Alive!,* 53.

263 *"head made of rock":* "Teenage Frankenstein," Alice Cooper.

CHAPTER TEN: TAKING THE MONSTER SERIOUSLY

Since I was a graduate student in English during the transitional years
1974–1978, many comments about the spirit of those times vis-à-vis
Frankenstein come from personal experience. I thank members of the
online discussion list of the North American Society for Studies in Romanticism (NASSR-L), who reminisced about the novel's changing reputation
during their own careers. Michael Rodemeyer helped me tremendously in
tracking and understanding the science and politics of "Frankenfoods."
Thorough agendas, transcripts of discussions, and papers presented before
the President's Council on Bioethics are archived on the U.S. Government
Web site created to reflect the council's work, http://www.bioethics
.gov/. Paul Cantor kindly offered personal recollections about his presentation to the President's Council on Bioethics.

264 *had led "to the unraveling . . .":* "Clue to Chemistry of Heredity Found,"
    New York Times, 13 June 1953, 17.
265 *Haldane explored the role:* Haldane, "Biological Possibilities for the
    Human Species in the Next Ten Thousand Years," published online at
    http://www.transhumanism.org/resources/Haldanebioposs.htm/.
265 *"New possibilities of clonal reproduction . . .":* Lederberg, "Unpredictable
    Variety Still Rules Human Reproduction," *Washington Post,* 30 Sep-
    tember 1967.
266 *a young biochemist:* Kass, "Genetic Tampering," Letters to the Editor,
    Washington Post, 3 November 1967.
266 *"If the attempts to clone . . .":* Ibid.
267 *"Scientists hailed the virus work . . .":* Schmeck, "Scientist Doubts Genetic
    Abuse; Calls Research the Best Defense," *New York Times,* 9 March 1968.
267 *"How the human species . . .":* Quoted in ibid.
268 *"The notion that man might . . .":* Watson, "Moving Toward the Clonal
    Man," *The Atlantic,* May 1971.
268 *a three-year-old center:* As stated in "Studies in Revolution," a sidebar to
    Gaylin, "We Have the Awful Knowledge to Make Exact Copies of
    Human Beings," *New York Times Magazine,* 5 March 1972.
269 *"The Frankenstein myth becomes . . .":* Gaylin, "We Have the Awful Knowl-
    edge to Make Exact Copies of Human Beings," *New York Times Maga-
    zine,* 5 March 1972.
270 *"The tragic irony is not that . . .":* Ibid., 49.

270 *one participant remembers:* Fredrickson, *The Recombinant DNA Controversy, A Memoir,* 13–14.

271 *One among them is reported:* Ibid., 15, 16.

271 *"One aim of the meeting . . .":* Berg, "Asilomar and Recombinant DNA," Berg's Nobel Prize acceptance speech, delivered 26 August 2004 and published on the Noble Prize Web site at http://nobelprize.org/ nobel_prizes/chemistry/articles/berg/index.html/.

271 *"The new techniques . . .":* McElheny, "World Biologists Tighten Rules on 'Genetic Engineering' Work," *New York Times,* 28 February 1975.

271 *"rare in the history of science":* Ibid.

272 *"Are we really that much farther along . . .":* Quoted in Kolata, *Clone,* from *Science,* 15 October 1976.

273 *"the greatest horror story . . .":* Jacket copy, Shelley, *Frankenstein* (Lion Books, 1953).

275 *"his glare turned to venom . . .":* *Monsters,* 10.

275 *"he saw the dull yellow eye . . .":* *Frankenstein, Based on the Novel by Mary Shelley,* adapted by Dale Carlson, 11, 141.

276 *"My name is Victor Frankenstein. . . .":* Shelley, *Frankenstein,* adapted by Larry Weinberg, 7.

277 *"Shelley's eighteen-year-old mistress . . .":* "Note on the Text," in Shelley, *Frankenstein; or, The Modern Prometheus: The 1818 Text,* ed. Rieger, xliii.

277 *"Myths are neither validated nor invalidated . . .":* "Introduction," in ibid., xxxiv.

277 *"If the myth has become tawdry . . .":* Ibid., xxxvi.

277 *"not a work of scholarship . . .":* Small, *Mary Shelley's Frankenstein: Tracing the Myth,* 9.

278 *"The motion-picture viewer . . .":* Bloom, "Afterword," in Shelley, *Frankenstein, or The Modern Prometheus* (Signet Classic), 212.

278 *"what makes* Frankenstein *an important book . . .":* Ibid., 215.

279 *"Happy 150th . . .":* Front cover, *Life,* 15 March 1968.

279 *"I settled back as its pseudodocumentary . . .":* Rosenberg, "The Horrible Truth About Frankenstein: Happy Sesquicentennial, Dear Monster," *Life,* 15 March 1968, 74D, 84.

281 *"If ever there was a time . . .":* Moers, *Literary Women: The Great Writers,* xi, xiii.

281 *"A baby at birth is usually . . .":* Ibid., 91.

281 *a new feminist definition of the Gothic:* Ibid., 92.

281 *"early and chaotic experience . . ."*: Ibid.

282 *"No outside influence . . ."*: Ibid., 97.

282 *"When several of us discovered . . ."*: Levine and Knoepflmacher, "Preface," *The Endurance of Frankenstein*, xi–xii.

283 *"Everybody talks about* Frankenstein *. . ."*: Levine, "The Ambiguous Heritage of *Frankenstein*," in ibid., 3.

283 *"Of all the imaginary monsters . . ."*: Gray, "The Man-Made Monster," *Time*, 23 July 1979, 86–87.

284 *"come forth from the hands of God . . ."*: Shelley, *Frankenstein*, 87.

284 *"I ought to be thy Adam . . ."*: Ibid., 66, 87.

285 *nowhere in the section's ten pages*: The Norton Anthology of English Literature (3rd ed.), vol. 2.

285 *An introduction called* Frankenstein: *The Norton Anthology of English Literature* (4th ed.), vol. 2, 880.

285 *remembers that*: Comment posted to NASSR-L, 8 March 2006.

285 *A 1991 statistical study*: Linkin, "The Current Canon in British Romantics Studies," *College English*, vol. 53, no. 5 (September 1991).

286 *"the canon in British Romanticism . . ."*: Ibid., 560.

286 *had made it into the ivory tower*: Although, ironically, by 2006, one scholar reported deliberately not putting *Frankenstein* on her graduate seminar reading list because "it's overdone by the graduate level" and because she "wanted to show that the Romantic era consists of more than 6 authors and 1 woman who had a nightmare" (Katherine D. Harris, San Jose State University, NASSR-L discussion list, 21 May 2006).

286 *"A live, human-made micro-organism . . ."*: Diamond v. Chakrabarty, 447 U.S. 303 (1980).

286 *"present a gruesome parade of horribles . . ."*: Ibid.

287 *"Would a specific type of genetic alteration . . ."*: Quoted in Charles, *Lords of the Harvest*, 56.

288 *encouraging "wider public debate . . ."*: As quoted on His Majesty the Prince's Web site, http://www.princeofwales.gov.uk/speeches/agriculture_01061999 .html/.

288 *"Ever since Mary Shelley's baron . . ."*: Lewis, Letter to the Editor, *New York Times*, 16 June 1992. For more on Lewis and his influential coinage, see Metcalf, *Predicting New Words*.

288 *proof that the public is "uneasy"*: O'Neill, "Geneticists' Latest Discovery: Public Fear of 'Frankenfood,'" *New York Times*, 28 June 1992.

289 *"CLONING BRINGS FACTORY PRECISION ...":* Schneider, "Cloning Brings Factory Precision to the Farm," *New York Times,* 17 February 1988.

289 *"Lawmakers must be vigilant ...":* "Life, Industrialized," *New York Times,* 22 February 1988, 18.

291 *"Now there are no boundaries. ...":* Quoted in Kolata, *Clone,* 221.

291 *"SCIENTISTS SOUND WARNING ...":* Laurance and Hornsby, "Scientists sound warning on 'human clones,'" *The [London] Times,* 24 February 1997, 1.

292 *"opened up the theoretical prospect ...":* Ibid.; Hawkes, "Legal barriers will prevent apocalypse now, if not later," *The Times,* 26 February 1997, 3.

292 *"the debate was metaphorical ...":* Hellsten, "Dolly: Scientific Breakthrough or Frankenstein's Monster? Journalistic and Scientific Metaphors of Cloning," *Metaphor and Symbol* (2200), 213.

292 *"carbon-copy people" and "extra organ factories":* Quoted in ibid., 217.

292 *"Science marches on ...":* Ibid.

292 *"Frankenstein's alarmists"; "Dolly, Adolf Hitler and Frankenstein":* Purves, "Like a wolf on the fold," *The Times,* 25 February 1997; as quoted in Butler and Wadman, "Putting the lid on Pandora's box of genetics," *Nature,* 386(6620), 9.

292 *"The most immediate medical consequence ...":* Trafford, "Fear of Cloning and the Ewe To-do," *Washington Post,* 11 March 1997.

293 Fears about cloning *"mirror those . . .":* Morris Sullivan, "Modern Prometheus or Frankenstein's Monster," Impact Press Web site, February–March 1998, http://www.impactpress.com/articles/febmar98/clone.htm/.

293 *"Western culture is replete with myths ...":* Shapiro, Long, and Gideon, "To Clone or Not to Clone," *New York University Journal of Legislative and Public Policy,* 23–34.

294 *"Hollywood knows only one theme ...":* Gould, "The Monster's Human Nature," in *Dinosaur in a Haystack,* 60. This essay was first published in *Natural History* in 1994.

295 *"In the forums that count ...":* Celia Hooper, e-mail correspondence, 23 May 2005.

295 *"I was hooked":* Donald A. B. Lindberg, M.D., "Director's Introduction," in *Frankenstein: Penetrating the Secrets of Nature* [exhibition guidebook], vi.

297 *"Why would the National Institutes ...":* Fee, "Prologue," in ibid., ix.

297 *"on bioethical issues that may emerge ...":* Executive Order 13237, 28 November 2001, *Federal Register,* 66 FR 59851.

298 *"New biomedical technologies . . .":* Kass, "Making Babies: The New Biology and the 'Old' Morality," *The Public Interest,* no. 26 (Winter 1972), 18–19.

298 *He urged discussion:* Ibid., 55.

299 *"prearticulate human moral sense":* Kass, "The Wisdom of Repugnance," in Kass and Wilson, *Ethics of Human Cloning,* 79.

299 *"People are repelled . . .":* Ibid., 17–18.

299 *"They recoil . . .":* Ibid., 19.

300 *"as the last crimson tint . . .":* Hawthorne, "The Birthmark," *Mosses from an Old Manse,* 43.

300 *"our human aspiration . . .":* President's Council on Bioethics, Transcript: First Meeting, Session 2, 17 January 2002, http://www.bioethics.gov/.

301 *"the question of the meaning of suffering . . .":* Ibid.

301 *"The council, under my chairmanship . . .":* Kass, e-mail correspondence, January 2006.

302 *"We may have at one point discussed . . .":* Ibid.

302 *"The Romantics were the first poets . . .":* Cantor, "The Scientist and the Poet," *The New Atlantis,* 76. This essay is a later published version of the talk given at the Council event, provided to me by Professor Cantor as the closest thing available to a transcript of the talk, which was neither written down nor recorded.

302 *"If there is one imaginative work . . .":* Ibid., 81, 82, 84.

303 *As Cantor says today:* Cantor, personal conversation, July 2006.

THE MONSTER AND HIS MYTH TODAY

Sara Karloff and Barbara Field generously spoke with me on the phone about their various interactions and relationships with the monster and his myth. I could not have been so thorough—nor so thoroughly amused—in tracking the abundant media appearances of Frankenstein without Google and eBay. Thank you to Charles Robinson for telling me about Barbara Field's play, *Playing with Fire.* I appreciate the helpfulness of librarians at the Huntington Library in Santa Monica, California, who searched through their Christopher Isherwood correspondence archives to find any letters related to the teleplay that he and Don Bachardy wrote, modernizing the myth.

305 *as cartoonist Edward Sorel depicted:* Cover image, *The New Yorker,* 17 February 1997.

306 *"How can we keep the government . . .":* Friedman, *Capitalism and Freedom,* 2.

306 *"and now we are creating for it . . .":* Raimondo, "Frankenstein in London," http://www.antiwar.com/blog/comments/, posted 9 July 2005.

306 *"China is the Frankenstein . . .":* Quoted in Kin-Ming Liu, "Panda Huggers on Alert," *New York Sun,* 16 January 2006.

306 *"a Frankenstein's monster, killing anyone . . .":* "Killers on Probation," *Sacramento [Calif.] Bee* online, http://www.sacbee.com/, 19 July 2005.

306 *"a Frankenstein's monster which is completely . . .":* Mulholland, "MP: Councillor conduct watchdog is out of control," *Guardian Unlimited,* http://www.guardian.co.uk/, 27 July 2005.

306 *"a political Frankenstein":* "Political Frankenstein Born in Parliament—Nationalist Leader," http://www.novinite.com/, 27 July 2005.

306 *"a Frankenstein monster that devours . . .":* Ajaz ul-Haque, "Public or Republic," http://www.greaterkashmir.com/, posted 29 January 2006.

306 *"fast food's first edible Frankenstein":* Horovitz, "Restaurant Sales Climb with Bad-for-You Food," *USA Today,* 13–15 May 2005, 1.

307 *"a McFrankenstein creation":* As cited in *Super Size Me,* written and directed by Morgan Spurlock, 2004.

307 *"FRANKEN-SWINE! FARMER USES . . .":* Cover headline, *Weekly World News,* 17 October 2005.

307 *A nine-year-old boy in Virginia:* "Boy's Biopsy Is Set for Today," *Richmond Times-Dispatch,* 2 February 2005; Jablon, "Boy Who Fought 'Frank the Tumor' Gets Clean Bill of Health," *Richmond Times-Dispatch,* 14 April 2006.

309 *"I used to be known as a big stiff . . .":* The television ad is used as a corporate sample on Cycle Media's Web site, http://www.cyclemedia.net/. Thanks to Ben Varner of the University of Northern Colorado for showing the site to me.

310 *"Now, we all know the story . . .":* Jobling, *Frankenstein's Cat,* n.p.

310 *"monstrous poems and pictures":* Cover text, McNaughton, *Making Friends with Frankenstein.*

310 *"When I am feeling lonely . . .":* McNaughton, *Making Friends with Frankenstein,* 32. Used with permission from Walker Books.

311 *"I might be a monster . . .":* Graves, *Frank Was a Monster Who Wanted to Dance,* n.p.

311 *California after-school art teacher:* Miller, "Everybody's a Comic Book Artist," *Daily Pilot* (Newport Beach and Costa Mesa, CA), 15 November 2005.

311 *"the fantasy film fan event . . .":* As printed on the convention poster, recently displayed on eBay.

312 *"deceased personality's name . . .":* California Civil Code Section 990, "Practitioner's Guide to California Right of Publicity Law."

313 *According to Sara Karloff:* Ms. Karloff's report of these events has been conveyed to me through personal and telephone conversations and e-mail correspondence, June 2005 through May 2006.

314 *"124,000 educational and entertaining . . .":* *Classic Movie Monsters Stamps Media Kit,* United States Postal Service, October 1997.

315 *"They promised that they would buy . . .":* Karloff, personal and telephone conversations.

318 *An early book of poems by Margaret Atwood:* A copy is held by the Pforzheimer Library in New York, from which I quote.

319 *"I thought the idea was gigantic . . .":* Barbara Field, telephone conversation, May 2006.

319 *"Why do you hate me? . . .":* Field, *Playing with Fire,* in *New Classics from the Guthrie Theater,* 309.

319 *"There is no good and evil . . .":* Ibid., 344.

319 *"Our intent was always . . .":* Branagh, *Mary Shelley's Frankenstein,* 9, 22

321 *"collective depression narrative":* Goodson, "Frankenstein in the Age of Prozac," *Literature and Medicine,* 30.

321 *"Armed with a scalpel . . .":* Liner notes, Francis Dhomont, *Frankenstein Symphony* (CD).

323 *"Neither Don Bachardy nor I are in favor . . .":* Letter from Christopher Isherwood to Ms. Judith Weber, 16 November 1973, courtesy of Huntington Library.

323 *The very "plasticity" of the novel:* Rose, "Custody Battles: Reproducing Knowledge about *Frankenstein,*" *New Literary History,* 809.

324 *"the simple, primordial human being . . .":* Kass, *The Beginning of Wisdom,* 61.

325 *"Begone! relieve me from the sight . . .":* Shelley, *Frankenstein,* 67.

BIBLIOGRAPHY

BOOKS, PLAYS, AND WEB SITES

Forrest J. Ackerman, ed., *The Frankenscience Monster*. New York: Ace Publishing Corp., 1969.

Charles Addams, *Drawn and Quartered: An Album of Drawings*. New York: Random House, 1942.

Aeschylus, *Prometheus Unbound,* translated by Elizabeth Barrett Browning. New York: The Liberal Arts Press, 1950.

Brian W. Aldiss, *Billion-Year Spree*. New York: Doubleday & Co., 1973.

Richard J. Anobile, ed., *Frankenstein*. New York: Darien House/Avon Books, 1974.

Chris Baldick, *In Frankenstein's Shadow: Myth, Monstrosity, and Nineteenth-Century Writing*. Oxford: Clarendon Press, 1987.

Betty T. Bennett and Charles E. Robinson, eds., *The Mary Shelley Reader*. New York and Oxford: Oxford University Press, 1990.

J. D. Bernal, *Science in History, Vol. 2: The Scientific and Industrial Revolutions*. Cambridge, Mass.: MIT Press, 1969 (third edition).

[William Blake], *Blake Complete Writings,* ed. Geoffrey Keynes. London: Oxford University Press, 1966.

Harold Bloom, ed., *Mary Shelley's Frankenstein*. New York/New Haven/Philadelphia: Chelsea House Publishers, 1987.

Louise Schutz Boas, *Harriet Shelley: Five Long Years*. London: Oxford University Press, 1962.

Richard Bojarski and Kenneth Beale, *The Films of Boris Karloff*. Seacaucus, NJ: The Citadel Press, 1974.

Asa Briggs, *The Power of Steam: An Illustrated History of the World's Steam Age*. Chicago: University of Chicago Press, 1982.

George Gordon, Lord Byron, *Byron's Poetry,* ed. Frank D. McConnell. New York and London: W. W. Norton, 1978.

Joseph Campbell, *The Hero with a Thousand Faces.* Princeton, New Jersey: Princeton University Press (Bollingen Series XVII), 1949.

Paul Cantor, *Creature and Creator: Myth-Making and English Romanticism.* Cambridge, U.K.: Cambridge University Press, 1984.

Karel Čapek, trans. Paul Selver, *R.U.R. (Rossum's Universal Robots).* Garden City, NY: Doubleday, Page & Co., 1925.

————, "The Author of the Robots Defends Himself," trans. Cyril Simsa, *Science Fiction Studies* 68 (vol. 23, part 1), March 1996.

Daniel Charles, *Lords of the Harvest: Biotech, Big Money, and the Future of Food.* Cambridge, Mass.: Perseus Publishing, 2001.

[Claire Clairmont], *The Journals of Claire Clairmont,* ed. Marion Kingston Stocking. Cambridge, Mass.: Harvard University Press, 1968.

The Clairmont Correspondence: Letters of Claire Clairmont, Charles Clairmont, and Fanny Imlay Godwin, vol. I, ed. Marion Kingston Stocking. Baltimore and London: The Johns Hopkins University Press, 1995.

Classic Movie Monsters Stamps Media Kit, United States Postal Service, October 1997.

Debbie Dadey and Marcia Thornton Jones, *Frankenstein Doesn't Plant Petunias.* New York: Scholastic, 1993.

Sharon Darrow, *Through the Tempests Dark and Wild: A Story of Mary Shelley, Creator of* Frankenstein. Cambridge, Mass.: Candlewick Press, 2003.

Erasmus Darwin, *The Temple of Nature.* In vol. III, *The Poetical Works of Erasmus Darwin.* London: J. Johnson, 1806.

Humphry Davy, *A Discourse Introductory to a Course of Lectures on Chemistry* and *Syllabus of a Course of Lectures on Chemistry, delivered in the Theatre of the Royal Institution, on the 21st of January, 1802,* in vol. II of *The Collected Works of Sir Humphry Davy,* ed. John Davy. London: Smith, Elder & Co. Cornhill, 1839.

Charles Dickens, *Great Expectations*, ed. Edgar Rosenberg. New York and London: W.W. Norton, 1999.

R. H. W. Dillard, *Horror Films.* New York: Simon & Schuster, 1976.

Carl Fallberg, *Frankenstein, Jr.: The Menace of the Heartless Monster.* Racine, Wisc.: Whitman Publishing Co., 1968.

[Barbara Field], *New Classics from the Guthrie Theater: Classic Adaptations for the American Stage by Barbara Field.* Hanover, New Hampshire: Smith and Kraus, 2003.

Radu Florescu, *In Search of Frankenstein.* New York: Warner Books, 1976.

Frankenstein, Based on the Novel by Mary Shelley, adapted by Dale Carlson. Racine, Wisc.: Golden Press/Western Publishing Co., 1968.

Frankenstein: Penetrating the Secrets of Nature (exhibition catalog). New Brunswick, New Jersey, and London: Rutgers University Press, 2002.

Donald S. Fredrickson, M.D., *The Recombinant DNA Controversy, A Memoir: Science, Politics, and the Public Interest 1974–1981.* Washington, D.C.: ASM Press, 2001

Milton Friedman, *Capitalism and Freedom.* Chicago and London: The University of Chicago Press, 1982.

Tim Fulford, Debbie Lee, and Peter J. Kitson, *Literature, Science and Exploration in the Romantic Era: Bodies of Knowledge.* Cambridge: Cambridge University Press, 2004.

Denis Gifford, *Karloff: The Man, the Monster, the Movies.* New York: Curtis Books, 1973.

————, *A Pictorial History of Horror Movies.* London, New York, Sydney, Toronto: Hamlyn, 1973.

David D. Gilmore, *Monsters: Evil Beings, Mythical Beasts, and All Manner of Imaginary Terrors.* Philadelphia: University of Pennsylvania Press, 2003.

Donald F. Glut, *The Frankenstein Archive: Essays on the Monster, the Myth, the Movies, and More.* Jefferson, N.C., and London: McFarland & Co., 2002.

Harry Goldman, *Kenneth Strickfaden: Dr. Frankenstein's Electrician.* Jefferson (North Carolina) and London: McFarland & Company, Inc., 2005.

Stephen Jay Gould, *Dinosaur in a Haystack: Reflections in Natural History.* New York: Harmony Books, 1995.

Fritz Graf, trans. Thomas Marier, *Greek Mythology.* Baltimore and London: Johns Hopkins University Press, 1993.

Elaine L. Graham, *Representations of the Post/Human: Monsters, Aliens and Others in Popular Culture.* New Brunswick, N.J.: Rutgers University Press, 2002.

Keith Graves, *Frank Was a Monster Who Wanted to Dance.* San Francisco: Chronicle Books, 1999.

Peter Haining, ed. *The Frankenstein File.* London: New English Library, 1977.

————. *The Frankenstein Omnibus.* Edison, NJ: Chartwell Books, 1994.

T. C. Hansard, ed. *The Parliamentary Debates,* vol. X. London: T. C. Hansard at the Pater-Noster Press, 1824.

Nathaniel Hawthorne, *Mosses from an Old Manse,* New York: Modern Library, 2003.

Hesiod, trans. Richmond Lattimore, *The Works and Days;Theogony;The Shield of Herakles*. Ann Arbor: The University of Michigan Press, 1959.

Richard Holmes, *Shelley: The Pursuit*. London: Quartet Books, 1976.

Maurice Horn, ed. *The World Encyclopedia of Comics,* vol. I. New York: Chelsea House Publishers, 1976.

Peter Hutchings, *Hammer and Beyond: The British Horror Film*. Manchester and New York: Manchester University Press, 1993.

Christopher Isherwood and Don Bachardy, *Frankenstein: The True Story*. New York: Avon Books, 1973.

Paul M. Jensen, *The Men Who Made the Monsters*. New York: Twayne Publishers, 1996.

Curtis Jobling, *Frankenstein's Cat*. New York: Scholastic, 2001.

Stephen Jones, *The Frankenstein Scrapbook*. New York: Carol Publishing Group, 1995.

William B. Jones, *Classics Illustrated: A Cultural History, with Illustrations*. Jefferson, N.C., and London: McFarland & Company, Inc., 2002.

Carl Gustav Jung, *Psychology & Religion*. New Haven and London: Yale University Press, 1938.

Leon R. Kass, *The Beginning of Wisdom: Reading Genesis*. New York: Free Press, 2003.

Leon R. Kass and James Q. Wilson, *The Ethics of Human Cloning*. Washington, D.C.: The AEI Press, 1998.

John Keats, *Letters of John Keats,* ed. Robert Gittings. London, Oxford, New York: Oxford University Press, 1970.

C. Kerenyi, trans. Ralph Manheim, *Prometheus: Archetypal Image of Human Existence*. New York: Bollingen Foundation/Pantheon Books, 1963.

Joseph Kesselring, *Arsenic and Old Lace*. New York: Dramatists Play Service, 1942.

Jackson King, Monsters in Animation Web site, http://www.JimHillMedia.com.

Gina Kolata, *Clone: The Road to Dolly and the Path Ahead*. New York: William Morrow and Co., 1998.

[Charles and Mary Lamb], *The Letters of Charles and Mary Anne Lamb* (3 vols.), ed. Edwin W. Marrs, Jr. Ithaca and London: Cornell University Press, 1975, 1976, 1978.

Christopher Lee, *Tall, Dark and Gruesome: An Autobiography*. London: W. H. Allen, 1977.

George Levine and U. C. Knoepflmacher, *The Endurance of Frankenstein: Essays on Mary Shelley's Novel.* Berkeley, Calif.: University of California Press, 1979.

Cynthia Lindsay, *Dear Boris: The Life of William Henry Pratt A.K.A. Boris Karloff.* New York: Alfred A. Knopf, 1975.

Charles J. Lumsden and Edward O. Wilson, *Promethean Fire: Reflections on the Origin of Mind.* Cambridge, Mass., and London: Harvard University Press, 1983.

Fiona MacCarthy, *Byron: Life and Legend.* Farrar, Straus and Giroux, 2002.

D. L. MacDonald, *Poor Polidori: A Critical Biography of the Author of* The Vampyre. Toronto, Buffalo, London: University of Toronto Press, 1991.

Gregory William Mank, *It's Alive! The Classic Cinema Saga of Frankenstein.* San Diego and New York: A. S. Barnes & Co., Inc., 1981.

Tim Marshall, *Murdering to Dissect: Grave-Robbing,* Frankenstein *and the Anatomy Literature.* Manchester and New York: Manchester University Press, 1995.

Colin McNaughton, *Making Friends with Frankenstein.* London: Walker Books, 1993.

Allan Metcalf, *Predicting New Words: The Secrets of Their Success.* Boston and New York: Houghton Mifflin Co., 2002.

John Milton, *Paradise Lost,* ed. Gordon Teskey. New York: W. W. Norton, 2005.

Ellen Moers, *Literary Women: The Great Writers.* Garden City, NJ: Doubleday, 1976.

"The Monster Made by Man," in Franz J. Potter, ed., *The Monster Made by Man: A Compendium of Gothic Adaptations.* Zittaw Press, 2004.

Monsters: Three Famous Spine-Tingling Tales, adapted and abridged by Walter Gibson. New York: Wonder Books, 1965.

Timothy Morton, ed., *A Routledge Literary Sourcebook on Mary Shelley's* Frankenstein. London and New York: Routledge, 2002.

Iwan Rhys Morus, *Frankenstein's Children: Electricity, Exhibition, and Experiment in Early-Nineteenth-Century London.* Princeton: Princeton University Press, 1998.

William R. Newman, *Promethean Ambitions: Alchemy and the Quest to Perfect Nature.* Chicago and London: University of Chicago Press, 2004.

Ashton Nichols, ed., *Romantic Natural Histories.* Boston and New York: Houghton Mifflin, 2004.

The Norton Anthology of English Literature (3rd ed.), vol. 2, ed. M. H. Abrams. New York: W. W. Norton, 1974.

The Norton Anthology of English Literature (4th ed.), vol. 2, ed. M. H. Abrams. New York: W. W. Norton, 1979.

Sal Piro, "It Was Great When It All Began," from *Creatures of the Night,* reprinted on The official Web site of The Rocky Horror Picture Show, http://www.rockyhorror.com/.

[John William Polidori], *The Diaries of Dr. John William Polidori, 1816,* ed. William Michael Rossetti. London: Elkin Mathews, 1911.

John William Polidori, *The Vampyre* and *Ernestus Berchtold; or, The Modern Oedipus,* ed. D. L. Macdonald and Kathleen Scherf. Toronto, Buffalo, London: University of Toronto Press, 1994.

President's Council on Bioethics Web site, http://www.bioethics.gov/.

Joseph Priestley, *The History and Present State of Electricity with Original Experiments.* Reprinted from the 3rd ed., London, 1755. New York and London: Johnson Reprint Corporation, 1966.

Peter Pringle, *Food, Inc.* New York: Simon & Schuster Paperbacks, 2003.

Paul Ramsey, *Fabricated Man: The Ethics of Genetic Control.* New Haven and London: Yale University Press, 1970.

Philip J. Riley, ed., *Abbott and Costello Meet Frankenstein.* Absecon, NJ: MagicImage Filmbooks, 1990.

Rocky Horror Picture Show, The official web site, http://www.rockyhorror.com/.

Rocky Horror Show Web site, http://www.rockyhorror.co.uk/.

Jimmy Sangster, *Do You Want It Good or Tuesday? From Hammer Films to Hollywood! A Life in the Movies.* Baltimore: Midnight Marquee Press, 1997.

Steven Shapin and Simon Schaffer, *Leviathan and the Air-Pump: Hobbes, Boyle, and the Experimental Life.* Princeton, NJ: Princeton University Press, 1985.

Roger Shattuck, *Forbidden Knowledge: From Prometheus to Pornography.* New York: Harcourt, 1997.

George B. Shaw, ed. *Fabian Essays in Socialism.* London: The Walter Scott Publishing Co., 1908.

Mary Wollstonecraft Godwin Shelley, *Frankenstein, or, The Modern Prometheus.* New York: Grosset & Dunlap, n.d. [1932].

———, *Frankenstein; or, The Modern Prometheus,* with illustrations by Nino Carbe. New York: Illustrated Editions Co., Inc., n.d. [1932].

————, *Frankenstein; or, The Modern Prometheus.* New York: Harrison Smith and Robert Haas, 1934.

————, *Frankenstein; or, The Modern Prometheus,* with an introduction by Edmund Lester Pearson and illustrations by Everett Henry. New York: The Limited Editions Club for the George Macy Companies, Inc., 1934.

————, *Frankenstein.* Editions for the Armed Services, n.d. [1945?].

————, *Frankenstein.* New York: Lion Books, 1953.

————, *Frankenstein.* New York: Airmont Publishing, 1963.

————, *Frankenstein; or, The Modern Prometheus,* ed. Harold Bloom. New York: Signet Classic, 1963 (rpt. with Afterword, 1965; rpt. with Bibliography, 1983).

————, *Frankenstein; or, The Modern Prometheus: The 1818 Text,* edited, with variant readings, an Introduction, and Notes, by James Rieger. Chicago and London: The University of Chicago Press, 1974.

————, *Frankenstein,* adapted by Larry Weinberg. New York: Random House (A Stepping Stone Book Classic), 1982.

————, *Frankenstein,* ed. J. Paul Hunter. New York & London: W. W. Norton, 1996.

————, *The Journals of Mary Shelley, 1814–1844,* ed. Paula R. Feldman and Diana Scott-Kilvert. Baltimore and London: The Johns Hopkins University Press, 1987.

————, *The Letters of Mary Wollstonecraft Shelley,* vol. I, "A part of the Elect," ed. Betty T. Bennett. Baltimore and London: The Johns Hopkins University Press, 1980.

————, *The Frankenstein Notebooks,* ed. Charles E. Robinson, vols. 1 and 2. New York and London: Garland Publishing, 1996.

————, *Transformation.* London: Hesperus Classics, 2004.

[Percy Bysshe Shelley], *The Letters of Percy Bysshe Shelley,* 2 volumes, ed. Frederick L. Jones. Oxford: Oxford University Press, 1964.

————, *Shelley Poetical Works,* ed. Thomas Hutchinson. London: Oxford University Press, 1967.

David J. Skal, *The Monster Show: A Cultural History of Horror* (revised edition). New York: Faber and Faber/Farrar, Straus & Giroux, 2001 (1993).

Christopher Small, *Mary Shelley's Frankenstein: Tracing the Myth.* Pittsburgh: University of Pittsburgh Press, 1973.

William St. Clair, *The Reading Nation in the Romantic Period*. Cambridge and New York: Cambridge University Press, 2004.

Emily W. Sunstein, *Mary Shelley: Romance and Reality*. Boston, Toronto, London: Little, Brown & Co., 1989.

Jon Turney, *Frankenstein's Footsteps: Science, Genetics and Popular Culture*. New Haven and London: Yale University Press, 1998.

Samuel Holmes Vasbinder, *Scientific Attitudes in Mary Shelley's* Frankenstein. Ann Arbor: UMI Research Press, 1984, 1976.

Mark A. Vieira, *Hollywood Horror from Gothic to Cosmic*. New York: Harry N. Abrams, 2003.

Constantin François Volney, *A New Translation of Volney's Ruins*, vols. 1 and 2 (reproduction of 1802 Paris edition). New York and London: Garland Publishing, 1979.

Stephen Wagner and Doucet Devin Fisher, *The Carl H. Pforzheimer Collection of Shelley and His Circle: A History, a Biography, and a Guide*. New York: New York Public Library, 1996.

Frederick C. Wiebel, Jr., *Edison's Frankenstein*. Hagerstown, Maryland: The Frederick C. Wiebel, Jr. Fine Arts Studio, 2003.

Gene Wilder, *Kiss Me Like a Stranger: My Search for Love and Art*. New York: St. Martin's Press, 2005.

Gaby Wood, *Edison's Eve: A Magical History of the Quest for Mechanical Life*. New York: Anchor Books, 2003.

I. Maurice Wormser, *Frankenstein, Incorporated*. New York and London: Whittlesey House, McGraw-Hill, 1931.

ESSAYS AND ARTICLES

"The Anniversary" [review of works including *Shelley's Posthumous Poems*, edited by Mary W. Shelley, and *Frankenstein*], *Knight's Quarterly Magazine*, vol. III, August–November 1824, pp. 178–99.

Nelson B. Bell, "Thoughts on Horror Era, Renaissance and Miss Ulric," *Washington Post*, 21 February 1932, A1.

Paul Berg, "Asilomar and Recombinant DNA," 26 August 2004, Nobel Prize Web site, http://nobelprize.org/nobel_prizes/chemistry/articles/berg/index.html/.

Darlene Berger, "A brief history of medical diagnosis and the birth of the

clinical laboratory," part 2. *Medical Laboratory Observer,* www.mlo-online
.com/.

Harold Bloom, "Afterword," in Mary W. Shelley, *Frankenstein, or, The Modern
Prometheus.* New York: Signet Classic, 1965.

Luciana Bohne, "Frankenstein's monster is on the loose," http://www
.onlinejournal.com/, posted 2 September 2005.

"Boy's biopsy is set for today," *Richmond Times-Dispatch,* 2 February 2005.

D. Butler and M. Wadman, "Putting the lid on Pandora's box of genetics."
Nature, 386(6620), 9.

"Child's Reactions to Movies Shown," *New York Times,* 28 May 1933, B7.

"Clue to Chemistry of Heredity Found," *New York Times,* 13 June 1953, 17.

Mitchell Dawson, "Frankenstein, Inc.," *The American Mercury*, March 1930,
274–80.

Martin Enserink, "Food Fight: Industry Response: Ag Biotech Moves to
Mollify Its Critics," *Science* 286, 5445 (26 November 1999), 1666–68.

"'Frankenstein' Finished," *New York Telegraph,* 11 October 1931.

George Garrett, "The Crossover Beard; or, the True Story of Frankenstein
Meets the Space Monster (Among Other Things)," *Virginia Quarterly
Review* 81, 1 (Winter 2005), 4–39.

Willard Gaylin, "We Have the Awful Knowledge to Make Exact Copies of
Human Beings," *New York Times Magazine,* 5 March 1972, 12–13, 41–43,
48–49.

"George Macy Companies: Limited Editions Club (1929–1985) & The
Heritage Press (1935–1970)," HRC Research Web site, Harry Ransom
Humanities Research Center at the University of Texas at Austin,
http://www.hrc.utexas.edu/research/fa/macy.html/.

A. C. Goodson, "Frankenstein in the Age of Prozac," *Literature and Medicine*
15, 1, (1996), 16–32.

Paul Gray, "The Man-Made Monster," *Time,* 23 July 1979, 86–87.

Mordaunt Hall, "Blue-Ribbon Pictures of 1931," *New York Times,* 3 January
1932, X5.

———, "A Man-Made Monster in Grand Guignol Film Story—
Lawrence Tibbett as a Singing Marine," *New York Times,* 5 December
1931, 21.

N. Hawkes, "Legal barriers will prevent apocalypse now, if not later." *The*
[London] *Times,* 26 February 1997, 3.

"Heart Transplant Keeps Man Alive in South Africa," *New York Times,* 4 December 1967, 1.

Marjorie Heins, "*The Miracle:* Film Censorship and the Entanglement of Church and State," University of Virginia Forum for Contemporary Thought, 28 October 2002, online at http://www.fepproject.org/.

Iina Hellsten, "Dolly: Scientific Breakthrough or Frankenstein's Monster? Journalistic and Scientific Metaphors of Cloning," *Metaphor and Symbol* 15(4), 213–21.

Bruce Horovitz, "Restaurant sales climb with bad-for-you food," *USA Today,* 13–15 May 2005, 1.

John Bressner Huber, "An Incredible Miracle of Surgery," *Washington Post,* 17 January 1915, MS8.

Wilson M. Hudson, "Jung on Myth and the Mythic," in Robert A. Segal, ed., *Psychology and Myth.* New York and London: Garland Publishing, 1996.

Robert Jablon, "Boy who fought 'Frank the Tumor' gets clean bill of health," *Richmond Times-Dispatch,* 14 April 2006.

"James Whale and 'Frankenstein,'" *New York Times,* 20 December 1931, X4.

Stefan Kanfer, "Frankenstein at Sixty," *Connoisseur,* January 1991, 41–42, 44, 47.

Boris Karloff, "Houses I Have Haunted," *Liberty,* 4 October 1941, 16–17.

———, "My Life as a Monster," *Films and Filming,* November 1957, 11, 34.

———, as told to Arlene and Howard Eisenberg, "Memoirs of a Monster," *The Saturday Evening Post* 235, 39 (3 November 1962), 77–80.

Leon R. Kass, M.D., "Genetic Tampering," Letters to the Editor, *Washington Post,* 3 November 1967, A20.

———, "Making Babies—The New Biology and the 'Old' Morality," *The Public Interest,* no. 26 (Winter 1972), 18–56.

"Killers on Probation," *Sacramento [Calif.] Bee* online, http://www.sacbee.com, 19 July 2005.

"Lansbury is cheered in attack on capital," *New York Times,* 8 September 1932.

J. Laurance and M. Hornsby, "Scientists sound warning on 'human clones.'" *The* [London] *Times,* 24 February 1997, 1.

Joshua Lederberg, "Unpredictable Variety Still Rules Human Reproduction," *Washington Post,* 30 September 1967, A17.

Paul Lewis, Letter to the Editor, *New York Times,* 16 June 1992.

"Life, Industrialized," *New York Times,* 22 February 1988.

Harriet Kramer Linkin, "The Current Canon in British Romantics Studies," *College English* 53, 5 (September 1991), 548–70.

Kin-Ming Liu, "Panda Huggers on Alert," *New York Sun,* 16 January 2006.

Victor K. McElheny, "World Biologists Tighten Rules on 'Genetic Engineering' Work," *New York Times,* 28 February 1975, 1, 38.

Helene Mulholland, "MP: Councillor conduct watchdog is out of control," *Guardian Unlimited,* http://www.guardian.co.uk/, 27 July 2005.

"Oh, You Beautiful Monster," *New York Times,* 29 January 1939, X4.

Molly O'Neill, "Geneticists' Latest Discovery: Public Fear of 'Frankenfood.'" *New York Times,* 28 June 1992, 1.

"Political Frankenstein Born in Parliament—Nationalist Leader," http://www.novinite.com, 27 July 2005.

"Prohibition's Frankenstein Monster Is Still Alive," *Washington Post,* 3 June 1934.

Justin Raimondo, "Frankenstein in London," http://www.antiwar.com/blog/comments/, posted 9 July 2005.

Rob Reel, "Boris Karloff, Colin Clive Deliver Fine Acting in State-Lake Thriller," *Chicago American,* 4 December 1931.

"Remarks on Frankenstein, or the Modern Prometheus; a Novel," *Blackwood's Edinburgh Magazine* II, xii (March 1818), 613–20.

"Revival of the Undead," *New York Times,* 16 October 1938, 160.

"Rialto," *Washington Post,* 28 November 1931, 14.

Ellen Cronan Rose, "Custody Battles: Reproducing Knowledge about *Frankenstein," New Literary History* 26, 4 (Autumn 1995), 809–32.

Samuel Rosenberg, "The Horrible Truth About Frankenstein: Happy Sesquicentennial, Dear Monster." *Life* 64, 11 (15 March 1968), 74B–84.

Harold M. Schmeck, Jr., "Scientist Doubts Genetic Abuse; Calls Research the Best Defense," *New York Times,* 9 March 1968, 29.

Keith Schneider, "Cloning Brings Factory Precision to the Farm," 17 February 1988, *New York Times,* 1.

"Scores Our 'Frenzy' as Threat to Race," *New York Times,* 10 December 1931.

E. Donald Shapiro, Jennifer Long, and Rebecca Gideon, "To Clone or Not to Clone," *New York University Journal of Legislative and Public Policy,* 2000–2001, 4(1), 23–34.

Susan Sontag, "Notes on 'Camp,'" *Partisan Review,* Fall 1964, 515–30.

[Glenn Strange], "My Life as a Monster," *Mad Monsters* 1, 4 (November 1962).

"Strong Men Gasp and Women Scream," *World Telegram,* 16 December 1931.

Morris Sullivan, "Modern Prometheus or Frankenstein's Monster," Impact Press Web site, February–March 1998, http://www.impactpress.com/articles/febmar98/clone.htm/.

Deborah Sussman, "Just for the Fun and Games of It: The Dramatic Writing of George Garrett." *The Southern Quarterly* 33, 2–3 (Winter–Spring 1995), 197–213.

"Terror of Nazism in Balkans Told," *New York Times,* 14 March 1942, 7.

Irene Thirer, "'Frankenstein' Weird Chiller," *Daily News,* 5 December 1931.

Abigail Trafford, "Fear of Cloning and the Ewe To-do," *Washington Post* (Health section), 11 March 1997, 6.

Ajaz ul-Haque, "Public or Republic," *Greater Kashmir Online,* http://www.greaterkashmir.com, posted 29 January 2006.

Henry R. Viets, "The London Editions of Polidori's *The Vampyre.*" *Papers of the Bibliographical Society of America* 63 (1969), 83–103.

Richard Watts, Jr., "'Frankenstein'—Mayfair," *New York Herald Tribune,* 12 December 1931.

James D. Watson, "Moving Toward the Clonal Man," *The Atlantic* 227, 5 (May 1971), 50–53.

"Weird Theme Pictured in Rialto Film," *Washington Post,* 22 November 1931, A1.

COMICS

Dick Briefer, "Frankenstein," *Prize Comics* 59 (May–June 1946).

———, "Frankenstein Meets Boris Karload, Master of Horror," *Frankenstein* 11 (January–February 1948), reprinted in *The Journal of Frankenstein* no. 5 (October 2001), 54–58.

———, "The Monster of Frankenstein," *The Monster of Frankenstein* 30 (April-May 1954).

Frankenstein, no. 2. New York: Dell Publishing Co., 1966.

Frankenstein by Mary W. Shelley [Classic Comics edition]. New York: Gilberton Company, 1945 (rpt. 1958).

Frankenstein: The Monster Is Back! no. 1. New York: Dell Publishing Co., 1963 (2nd printing, August–October 1964).

The Frankenstein Monster! no. 18 (September 1975). New York: Marvel Comics Group, 1975.

Gary Friedrich and Doug Moench, *Essential Monster of Frankenstein,* vol. 1. New York: Marvel Comics, 2004.

The Monster of Frankenstein, vol. 1, no. 1 (January 1972). New York: Marvel Comics Group, 1972.

ARCHIVAL MATERIALS

"Dramatic #287 Synopsis, *Frankenstein,*" 14 February 1910. From the Film Study Center, Museum of Modern Art, New York.

Executive Order 13237, 28 November 2001, *Federal Register,* 66 FR 59851.

"'Frankenstein': A Liberal Adaptation of the Classic Novel by Mary Shelley," *The Edison Kinetogram,* vol. 2, no. 4 (15 March 1910), reprinted by the Henry Ford Museum and Edison Institute, Dearborn, Michigan.

"Frankenstein, or the Modern Prometheus," in *The Quarterly Review,* vol. XVIII (October 1817 and May 1818), 379–85.

"Frankenstein; or, The Modern Prometheus," *La Belle Assemblée*; *or, Bell's Court and Fashionable Magazine,* March 1818, 139–42.

President's Council on Bioethics, Transcript: First Meeting, Session 2, 17 January 2002, http://www.bioethics.gov/.

"Production Data from Universal Studios: 'Son of Frankenstein.'" Issued 20 December 1938 by John Joseph, Director of Advertising and Publicity. From the Motion Picture and Television Reading Room, Library of Congress.

Production notes, "Return of Frankenstein," no. 6265 [Universal Studios]. From the Motion Picture and Television Reading Room, Library of Congress.

Peggy Webling, "Frankenstein" (play manuscript), 7 September 1928, Reel 2828, Copyright Drama Deposits, Manuscripts Division, U.S. Library of Congress.

AUDIO AND VIDEO MATERIALS

Boris Karloff: Frankenstein: The Legacy Collection, DVD set. Universal Studios, 2004.

Alice Cooper, "Ballad of Dwight Fry," *Love It to Death.* Warner Bros., 1971.

———, "Teenage Frankenstein," *Constrictor.* MCA, 1986.

Francis Dhomont, *The Frankenstein Symphony* (1997). Asphodel Records, 1997.

Edison's 1910 "Frankenstein," DVD. A.D. Ventures, 2003.

Frankenstein: Original 1932 Radio Broadcast (audiotape). Radio Spirits, 1998.

Frankenstein Tai Baragon (1965), DVD.

"Frankenstein" (telecast 18 January 1952), *Tales of Tomorrow,* Collection One of 1st Season Shows, DVD. Image Entertainment, 2004.

Frankenweenie (1984), VHS. Walt Disney Video, 1994.

Man-Made Monster (1941), DVD. Universal Pictures; reissued by Crypt-Flicks.

The Munsters, 1st and 2nd seasons, DVD. Universal Studios, 2004 and 2005.

New York Dolls, "Frankenstein," *New York Dolls,* CD. Polygram Records, 1973.

The Rocky Horror Picture Show (1975), DVD. Twentieth Century Fox, 2004.

Super Size Me (2004), DVD. Hart Sharp Video, 2004.

Young Frankenstein (1974), DVD. Twentieth Century Fox, 1998.

ILLUSTRATION CREDITS

INDEX

Page numbers in italic type refer to illustrations and captions.